C# 2012
Joes 2 Pros®

Common Object Oriented Programming Tutorial
in .NET using the C# Language

By

Vinay Chopra

EAN: 978-1-939666-19-2

INFO@JOES2PROS.COM

Table of Contents

About the Author

Vinay had his first interaction with a computer at the nascent age of nine and little did he know that computers would end up being a lifelong interest. He started programing simple games in BASIC for his classmates to enjoy and soon this hobby turned into a passion which motivated him to earn a masters degree in Computer Science from the University of Texas in Dallas. While in graduate school, Vinay started working with the beta bits of C# 1.0. Since that time he has accumulated more than 10 years of coding experience in the C# language. He is currently a senior software developer at Microsoft and works on highly scalable distributed systems. Vinay has been teaching C# and SQL part-time for many years.

Preface

Learning a programming language can sometimes be an arduous task, not because it requires something extraordinary, but due to the lack of a consolidated knowledge source. Over the years, I have had to learn programming by reading many books, online articles, blogs, and various other sources. The common pitfall of many of these books lies in their assumption that the reader possesses some level of basic knowledge about programming. Many of these sources can also swing towards the extremes and end-up being either too basic or too advanced. The few books that have helped me the most in the learning process have been the ones that cover a few core fundamentals which have enabled me to learn more on my own.

Acknowledgements

I have incorporated my teaching experience of many years into this one book that can serve as an easy to understand and extensive source of programming knowledge for people of various backgrounds. This book is a result of inspiration from my good friend Rick Morelan, author of the SQL Joes 2 Pros series and the support of my family and friends.

I would like to acknowledge and thank a few people who helped in making this a better book.

Editor: Tony Smithlin
Technical Review: Lori Stow
User Acceptance Testing: Sandra Howard,

Finally I would like to thank my lovely wife Naveta for her encouragement and support throughout this journey.

Introduction

This book aims is to be a reader's first introduction to the amazing world of programming. Keeping that in mind, the book has been designed so that individuals with no previous experience with programming can understand C# in a natural manner. Most of the programming fundamentals have been presented with analogies relating to everyday life making concepts easier to grasp and remember in the long term. There are a few carefully selected questions provided at the end of each chapter for the users to test their understanding of the material and also practice their newly learned skills. For a more hands-on experience, this book accompanies some videos (found at Joes2Pros.com) which walk the users through each section making the learning experience much more interactive.

The concepts presented in this book can be applied to many other object oriented programming languages making learning them much easier. This book will prove to be a powerful tool if you want to gain a sound understanding of core programming fundamentals and envision yourself working as a platform, web, or application developer.

How to Use the Joes 2 Pros web site with your book.

Clear content and high-resolution multimedia videos coupled with code samples will take you on this journey. To give you all this and save printing costs, all supporting files are available with a free download from www.Joes2Pros.com. The breakdown of the offerings from these supporting files is listed as follows:

Training videos: To get you started, the first four chapters are in video format for free downloading. Videos show labs and demonstrate concepts. Ranging from 3-18 minutes in length, they use special effects to highlight key points. You can go at your own pace and pause or replay within lessons as needed.

Answer Keys: The downloadable files also include an answer key. You can verify your completed work against these keys. These coding answers are available for peeking if you get really stuck.

Chapter 1 Visual Studio 2012 and .NET Framework

Most C# or .NET books will start off with a summarized explanation like this, "Visual Studio is a comprehensive tool for developing and debugging applications". This sounds good if we already know everything about Visual Studio and have working experience with the tool. Think of Visual Studio as a glorified version of Notepad for you to open up and just write whatever is on your mind. In this case what is on your mind will be like a letter written in C#.

If we can type C# code just as quickly with Notepad as with Visual Studio then what is the big difference? We can write a letter in Notepad but Microsoft Word helps us do better work with features like spell check, formatting, and indentation. Word makes a better development environment than Notepad for writing letters in our spoken language (like English). Word knows the rules of what you are trying to accomplish and helps you to write letters cleaner and faster than Notepad.

There is no law telling us we have to use a word processing program to write a letter. There is actually no mandated program we have to use to write in C# (or in any other language). If we really want we can use Notepad to write all our C# code. The tools in Visual Studio know the rules of programming and help us to write code faster and cleaner than using Notepad. It is one of the best development environments available to write C# applications.

So what is .NET? The next section will explain what .NET is and why we need it and won't leave you hanging with just a dictionary definition like "It is a framework that allows writing and running of applications written in C# and other .NET languages".

READER NOTE: *Before doing the steps in this section you need to have the following folder structure on your hard drive C:\Joes2Pros\C# 2012\Chapter 1. Within the Chapter 1 folder there should be two more folders called Lab 1.1 and Lab 1.2. In order to follow along with the examples, you will need to have some version of Visual Studio 2012 installed.*

1.1 C# and the .NET Framework

About a year after .NET was launched I saw it listed on many job openings showing high rates of pay. I knew it was a big deal and many companies used it. What I did not know was what .NET really meant and why it was so widely used. When I asked friends of mine in the .NET world what it was, they would just tell me "It's a framework". As much as I believed them, their simple explanation did not help me. They also said frameworks are good because they are language independent. Again this is good but what does that mean for me or the people who will pay me to know C# and .NET in the workplace?

What is a framework in general? A car is a good example. The first car I owned was made in Japan. Some of the workers who built my car may not even know how to speak English yet they were able to build it for an English speaking driver. All the levers, pedals, and even the steering wheel are in a place where I could operate the car just fine. If a friend from India were to drive my car it would not matter if he spoke English, Hindi, or Japanese. The car is a framework of known pedals, levers and buttons. We use them in similar fashion like any other car. The car does not care what language we speak. If we press the right pedal then the car takes action.

Imagine there are a set of levers (known as classes) that can be pushed to make the computer screen change color, make a sound, or show a button to click. No matter what language we use as long as we know where the buttons are we can drive the computer. Can we use C# to talk to the built-in classes of .NET? Yes! Can we use VB.NET (another .NET language) to talk to the .NET classes in the exact same way? Yes! Thanks to the .NET Framework, programming to it can be language independent.

Any computer with the .NET Framework installed will be able to run programs written from .NET languages. This is true regardless of the operating system. Many computers already have .NET installed. The .NET Framework is an important component of the Windows operating system which helps with the creation and running of applications written in .NET programming languages. In this section we will talk about important features of the .NET Framework.

Imagine a child's toy that would not work because of dead batteries. The buttons were still there but pressing them does no good. So we implicitly know that we need more than just buttons present for us to press. We really want the behavior to take place. Think of the set of buttons to press as the classes and the action it needs to take is to be run by the .NET Runtime engine. To get this desired action the two main features of the .NET Framework are the Common Language

Runtime (CLR) and Framework Class Library (FCL) which will be discussed in future sections.

We write code or instructions that tell our application what to do. The code we are writing is also known as source code. The source code turns into an application using compilers.

SOURCE CODE

Have you ever followed a recipe to make a meal for your guests? That recipe did not take any action (it was just a piece of paper). By following the steps on the piece of paper you created a meal. In this analogy the steps in a recipe are like the source code for an application. The source code contains the steps in which a program will follow to do its work.

Think of source code as the instructions that built an application, much like a blueprint creates a downtown skyscraper. The building's blueprint was executed via a construction process to create an actual building. Similarly, source code is executed in steps while running an application (in the .NET world it is also called the .NET assembly).

ASSEMBLIES

Most people are comfortable with the idea of using an application or program. I am continually impressed at how handy Microsoft Word is. It helps me create well written professional letters despite my mediocre grammar skills. This Word application actually has mini-applications as part of its whole composition. For example, the spell-checker appears to be part of Word but it is also part of PowerPoint and Outlook. This handy spell-checker assembly is a re-usable subset of a bigger program. Microsoft Word is really many assemblies that together run as a program. Big programs (like Word) are often many assemblies running together. Some smaller simple programs might just be made up of one assembly.

In short, all applications consist of one or more assemblies. An assembly is a deployable unit of .NET code. Sometimes an assembly is the entire application and sometimes it is a supporting part of a bigger application. Think again of the spell-checker in Microsoft Word. We can't run spell-checker without Word (or another Office application) open. Spell-checker can be an assembly that does not run on its own but instead supports another application. Updates can be made to the spell-checker without needing to make any changes to the Word program itself. If a new, improved spell-checker version is released, we can use it without having to change our Word application. In short, all applications consist of one or more assemblies. So when we said "An assembly is a deployable unit of .NET code" we used the example that we can make an update to the spell-checker without having to update the Word program.

Spell-checker is just one assembly but how many source files went into creating this assembly? Assemblies can be created from one file or multiple files. Assemblies created from one file are known as single-file assemblies. Assemblies created from more than one file are called multi-file assemblies.

COMPILERS

Imagine you are a caterer specializing in large parties. One party coming up has a French theme so you gather some French recipes in preparation. The size of this party means you need to hire a chef so you are free to handle the business side of the operation.

You give the French recipes to the French chef to cook the meal. The recipes act like the source code of steps to follow. The chef will look at the recipes and cook the meal. Tomorrow this same type party will happen again and again the same meals prepared. If you use the same chef he or she will not need to look at the recipes unless they changes. The chef compiled the information from the recipes into his or her brain so the work could be done. The chef is the equivalent of the assembly running, based on what the source code said. You must also ensure you give the chef the recipe in a language that he or she can understand.

How do you hire a chef who can turn recipes into meals? Hiring a chef who turns recipes into meal is similar to compiling the source code into an assembly or application. The compiler turns source code into a file or set of files that becomes a running application.

Just as a construction team in Germany would have blueprints written in German, a compiler would have code written in a specific language. For example, to turn C# code into a .NET assembly, we need a C# compiler.

Compilers are computer programs which turn source code into assemblies. An application is made up of one or more assemblies.

In future chapters, we will have a single assembly application to keep things simple.

COMMON LANGUAGE RUNTIME - CLR

Back when Windows 95 was in its heyday, 32-bit apps were used the most. The 32-bit compiler had to create the 32-bit executable (32-bit assembly) that the operating system (OS) could run. Not many compilers could do that. In other words, the assembly had to speak the language of the OS. Each new version of the OS (like from Windows 95 to Windows 98) might change its internals and cause the same application to not work or need patches to help it along.

Figure 1.1 This shows Legacy Application Execution.

With .NET, the CLR (also called the .NET Runtime) will do all the talking with the OS. The assembly just needs to talk to the CLR. The CLR works with any .NET assembly from any of the CLR languages like C#, VB.NET, etc. If the OS changes, the CLR will accept the same calls from the program as before and it will make sure the program still works. As long as the system has the CLR installed it does not matter what language we use or what OS we are running.

We do not refer to .NET Runtime as a translator, but rather as a "layer" between the top layer (the compiled program) and the bottom layer (the operating system). The .NET layer (CLR) lives between these two other layers. As data moves through the CLR, it gets translated (Figure 1.2) into calls to the OS. In other words, we compile the code to the CLR. The CLR is already installed in each machine. We only need one CLR to run all the .NET applications we want.

Figure 1.2 .NET Application Execution.

SOURCE CODE AND COMPILERS

So, if we have a .NET executable (application) on a computer with the CLR we are all set. But where do .NET programs come from? Let's go back to the 32-bit days for an example. When most of the traditional (non.NET) applications are written, a compiler was there to convert the source code into an executable file. If we write our code using Notepad and save it as text file, it is just a text file and nothing much can be done with the file other than opening the file and reading or editing it. If this text file contains valid program instructions and we compile it using any valid compiler (like C or C++), we will get back an application. The compiler took the source code and created a new file with a file extension as .exe, which can be executed like any other program or application.

Figure 1.3 Non .NET Compiler

In **Figure 1.3** the source code file is converted into an executable which the operating system (like Windows) can understand. Here the HelloWorld application is made up of program instructions in the operating system language (called native code) which can only be executed on a processor (CPU) and OS (operating system) of similar architecture.

Microsoft Intermediate Language

.NET applications have something very special; when the .NET application is compiled it stores instructions in the Microsoft Intermediate Language (MSIL). When C# code is run in Visual Studio the C# compiler generates an assembly in a universal language usable by .NET. The .NET layer can then translate MSIL to the specific OS (operating system) and processor on any given computer. In other words, MSIL instructions are the same on all .NET computers even if the OS is completely different. Another way to say this is that MSIL is agnostic (does not care) about the processor architecture and the OS (operating system). The .NET assembly does not directly talk to the OS or processor but instead talks to the CLR. At runtime intermediate language instructions from the assembly are compiled to native code using a process called just-in-time (JIT). It is this native code that is specific for a particular operating system and processor architecture.

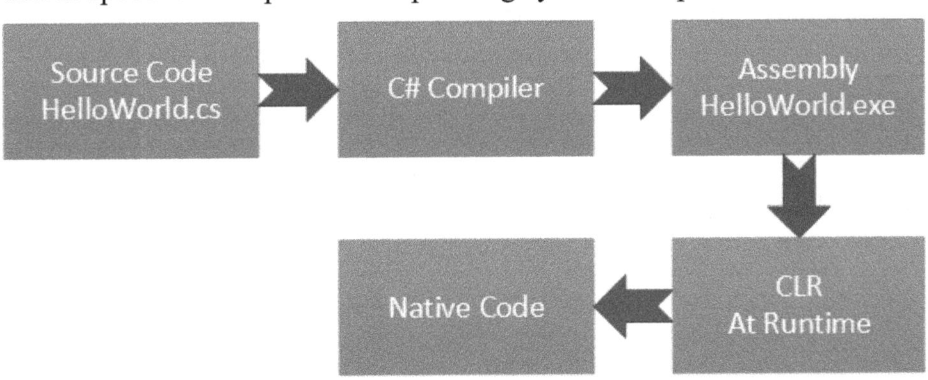

Figure 1.4 .NET Compiler

In **Figure 1.4** we see .NET source code of HelloWorld.cs is compiled through the C# compiler into a .NET assembly called HelloWorld.exe. The HelloWorld.exe will get JIT compiled by the CLR and the assembly's MSIL instructions will be turned into native code for the OS to run. The CLR prepares the code to run natively on the OS. The CLR does much more than compile at runtime. For example, it manages memory, code security, thread safety, etc.

Framework Class Library - FCL

There are thousands of things that can be done on our computer like write a letter, open a chat connection with friends, and save pictures to the hard drive. We don't have to write these applications on our own, we just use them. If we wanted to write these applications ourselves it would be tough as we will be required to know how to use native code to write to the file system, and open network connections. If we already have applications like Microsoft Word and Skype to do these things, then life is much easier. The .NET Framework Class Library (FCL) is a collection of reusable components for the programmer to build advanced applications without having to know the computer's native code.
The FCL helps developers to write different types of applications. An example can be Windows applications, web applications, or services. The FCL already knows what a web address looks like or how a port works. Therefore, a lot of common functionality is already written in these libraries so a developer can use these classes. This allows us to concentrate on the design flow and development of the actual business logic.

A few examples of features provided in the Framework Class Library are:

- String operations, like joining two strings, string matching, etc.
- File operations, like copy, paste, delete of files on hard drives, etc.
- Networking operations, like opening a connection, etc.
- Drawing operations, like drawing simple shapes to complex image manipulations.

In short, the FCL is a call to these pre-existing libraries which make our development better and more efficient.

Points to Ponder - .NET Framework

1. The .NET Framework is an integral part of the Windows operating system.
2. Two of the most important features of the .NET Framework are Common Language Runtime (CLR) and Framework Class Library (FCL).
3. An assembly is a deployable unit of .NET code.
4. An assembly can be a single-file assembly or multi-file assembly.
5. In the .NET world compilers are programs that convert source code into a .NET assembly.
6. CLR compiles the .NET assemblies at runtime into native code.
7. FCL provides the building blocks for .NET applications.
8. It is required to have different JIT compilers for different platforms (operating systems and processors).

1.2 Visual Studio 2012

Notepad has been included in every version of Windows and it is a very easy-to-use text editor program. As we talked about in the last section, Microsoft Word is a better application for writing letters. To put this in proper terms, Microsoft Word is a better Development Environment for writing documents. Similarly, Visual Studio makes our life easier by helping us to write faster, cleaner, and efficient applications. If we make a simple typing error in C# then Visual Studio is going to underline the error and make correction suggestions. This is the same way Microsoft Word underlines spelling or grammar errors we make when writing a document. Notepad never makes any helpful suggestions.

READER NOTE: *Before doing the steps in this section you need to have the following folder structure on your hard drive C:\Joes2Pros\C# 2012\Chapter 1\Lab 1.2. If you are familiar with Visual Studio 2012 and its basic features you can skip this chapter and go directly to the Skill Checks.*

Visual Studio 2012 Editions

Visual Studio 2012 comes in many editions like:

- Ultimate
- Premium
- Professional
- Express
    - For Web
    - For Windows 8
    - For Windows Desktop

Have you ever seen cars loaded with all the GT options? Putting these cool options on a car adds to the cost of the car. Often times the more we pay the more we get. This is also true with Visual Studio editions. These editions differ in the feature set offered to the developer. We will use some of the feature sets as we progress throughout the book.

Visual Studio Express 2012 is a free version which can be downloaded. Visual Studio Express 2012 is comprised of many components. For this book the free Visual Studio Express 2012 for Windows Desktop will work with all the examples and labs. If you prefer, you can use any of the higher editions as you follow our tutorial. The screen shots of this book will be using Visual Studio Ultimate 2012, but the videos on the Joes2Pros.com website will be shot using Visual Studio Express 2012 for Windows Desktop.

Installing VS Express 2012 for Windows Desktop

If you don't have the Professional or Ultimate edition of Visual Studio you can download Visual Studio Express 2012 for Windows Desktop from Microsoft's website. The most current location at the time of this writing is at the following URL:

http://www.microsoft.com/visualstudio/eng/downloads

For running Visual Studio, the following operating systems are currently supported:

- Windows 7 SP1 (x86 and x64)
- Windows 8 (x86 and x64)
- Windows Server 2008 R2 SP1 (x64)
- Windows Server 2012 (x64)

Understanding C# Syntax

Let's see how a simple command given in English works, "John, raise your right hand". In C# this can translate to **John.RightHand.Raise()**. Raise is an action. In C# an action is called a method (or function). Raise is a method on the object of type **RightHand**.

Another example can be "John, change your shirt color to blue", which translates to **John**.**Shirt**.**Color** = **Blue**. Here you are assigning the shirt color to blue. In C#, color is not an action but is called a property. Color is a property of the "Shirt" object.

Creating a C# Application

Let's start by opening Visual Studio 2012 (going forward we will be calling it Visual Studio). Once Visual Studio is open click **New Project** from the start page. Visual Studio will give us various choices for different types of projects. For this example choose **Console Application** from the list and name the project **HelloCSharp**.

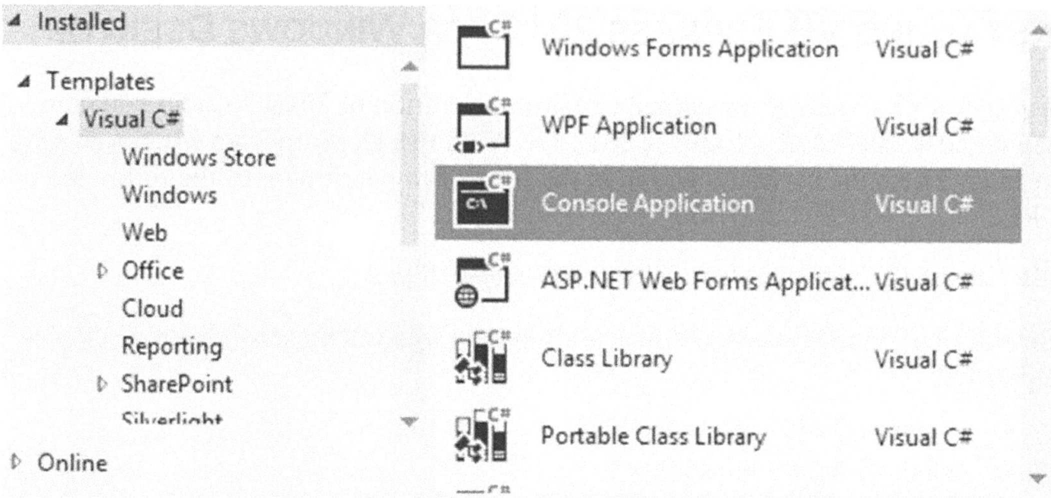

Figure 1.5 Creating a Console Application.

Save the Console Application in the **C:\Joes2Pros\C# 2012\Chapter 1\Lab1.2** folder, as shown in **Figure 1.6**.

Figure 1.6 HelloCSharp Save Location.

The first thing seen here is an empty **Main** method. Some of the code created for us should resemble the following:

```
class Program
{
  static void Main(string[] args)
  {
  }
}
```

There are some C# keywords in this code we have not talked about yet. The C# keywords turn a solid blue color. Later we will discuss what the `class` and `static` keywords mean. For now let's assume any code we want to write will be written inside the curly braces of the **Main** method.

A C# project can hold many source code files along with other types of files, as shown for project "HelloCSharp" in **Figure 1.7**.

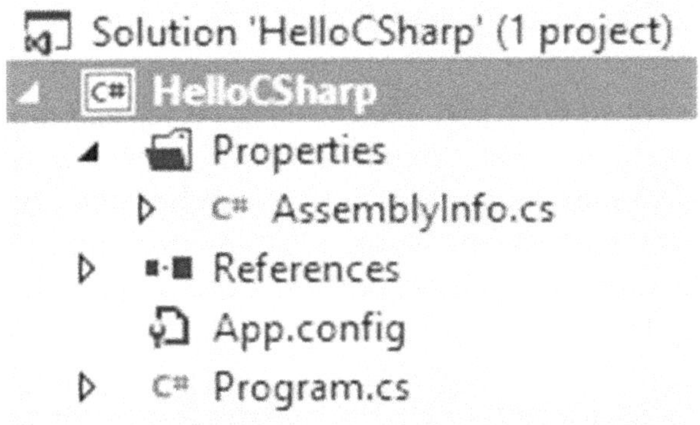

Figure 1.7 Project Files.

Since this is a Console Application let's test it out by printing some text on the console. The console is a black window which some people call a DOS window.

`Console` is an object (class) and `WriteLine` is the action (method) to be performed on the console. Notice in the following code example we have added two new C# statements inside the **Main** method. The first line inside the **Main** method writes text on the console window and the second line waits for us to press any key before closing the program. Here we are using the `Console` class and calling its `WriteLine` method to show text on the console. In the second line inside the **Main** method we see that `Console` has another method called `ReadKey`. This gets the console to wait until a key is pressed.

```
static void Main(string[] args)
{
    Console.WriteLine("Hello C Sharp");
    Console.ReadKey();
}
```

READER NOTE: *C# is a case-sensitive language and writing the code in the wrong case will result in errors. In* ***Figure 1.8*** *we use a lower case "r" in readKey and we get an error.*

```
Console.WriteLine("Hello C Sharp");
Console.readKey();
```

Figure 1.8 C# is Case Sensitive.

If we use a lower case "r" in `readKey` we get an error. To help us, Visual Studio put a red underline under `readKey` to identify the error. Notepad would not give us that type of help. Another thing to note here is that every C# statement should end with a semicolon. Let's fix this error by making the "R" upper case on `ReadKey`.

BUILDING AND RUNNING AN APPLICATION

This **HelloCSharp** project does just what we need it to do. One project might not solve all of our company's needs. For example, if this project needed to be deployed to many machines we could build a second project that would deploy the first project. Those two projects would make up one solution. This solution would just have a development project portion, but no fancy deployment project, so it will only deploy locally.

The **HelloCSharp** project is part of a solution which was created along with the project (Figure 1.7). A solution was created by default for us when we created the project. A solution is a container to store one or more projects.

When we choose to build a project or solution it converts the source code to an assembly. In this example the **HelloCSharp** project will be converted to the **HelloCSharp** application. In other words, the code will be compiled into an application.

We can build our solution by pressing the **F6** function key (or **F7** in Visual studio Express). We can also build this solution by clicking **Build Solution** under the Build menu. If no errors are found the program is ready to run. We can run the program by pressing the **F5** function key or clicking the green play button called **Start**, as shown in **Figure 1.9**.

Figure 1.9 Click Start to run the application.

In the last line of our program we specified `Console.ReadKey();`. This line will not run until the user presses any key, then the program reaches the end of **Main** and completes the execution. Right before the user pressed any key the program execution should look like Figure 1.10.

```
Hello C Sharp
```

Figure 1.10 Program Execution.

ANALYZING PROJECT FILES

When we create a Console Application project in Visual Studio a few files are created automatically to support the project. The most important file created is Program.cs. This file contains source code. There are other folders and files which are also created, as shown earlier in **Figure 1.7**. A similar folder structure is maintained on the computer's hard drive, as shown in **Figure 1.11**.

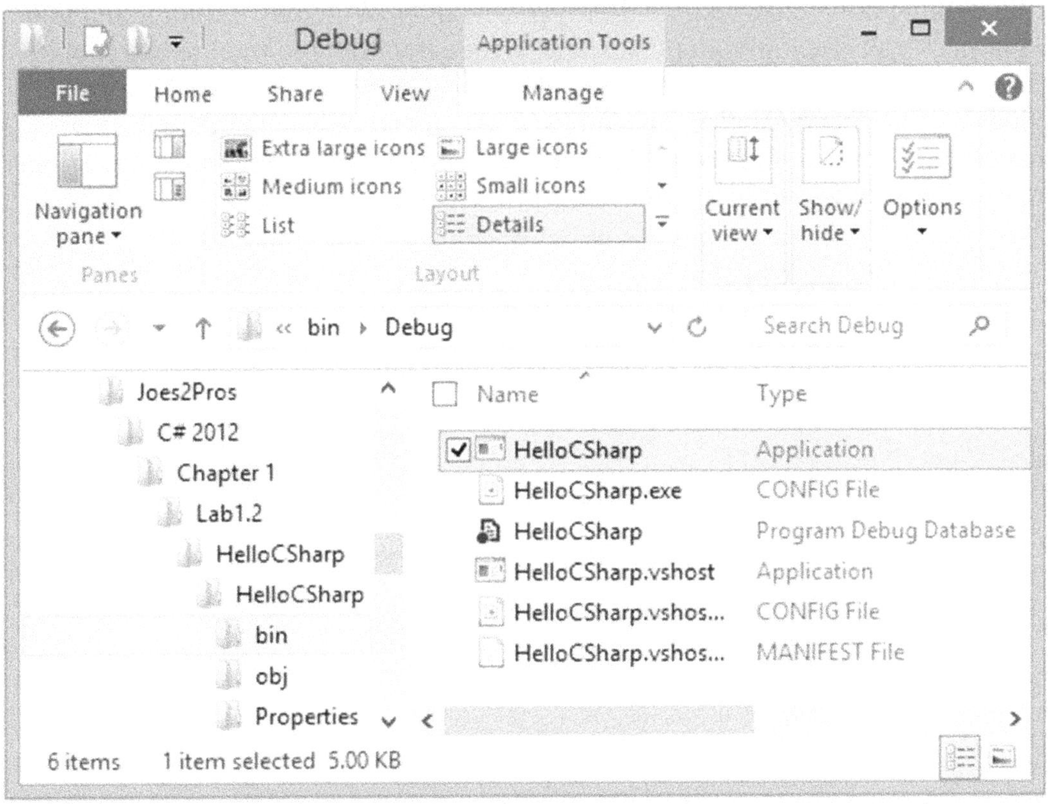

Figure 1.11 Project Folder Structure.

Since we have already built and run this project we will find our application "HelloCSharp.exe" under the bin\Debug folder. We can double click this file to run the application. Chances are high our application inside the debug folder is not showing the true file extension as ".exe". Notice in **Figure 1.11** the Application does not show the exe extension. This is because, by default, Windows hides file extensions for known file types. Therefore, HelloCSharp.exe shows as HelloCSharp, and HelloCSharp.exe.config is showing up as HelloCSharp.exe.

Go back to the Solution Explorer that is seen in **Figure 1.7**. If we expand the Properties folder we will find another file called AssemblyInfo.cs. Double click on the AssemblyInfo.cs file to open it. This file contains information like AssemblyTitle, AssemblyCompany, etc. These items are the properties for the application. Let's change the following values in this file:

```
[assembly: AssemblyCopyright("Joes2Pros Copyright © 2013")]
[assembly: AssemblyVersion("1.0.0.1")]
[assembly: AssemblyFileVersion("1.0.0.1")]
```

After making these changes, build the project. Open Windows Explorer and go to the project's bin\Debug folder. This time we are not going to run the exe file. Instead, right-click the application **HelloCSharp**, as seen in **Figure 1.11** in Windows Explorer and select Properties. Click the **Details** tab and notice the changes, as shown in **Figure 1.12**. Notice the copyright information and versions are exactly what we set in the AssemblyInfo.cs file.

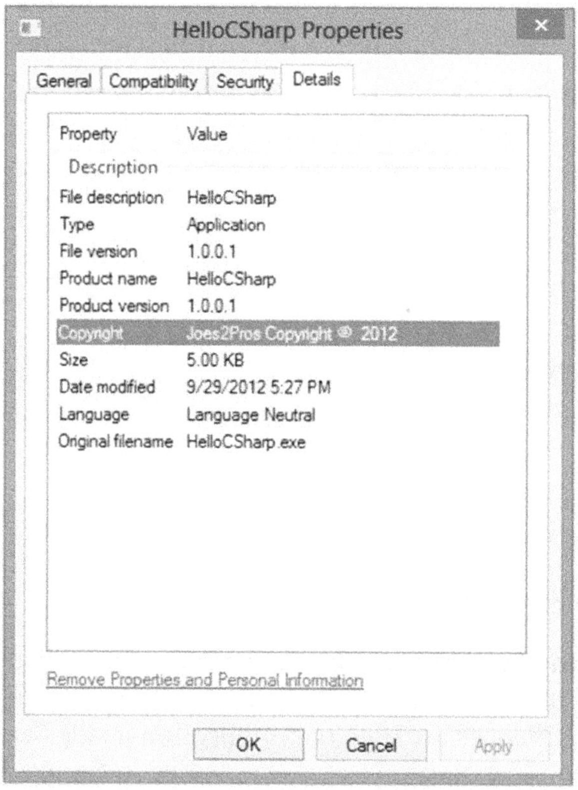

Figure 1.12 HelloCSharp Properties.

CODE COMMENTS

Old, classic movies utter this famous phrase, "Gentlemen, this is off the record". In movies this phrase is used when talking to the press and letting them know a certain comment or two will be said, however it is not meant for publication in the media. Sometimes, we want to use words or phrases within our code that we want the CLR runtime to ignore when executing the code.

The main purpose of commenting techniques is to allow us to write words or phrases that are often descriptive notes or warnings of what the code is doing, when to run it, and why it is necessary. This is a big benefit when other people (such as our team members, supervisors, or software testers) are reviewing the code for their own purposes. In other words, comments are commonly used as mini informational 'readme' notes. If you worked on a project and then went on vacation for two weeks, anyone working on that project while you were gone would understand your thoughts behind the code by reading your comments. This allows other people reading these comments to learn more about the code being used.

Why did we build this code? We can leave a comment using two forward slashes and then a message,, as seen in the following code:

```
static void Main(string[] args)
{
  // Testing a Console Message from Chapter1
  Console.WriteLine("Hello C Sharp");
  Console.ReadKey();
}
```

Run and test the code. It looks like we're done. We can see what we did and the program runs as expected. Notice it runs just the same. The CLR runtime is acting as if that comment is not even there. Comments are not executed by .NET and are only meant for us to read while in the source code.

Lab 1.2: Visual Studio 2012

Skill Check 1: Create a Console Application called **WelcomeToProgramming** to the **C:\Joes2Pros\C#2012\Chapter 1\Lab1.2** location. The application should write the messages shown in **Figure 1.13** to the console window using multiple `Console.WriteLine` statements. Make sure the application terminates after the user presses any key.

```
Welcome to C# Programming
C# is fun!!!
```

Figure 1.13 WelcomeToProgramming.

Skill Check 2: Make changes to the application created in Skill Check 1. Update the AssemblyInfo.cs file so that the application properties resemble the ones shown in Figure 1.14.

File description	WelcomeToProgramming
Type	Application
File version	2.0.0.0
Product name	WelcomeToProgramming
Product version	2.0.0.0
Copyright	Me
Size	5.00 KB
Date modified	9/29/2012 6:02 PM
Language	Language Neutral
Original filename	WelcomeToProgramming.exe

Figure 1.14 Application Properties.

Answer Code: The C# answer code for this lab is located in the downloadable files inside the Projects folder within the BeginningCS2012CompanionFiles.zip file.

Points to Ponder - Visual Studio 2012

1. Visual Studio is an IDE (Integrated Development Environment) designed to help create, debug, and execute .NET applications.
2. To save a C# file in Visual Studio go to the File > Save menu or Ctrl+S (Control and then the S key).
3. To save all the files in Visual Studio go to the File > Save All menu or Ctrl+Shift+S.
4. After making changes to the source code, rebuild the project for the executable to be updated.
5. We can run the executable directly from Visual Studio by pressing F5 or clicking the green play Start button on the tool bar.
6. Application properties (like version and application name) can be changed in the AssemblyInfo.cs file.
7. Assemblies in .NET can be an application just like our HelloCSharp.exe application or a supporting file for an application.
8. A C# project can hold multiple files.
9. A C# solution can hold multiple projects.
10. The Solution Explorer window shows the files that are part of the project and also the projects that are part of the solution.
11. C# is case-sensitive. Visual Studio will show a red underline error if the wrong case or spelling is in the source code.
12. Pressing **F7** in the Express Edition of Visual Studio builds the complete solution.
13. Pressing **F6** builds the complete solution, whereas **Shift+F6** just builds the current project in the Professional Edition of Visual Studio.
14. In Visual Studio Express use **F7** to build the solution.
15. The lines starting with // are comment lines.

Review Quiz - Chapter One

1.) A .NET assembly is something that is written in assembly language.

O a) TRUE
O b) FALSE

2.) Before you can run a C# application you must:

O a) Compile
O b) Export

3.) What it the name of the .NET runtime environment?

O a) Keyword List
O b) Common Language Runtime
O c) Framework Class Library

4.) What is a .NET compiler?

O a) The runtime that turns MSIL code into native code.
O b) A utility that turns source code into a file or set of files that becomes a running application.
O c) A library to extend the common type system (CTS).

5.) .NET code can be executed on an operating system other than Windows.

O a) TRUE
O b) FALSE

6.) Which file will you modify to set the version of your assembly or application?

O a) VersionInfo.cs
O b) VersionFile.cs
O c) AssemblyInfo.cs
O d) AssemblyFile.cs

Answer Key

1.) .NET assemblies are created using .NET languages and not using assembly language, making (b) the correct answer.

2.) Compilers turn source code into an executable (runnable) file. A compiler also checks for typing errors. Export means nothing in this context, making (a) the correct answer.

3.) The Framework Class Library defines usable classes which programs can use. The Common Language Runtime turns the MSIL code into native code which runs .NET applications, making (c) the right answer.

4.) The .NET runtime, CLR turns MSIL code into native code at runtime. Compilers turn source code into an assembly (runnable application). Here, (b) is correct since a compiler is not a library to extend CTS.

5.) The .NET code is compiled into Microsoft intermediate language (MSIL). CLR converts the MSIL code to native code (operating system specific). The correct answer is (a) since CLR can be written for platforms other than Windows.

6.) The AssemblyInfo.cs file stores the version information for the assembly, making (c) correct.

[NOTES]

Chapter 2 Variables and Data Types

When you go for a long jog or hike it is always considered a good practice to carry water with you. To bring your water you will need a water bottle to store the water. Your water bottle works as a storage container to carry the water. If you like, you can carry juice or milk instead. Your water bottle acts as a container to carry various liquids. As you will see, variables are like containers in that you can choose what you store in them.

When we want to add two numbers on a calculator we enter the first number, then press the plus + button and then enter the second number before hitting the equal (=) button. How does the calculator do the calculations and store these numbers? After you entered the first number, the calculator stores that value in its memory and also keeps track of which operation (+ - * /) you selected, and then it stores the second number into memory. After both the numbers and the plus + operator are in memory, the calculator adds the numbers.

Your calculator's memory acts like two different water bottles to store numbers (water bottle x and water bottle y). Just like your water bottle can carry different liquids, a calculator's memory can store different numbers.

In .NET and most programming languages, if we want to store data in a computer's memory we use these similar memory containers which are called variables.

Water bottles are great for storing liquids but they won't carry school supplies. A backpack does a better job of carrying school supplies, but does not store liquids. Different types of containers can hold different types of cargo. Variables can also be of different types to store different types of data. For example, integer data types can store whole numbers, and string data types can store text data. C# (and other .NET languages) supports different data types which are what we will demonstrate in this chapter.

READER NOTE: *Before doing the steps in this section you need to have the following folder structure on your hard drive C:\Joes2Pros\C# 2012\Chapter 2. Within the Chapter 2 folder there should be three more folders called Lab 2.1, Lab 2.2, and Lab 2.3.. In order to follow along with the examples, you will need to have some version of Visual Studio 2012 installed.*

2.1 Data Types

The .NET Framework provides us with different data types to store different kinds of data. These data types are common to all .NET languages and not just C#. What an integer can do in C# is identical to what an integer can do in VB.NET. This is because the library of the integer data types lives in .NET and C# is just using it. Therefore, if we write an assembly in C# and our VB.NET friend wants to use this C# assembly in VB.NET, they can do that. All these common .NET data types belong to something known as Common Type System (CTS). The CTS is a part of .NET that defines the data types. The .NET provided data types are also known as standard or simple types.

Numeric Data Types

How big is your water bottle? Bigger bottles are heavier but they can hold more liquid. These days we hear lots of people talking about things like “my new laptop supports 64-bit Windows but my old desktop only supports 32-bit Windows”. So what is meant by 32-bit or 64-bit? It means the new 64-bit laptop can handle larger sized address numbers than the old 32-bit system. The more the bits, the larger the number it can store. A 16-bit variable can store more numbers than an 8-bit variable and a 32-bit variable can store a larger number than a 16-bit variable.

If we want to write a simple calculator application where we will be storing our numbers to add or subtract, we can use any of the numeric data types supported by the .NET Framework. Based on what features we are creating for our calculator we can choose any number of data types, that are shown in Figure 2.14:

Name	Alias	.NET Type	Range	Size
Signed Byte	sbyte	SByte	-128 to 127	8 Bit
Byte	byte	Byte	0 to 255	8 Bit
Short	short	Int16	-32,768 to 32,767	16 Bit
Unsigned Short	ushort	UInt16	0 to 65535	16 Bit
Integer	int	Int32	-2,147,483,648 to 2,147,483,647	32 Bit
Unsigned Integer	uint	UInt32	0 to 4,294,967,295	32 Bit
Long	long	Int64	-9,223,372,036,854,775,808 to 9,223,372,036,854,775,807	64 Bit
Unsigned Long	ulong	UInt64	0 to 18,446,744,073,709,551,615	64 Bit

Figure 2.1 This figure shows the different numeric data types.

If our calculator only supports small numbers (like 32,767 down to negative 32,768) we can use the `short` data type. If our calculator only supports positive numbers we can use the unsigned short or `ushort` data type. The `ushort` data type ranges from 0 to 65,535. Both the `short` and `ushort` are the same size. Unsigned numbers can store larger positive numbers than their signed counterpart while using the same amount of memory space. If we want to design a calculator which deals in very large numbers (positive and negative) we can use the `long` data type to store the numbers.

The `short` data type is basically a small integer and the `long` data type is a very big integer. What about a regular sized integer? Integer (known as `int`) is the most commonly used data type when dealing in numbers. It supports both positive and negative numbers and ranges from about negative 2.1 billion to positive 2.1 billion.

How about the number 5.75? This number is between negative 2.1 billion and positive 2.1, billion but it will not work with an `int`. If our calculator supports numbers with decimals then the `int` data types mentioned previously will not work. We need to select other numeric data types, as shown in Figure 2.2.

Alias	.NET Type	Approximate Range	Precision	Size
float	Single	-3.4×10^{38} *to* $+3.4 \times 10^{38}$	7 Digits	32 Bit
double	Double	$\pm 5 \times 10^{-324}$ *to* $\pm 1.7 \times 10^{308}$	15-16 Digits	64 Bit
decimal	Decimal	$(-7.9 \times 10^{28}\ to\ 7.9 \times 10^{28}) / 10^{0\ to\ 28}$	28-29 Digits	128 Bit

Figure 2.2 This shows the different decimal data types.

5.0999999 is not larger than 5.1, but it is more precise and might take up more memory space. These common types differ in the amount of data and precision they support. If we want to store very large numbers with decimal points we can use the `double` data type as it holds more digits than the `single` type. If we want very high precision then we should go beyond the double and use the `decimal` data type. Data types with decimal points are also known as floating point data types.

Other Simple Data Types

In our calculator example, we know that we are dealing with numbers so we can use numeric data types. What data type should we use if we want to store things like someone's name? For storing a name or other text data we can use the `string` data type.

For storing just one character (like the letter 'V') we can use the `char` data type. The character (known as `char`) data type is a special kind of numeric data type where each character (like a, b, or c) is stored as a number ranging from 0 to 65,535 or in a hexadecimal system from 0000 to FFFFF. The `char` data type is also known as a Unicode 16-bit character.

Sometimes we go to any website and it asks us questions like, "Do you want to change your password?" or "Are you married?" All of these questions can be answered in a simple Yes/No or True/False fashion. In .NET, to store data in True/False format it uses the Boolean (known as `bool`) data type. There are only two values that can be stored in the Boolean data type (`true` or `false`).

Alias	.NET Type	Values
string	String	Sequence of characters
char	Char	A single Unicode character. Stored as a number from 0 to 65535 or 0000 to FFFF
bool	Boolean	true or false

Figure 2.3 This shows the String, Char and Boolean data types.

DECLARING VARIABLES

To declare any variable in C# we need to specify the data type followed by the variable name. Every C# statement should end with a semicolon.

```
<DataType> <VariableName>;
```

If we want to declare an integer variable we can type the following code:

```
int myFirstIntegerVariable;
```

Creating that empty variable was like getting an empty bottle. If we want to set this variable to have a value of 1000 we can initialize the variable in the next statement. The code sample to do this is on the second line of the following code:

```
int myFirstIntegerVariable;
myFirstIntegerVariable = 1000;
```

That last example was like buying an empty bottle and then filling it. When we go to the store to buy a bottle of soda we want it to be already filled with soda. Just like buying a bottle of soda, we can declare and 'fill' a variable at the same time. We declare and initialize a variable in one statement with the following code:

```
int myFirstIntegerVariable = 1000;
```

If we want to declare other variables, they can look like the following code examples:

```
string username = "John Doe";
//string uses double quotes

bool userMarried = true;
char firstCharacterOfName = 'J';
//char uses single quotes

int i,j;
//Two or more variables can be declared together
```

```
int a, b = 10;
//a & b are declared with b initialized to 10
```

VARIABLE NAMING

It is common in most countries for married couples to have the same last name. Some countries don't do this. In Russian speaking countries they have a similar naming convention where Mr. Petrov would be married to Mrs. Petrova. The ending "a" sound marks a feminine way to distinguish the wife's name from the husband's.

Just like every culture and country has different types of names, C# also follows some variable naming conventions and rules. In the previous example the variable names we created followed a particular variable naming style. In our style they start with a lower case letter and then every subsequent word's first character is capitalized. Here is a variable called **`theseAreFourWords`** where all words in the name have the first letter capitalized except for the first word. This is the most common way to name variables in C# and is called Camel casing. It looks a lot like a camel where the hump in the middle is the highest. When we use a two word variable name like firstName the big letter in the middle makes it very easy to see why it's called Camel casing.

Variable names can be very big or as small as a single letter. There are some limits to what names we can give to a variable. The following variable naming rules are required to be followed to define a variable:

- Variable names cannot have spaces.
- Variable names can only start with a letter, underscore, or @ symbol.
- Other than the first character, the only allowed characters are letters, underscores or numbers.

The following variable names are not allowed in C#:

- 123firstName
- _lastName@company
- user lastName

Since C# is case-sensitive, variables used in the same code with the names `FirstName` and `firstName` can both be created without errors. This looks confusing and makes it hard to keep track of their true meaning. It is not a good practice to use two variables with the same name but have a different case.

WORKING WITH VARIABLES

Now that we know what the different types of simple data types (or .NET provided data types) are let's do some practice together. Let's start by opening Visual Studio 2012 and click **New Project** from the start page. Visual Studio will give us various choices for different types of projects. For this example choose **Console Application** from the list and name the project **Working With Variables**. Going forward we will expect you to know the steps to create a Console Application and we will shorten the guidance to something like the following:

Create a Console Application and name it **Working with Variables**.

Our first goal is to create two `int` variables with initial values of 20 and 30 respectively. Then create a third variable to store the sum of both these variables. As always, we will write our code in the **Main** method.

```
static void Main(string[] args)
{
  int firstNumber = 20;
  int secondNumber = 30;
  int total;
}
```

Here we have initialized the `firstNumber` and `secondNumber` variables at the declaration time with the values 20 and 30. We did not initialize the variable named `total` at its declaration time. We must assign it a value before we can use it. We will assign the sum of `firstNumber` and `secondNumber` to the variable `total`.

READER NOTE: *Notice as we add each step we will bold the new code for emphasis.*

```
int firstNumber = 20;
int secondNumber = 30;
int total;

total = firstNumber + secondNumber;
```

If we execute this program we are going to get a value of 50 in the variable `total` but nothing will be shown to the user. To display this value on the console we should add `Console.WriteLine()`.

```
int firstNumber = 20;
int secondNumber = 30;
int total;
total = firstNumber + secondNumber;
Console.WriteLine(total);
```

The code in that last example will just print the value of the total on the console. If we want a nice message along with the variable values, we can use variable placeholders with the following code:

```
int firstNumber = 20;
int secondNumber = 30;
int total;
total = firstNumber + secondNumber;
Console.WriteLine("Sum of {0} and {1} is {2}", firstNumber,
    secondNumber, total);
```

Here {0}, {1}, and {2} are acting like placeholders for the variables `firstNumber`, `secondNumber`, and `total`. The previous statement could also have been written in the following way:

```
Console.WriteLine("Sum of " + firstNumber + " and " +
    secondNumber +" is " + total);
```

This second way is more cumbersome than the placeholder approach. Keep in mind the first index in the placeholder approach starts with 0 and not 1.

This program ran too quickly. Once execution reaches the end of **Main** the program terminates. It does not take a modern computer very long to run a few simple lines of code. We need this application to pause at the end and wait for the user to hit any key. This is easy to fix, but will require one more line of code. Make sure to add `Console.ReadKey()` as the last statement or else the application will exit without waiting for the user. The code inside the **Main** method should now look like the following:

```
int firstNumber = 20;
int secondNumber = 30;
int total = firstNumber + secondNumber;
Console.WriteLine("Sum of {0} and {1} is {2}", firstNumber,
secondNumber, total);
Console.ReadKey();
```

Build (F6 for VS Professional or F7 for VS Express) the application to verify no errors are reported. Execute (F5) the application and the screen should look like the one shown in **Figure 2.4**.

```
Sum of 20 and 30 is 50
```

Figure 2.4 Adding Two Numbers.

We are going to make the program bigger by adding more code that uses more common types. Let's personalize this application with some names. We're going to add a string concatenation example below our number example. Here we will be adding a few statements right before the `Console.ReadKey();`. Now define two string variables of `firstName` and `lastName` with the values "John" and "Doe". Display the full name stored in a third variable called `fullName` to the console. In this example we are joining strings (string concatenation) together as one using the + operator. Also declare a `char` variable to store the first initial of the first name.

Our string concatenation example is below the number example. The full code is inside the **Main** method and should look like the following:

```
// *** Adding Two Numbers Example ***

int firstNumber = 20;
int secondNumber = 30;
int total;
total = firstNumber + secondNumber;

Console.WriteLine("Sum of {0} and {1} is {2}",
    firstNumber, secondNumber, total);
    Console.ReadKey();

// *** String Concatenation Example ***

char firstInitial = 'J';
string firstName = "John";
string lastName = "Doe";
string fullName = firstName + " " + lastName;

Console.WriteLine("Initial:{0} fullName: {1}", firstInitial,
    fullName);

Console.ReadKey();
```

Build (F6 for VS Professional or F7 for VS Express) and then execute (F5) the program. The output should look like the one shown in **Figure 2.5.**

```
Sum of 20 and 30 is 50
Initial:J Fullname: John Doe
```

Figure 2.5 String Concatenation.

Remember that the lines starting with `//` are comment lines and are ignored by the compiler during execution of the application.

Lab 2.1: Data Types

Skill Check 1: Create a Console Application and call it **Job Seeker**. Define four variables to store the following information:

- **Name** (`string`)
- **Address** (`string`)
- **Gender** (`char`) [The character data type uses single quotes and not double quotes like string]
- **YearsOfExperience** (`byte`)

Use the values shown in **Figure 2.6** to assign them at variable declaration time. Show the variable values on the console window, as shown in **Figure 2.6**.

```
Name: John Doe
Address: 123 Tech Street, WA
Gender: M
Years of Experience: 7
```

Figure 2.6 Job Seeker.

Skill Check 2: Create a Console Application and call it **My Calculator**. Declare and initialize three variables called **num1**, **num2**, and **num3** of type `double` and initialize to values 33.33, 33.33 and 33.34 respectively. Create a fourth variable of type `double` called **total**. Assign the sum of the first three variables to total. Your output on the console should look like the one shown in **Figure 2.7**.

```
First: 33.33
Second: 33.33
Third: 33.34

33.33 + 33.33 + 33.34 = 100
```

Figure 2.7 My Calcualtor.

Answer Code: The C# answer code for this lab is located in the downloadable files inside the Projects folder within the BeginningCS2012CompanionFiles.zip file.

Points to Ponder - Data Types

1. All the common .NET data types belong to the CTS (Common Type System).
2. The higher the bits in the numeric data type, the larger the number it can hold.
3. Unsigned numbers can only store positive numbers and zero.
4. Floating point data types can store numbers that contain decimal digits.
5. If we want very high precision (more digits after the decimal point) use the decimal data type to store our needed numbers.
6. If a variable is not assigned a value at declaration time it needs to be assigned some value before it can be used.
7. Variable names can start with letters, _ or @.
8. Placeholders to display variable values in `Console.WriteLine()` start with the value 0, not 1.
9. If we want to declare a `float` variable we can also define it using the `single` data type, as shown here:

   ```
   Single floatData = 2.34F;
   ```

10. Suffix **F** after the value explicitly tells the compiler it is a `float` type value and not a `double` type value.

2.2 Operators and Expressions

In school we learned how to add, subtract, multiply, and divide numbers.

If we wanted to add two numbers we can write it as a formulate as follows:

2 + 4 = 6

In our formula there are two numbers and a + operator. The + operator works great and C# supports many different operators. A formula is called an expression in programming languages.

In programming, we don't write the computed value of the expression on the right side but we assign that expression to a variable. The following code adds 10 to 20 and assigns the expression value of 30 to the `k` variable:

```
int k = 10 + 20;
```

The computation is on the right and the result (the computed value) is on the left. Variable `k` now has a value of 30 assigned to it. If the numbers 10 and 20 are stored in variables our statement would look like the following code:

```
int i = 10;
int j = 20;
int k = i + j;
```

Since two variables or values are required for the + operator, + is called a binary operator. Binary means two and the + operator only works if there are two values (one on either side). This is why the + operator is called a binary operator.

Binary Operators

There are other binary operators supported by C# and .NET. Some of those binary operators are as follows:

Operator	Alias	Example	Description
+	Add	C = A + B	C is assigned a value that is the sum of A and B
–	Subtract	C = A - B	C is assigned a value that is B subtracted from A
*	Multiply	C = A * B	C is assigned a value that is A multiplied by B
/	Divide	C = A / B	C is assigned a value that is A divided by B
%	Mod	C = A % B	C is assigned a value that is remainder of A divided by B

Figure 2.8 This shows a list of the binary operators.

Let's create a new C# Console Application and call it **Binary Operators**. In the **Main** method declare two integer variables and initialize them with the values 13 and 5.

```
static void Main(string[] args)
{
    int a = 13;
    int b = 5;}
```

We will write the output to the console window after creating expressions using the binary operators we learned. Write the following code inside the **Main** method:

```
static void Main(string[] args)
{
    int a = 13;
    int b = 5;

    Console.WriteLine("{0} + {1} = {2}", a, b, a + b);
    Console.WriteLine("{0} - {1} = {2}", a, b, a - b);
    Console.WriteLine("{0} * {1} = {2}", a, b, a * b);
    Console.WriteLine("{0} / {1} = {2}", a, b, a / b);
    Console.WriteLine("{0} % {1} = {2}", a, b, a % b);

    Console.ReadKey();
}
```

Build (F6 for VS Professional or F7 for VS Express) and then run (F5) the application. The output should look like the one shown in Figure 2.9.

```
13 + 5 = 18
13 - 5 = 8
13 * 5 = 65
13 / 5 = 2
13 % 5 = 3
```

Figure 2.9 Binary Operators.

In the previous binary operator example, we used two different variables of **a** and **b** to create an expression. The **a** and **b** values were shown in the {0} and {1} placeholders for the varialbes in the first and second position of the `WriteLine` method. The value for the third position was not a hand typed number or a single variable. It was intstead an expression value which was displayed to the console using the placeholder {2}.

Here is a formula that a math teacher will tell us is impossible:

```
35 = 35 + 1
```

Now consider what happens to a 35 year old person on their next birthday. We know that whatever their age is now it will go up by one year. Let's set their age to 35 and then give them a birthday.

```
age = 35;
age = age + 1;
```

The single equal sign in C# is creating or replacing a new value. The equal sign is not a test or a check for accuracy. The equal sign takes the value of an expression and assigns it to a variable.

Here is one more example. Numbers in our life are constantly changing. If someone told you to please drive 10 kilometers faster, they want you to assign a new value to your current driving speed. That formula in C# would look like this:

```
driveSpeed = driveSpeed + 10;
```

If we need to add the value of variable **a** to variable **b** (**b+a**) and then assign the expression value back to variable **b** itself, that statement will look like the following:

```
b = b + a;
```

There is a shortcut method to achieve the same functionality using another type of operator. To add `b` and `a` together (and re-assign the value to `b`) would be with the += operator. The code example for this is as follows:

```
b += a;
```

If we want to multiply a and b, and then assign the value to b we can use the *= binary operator.

```
b *= a;
```

The following table shows some more types of binary operators:

Operator	Alias	Example	Also Means
=	Equals	B = A	B = A
+=	Add	B += A	B = B + A
–=	Subtract	B –=A	B = B - A
*=	Multiply	B *=A	B = B * A
/=	Divide	B /=A	B = B / A
%=	Mod	B %=A	B = B % A

Figure 2.10 Shorthand binary operators.

UNARY OPERATORS

What is the opposite of night? Yes, it is day! What is the opposite of cold? It is hot. Similarly, what is the negative equivalent of 10? We will say it is -10.

If we need to find out the negative equivalent of 10 using code we can do this by multiplying −1 with 10 to get −10.

```
int i = 10;
int j = i * -1;
```

There is another way to do this, we can write the code to look like the following:

```
int i = 10;
int j = -i;
```

We added - (negative sign) right before the variable **i** to negate the value stored in variable **i** and then assigned the value to variable **j**. The value of variable **i** did not change. The value of **i** with a changed sign got assigned to variable **j**. In other words, **i**'s value is still 10 and **j**'s value is -10.

These kinds of operators, where only one variable is involved in the expression, are called unary operators. The variable **i** is now 10 but we want to increment it by 1 to make it 11. To increase the value of **i** by 1 we can use the ++ unary operator.

```
i++;
```

Here, the value of **i** got changed to 1 more than its previous value. If the value of **i** was 23 before the **i**++; statement, the value of **i** will become 24 after the statement gets executed.

If **i** started off at 10 and we wanted to decrement it to 9 then we would use this expression:

```
i--;
```

Operators ++ and − − work a little different depending on whether they are placed before or after the variable getting assigned to another variable.

```
int a = 100;
int b = --a;
int c = 100;
int d = c--;
```

In the previous example, **a** will be decremented and then assigned to **b**. This way the value of **b** will become 99 and the value of **a** will be 99 as well. In the case of **c** and **d**, the value of **c** gets assigned to **d** and then **c** is decremented. This way the value of **d** will be 100 and the value of **c** will be 99.

The following table talks about various unary operators:

	Example	Description
+	B= +A	A is assigned to B
−	B= −A	Negative value of A is assigned to B
++	A++	A is incremented by 1
++	++A	A is incremented by 1
++	B= ++A	A is incremented by 1 and then the value is assigned to B
++	B= A++	A is assigned to B and then value of A is incremented by 1
− −	A− −	A is decremented by 1
− −	− −A	A is decremented by 1
− −	B= − −A	A is decremented by 1 and then the value is assigned to B
− −	B= A− −	A is assigned to B and then value of A is decremented by 1

Figure 2.11 This is a list of unary operators.

EVALUATING EXPRESSIONS

This might sound like a word game at first but follow along anyway. When somebody asks you to add 10 to 20 and then add 40 and then subtract 20, we can do the math in our mind by adding 10 to 20 to get 30, and then add 40 to 30 to get 70, and then subtract 20 from 70 to get 50. That means we were taking two numbers at a time and then evaluating the expression. The expression would look like this:

20 + 10 + 40 - 20

The first thing that happens in the computer memory is the 20 + 10 becomes 30, as shown here:

30 + 40 - 20

Next, the 30 and 40 are added to make 70 as a value and the expression now looks like the following:

70 - 20

The final result is 50:

50

To solve it we added mental braces around the numbers just like the ones shown here:

((20 + 10) + 40) - 20)

This is very easy if all we are doing is adding or subtracting numbers. We go left to right until all the numbers are added or subtracted. Now, if we want to evaluate the following expression things will be a little different:

20 × 4 + 10 ÷ 2

We can get confused here when trying to determine which operation should be evaluated first. Should I multiply 20 by 4 first or add 4 to 10 first? In expressions, the × and ÷ operators take precedence over + operators. Following this logic the previous expression can be rewritten as follows:

(20 × 4) + (10 ÷ 2)

In essence, the addition will only run after all the multiplication and division operators have run. Once it gets to the addition, the half completed processing of the expression multiplied the 20 and 4 to get 80, and the 10 ÷ 2 to get 5. Of the three lines below, the first two are expressions. All three lines will resolve to the same values:

(20 × 4) + (10 ÷ 2)
(80) + (5)
(85)

Now let's replace the actual numbers with variables a, b, c and d. These variables can have any value.

$e = a \times b + c / ++d$

++d is the prefix that increments. It takes precedence over any binary operator and × and / takes precedence over +. Using these rules we can write the expression as

$e = (a \times b) + (c / (++d))$

Now let's give some values to the variables as a = 10, b = 4, c = 40 and d = 9.

$e = (a \times b) + (c / (++d))$
$e = (10 \times 4) + (40 / (++9))$
$e = 40 + (40 / 10)$
$e = 40 + 4$
$e = 44$

We can use the following table to determine which operator takes precedence over the other operators. Operators in the same row have equal precedence.

Type	Operator
Unary (Highest)	+, −, Prefix ++, Prefix − −
Binary	*, /, %
Binary	+, −
Binary	=, +=, −=, *=, /=
Unary (Lowest)	Suffix ++, Suffix − −

Figure 2.12 Operators listed in order by algebraic hierarchy.

Lab 2.2: Operators and Expressions

Skill Check 1: Create a Console Application and call it **Binary Assignment Operators**. Declare and initialize two integer (`int`) variables.

```
int a = 100;
int b = 20;
```

Using binary operators, write the code to show the calculations, as shown in **Figure 2.13**. The expression should be calculated before printing the values. The first two lines in the figure can be displayed using the following code:

```
Console.WriteLine("Initial values a={0} b = {1}", a, b);
a += b;
Console.WriteLine("After a +=b; a={0} b = {1}", a, b);
```

```
Initial values a=100 b = 20
After a +=b; a=120 b = 20
After a -=b; a=100 b = 20
After a *=b; a=2000 b = 20
After a /=b; a=100 b = 20
```

Figure 2.13 Binary Assignment Operators.

Skill Check 2: Create a Console Application called **Expression Solver**. Declare and initialize the four `double` variables of **a**, **b**, **c** and **d** with values as 10, 20, 30 and 40. Declare a `double` variable **e** and initialize it to 0. Display the initial values of the five variables on the console and then assign the following expression to **e**.

```
e = ++a * b - d / c--;
```

Display the new values of these variables on the console, as shown in **Figure 2.14**.

```
Initial Values
a=10, b=20, c=30, d=40, e=0

Values after the expression
a=11, b=20, c=29, d=40, e=218.666666666667
```

Figure 2.14 Expression Solver.

Answer Code: The C# answer code for this lab is located in the downloadable files inside the Projects folder within the BeginningCS2012CompanionFiles.zip file.

Points to Ponder - Operators and Expressions

1. C# supports different types of operators like +, −, *, etc.
2. Operators that involve two variables or values in the expression are called binary operators.
3. Operators that involve one variable or value in the expression are called unary operators.
4. Every operator has precedence when evaluating the expression. For example, a multiplication (*) operation will take place before an addition (+) operation.
5. If we want addition (+) to take precedence over multiplication (*) then we can use braces. The following example will add 3 + 5 to get 8 and then multiply that by 10:

   (3 + 5) * 10

2.3 Capturing User Input

Until now we have been initializing variables at declaration time or later with some defined (hard-coded) values, as seen in the following statement:

```
string name = "John Doe";
```

Often we don't know the values of variables at declaration time and we need to get the values from the user at program execution time (runtime).

STRING INPUT

We have already learned that to write a statement on the console we can use the following statement:

```
Console.WriteLine("Hello there!");
```

To take input from the user we don't need to write something on the console, but instead we read user input from the console. We can use the `ReadLine()` method of the Console class. The method will take keystrokes from the user.

```
Console.ReadLine();
```

Using the `ReadLine()`method will pause the execution of the program until the user presses the Enter key. We can input many keystrokes and then press the Enter key. To capture user input in a variable, assign the value of the `ReadLine()` method statement to the `string` variable called `name`. An example of this is shown here:

```
string name = Console.ReadLine();
```

Now create a Console Application and call it **String Input**. Here we will start by asking for the user name and then we will display it on the console. Write the following statements inside the **Main** method.

```
static void Main(string[] args)
{
    Console.WriteLine("Please enter your name:");
    string name = Console.ReadLine();

    Console.WriteLine("Your name is: {0}", name);

    Console.ReadKey();

}
```

Build and execute the application. An example of the output can look like the one shown in **Figure 2.15**.

```
Please enter your name:
John Doe
Your name is: John Doe
```

Figure 2.15 String Input.

On the first line we can see that the user entered "John Doe" and pressed Enter. This caused the value "John Doe" to be stored in the variable called `name`. We used the value stored in the `name` variable to display it back to the console.

WRITELINE() AND WRITE()

The `WriteLine`() method writes a message and then moves the focus to the next line. If we had three `WriteLine`() statements then there would be three messages, each starting with their own line. Many times when taking input from a user we want the input to be on the same line as the question. An example of this is shown in **Figure 2.16**.

```
Please enter your name:John Doe
Your name is: John Doe
```

Figure 2.16 String Input Same Line.

Notice the user input of "John Doe" starts at the end of the first line instead of starting on a new line. We want to write a message but not drop down to the next line. We can achieve this by changing `Console.WriteLine` to `Console.Write` in the first statement inside **Main** method as seen here:

```
Console.Write("Please enter your name:");
string name = Console.ReadLine();
Console.WriteLine("Your name is: {0}", name);
Console.ReadKey();
```

The `Console.WriteLine` method moves the cursor to the next line but the `Console.Write` method keeps the cursor on the same line.

To illustrate the difference between Write() and WriteLine() even more clearly, let's create another Console Application and call it **Person Details**. Here we will store personal information like name, address, and age from the user.

To do this we will write the following code inside the **Main** method of the **Person Details** project:

```
string name, address, age;
Console.Write("Please enter your name: ");
name = Console.ReadLine();
Console.Write("Please enter your address: ");
address = Console.ReadLine();
Console.Write("Please enter you age: ");
age = Console.ReadLine();

Console.WriteLine();

Console.WriteLine("{0} {1} lives at {2}", name, age,
address);

Console.ReadKey();
```

Build (F6 for VS Professional or F7 for VS Express) and execute (F5) the project. The output should look like the one shown in **Figure 2.17**.

```
Please enter your name: John Doe
Please enter your address: 123 Tech Street, WA
Please enter you age: 23

John Doe 23 lives at 123 Tech Street, WA
```

Figure 2.17 Person Details.

In the previous example we are storing the age as a `string` since the `Console.ReadLine` returns user input as a `string`.

Lab 2.3: Capturing User Input

Skill Check 1: Create a Console Application called **My Favorites** to ask the following questions to the user:

- What is your favorite color?
- Which is your favorite cuisine?

The user should answer on the same line as the question. The output should look like the one shown in **Figure 2.18**.

```
What is your favorite color? Blue
Which is your favorite cuisine? Mexican
Favorite Color: Blue
Favorite Cuisine: Mexican
```

Figure 2.18 My Favorites.

Answer Code: The C# answer code for this lab is located in the downloadable files inside Projects folder within the BeginningCS2012CompanionFiles.zip file.

Points to Ponder - Capturing User Input

1. User input can be captured using a `Console.ReadLine` statement.
2. To capture user input in a variable assign a `string` variable to the return value of `Console.ReadLine`.
3. `Console.WriteLine` moves the cursor to next line.

Review Quiz - Chapter Two

1.) When can you use a variable without declaring it first?

O a) Never
O b) Anytime
O c) Only in the Main method
O d) Only in a static method

2.) What determines what a variable can store?

O a) Data Identifier
O b) Data Type
O c) Data Scope
O d) Input Method

3.) Which statement will assign a string value to the s1 variable?

O a) s1 = "Hello";
O b) s1 = = "Hello";
O c) s1 != "Hello";

4.) You want to declare an integer type that cannot hold negative numbers and can hold numbers up to 65,000. You decided to declare an unsigned short type using the ushort keyword. What is the underlying type of ushort?

O a) System.Int16
O b) System.UInt16
O c) System.Int32
O d) System.UInt32

5.) Which number cannot be stored in a byte data type?

O a) 23
O b) 0
O c) 240
O d) 256

6.) A bool type can be assigned which value?

O a) yes
O b) no
O c) boolean
O d) false
O e) "yes"

7.) Which of the following variable names is not valid?

O a) @lastname
O b) 2lastname
O c) _lastname
O d) @last_name

8.) Will the following code compile?
uint i = -3;

O a) Yes
O b) No

9.) What will be the value of the maxByte variable after the following code executes?

```
byte maxByte = 255;
maxByte++;
```

O a) 256
O b) 0
O c) 255
O d) 254

Answer Key

1.) All variables must be declared before you can use them, therefore, (b), (c) and (d) are all incorrect. Since you can never use a variable without declaring it first, (a) is the right answer.

2.) Data Identifier (name) is used to refer certain data. It doesn't define what is stored in a variable, hence option (a) is incorrect. Data scope of variable defines the lifetime of a variable, making option (c) incorrect. The Data Type is what determines the type of data that can be stored in a variable, so (b) is the correct answer.

3.) The = = and != operators are used as comparisons therefore, option (b) and (c) are incorrect. The = operator, assigns values to a variable, making (a) the correct answer.

4.) A short type is the same as System.Int16. Similarly, ushort will be System.UInt16, where "u" is used for unsigned, making option (b) the correct answer.

5.) The byte data type can hold numbers from 0 to 255, making choices (a), (b) and (c) valid. The number 256 is greater than 255, making choice (d) the correct answer.

6.) The bool data type can only store true or false. Choices other than (d) are invalid values for a bool type. The correct answer is (d) which is false.

7.) A variable name can start only with a letter, an underscore(_) or at sign (@). Option (b) 2lastname starts with a number, which is not allowed. All options other than (b) start with a valid character, making option (b) the correct answer.

8.) An unsigned number variable can only store positive numbers so the correct answer is (b).

9.) A byte type stores numbers from 0 to 255. When we started, the maxByte variable stored 255, adding 1 to it using ++ will make it overflow. When a variable overflows it starts with 0 again, making option (b) the correct answer.

[NOTES]

Chapter 3 Custom Data Types

In Chapter 2 we talked about some of the .NET provided data types like `int`, `bool`, and `string`. In this chapter we will talk about some more data types that we can define for our program or for other programs to use. In a conversation two people might be saying the same thing but still not communicating. To get these two people on the same page we might need a third person who can moderate. When two people speak different languages a translator can convert one language into another. These scenarios are also common to computer programs where one data type is required to be converted to another data type.

READER NOTE: *Before doing the steps in this section you need to have the following folder structure on your hard drive C:\Joes2Pros\C# 2012\Chapter 3. Within the Chapter 3 folder should be more folders called Lab 3.1 and Lab 3.2.. In order to follow along with the examples, you will need to have some version of Visual Studio 2012 installed.*

3.1 Structures

The types of double, bool, and string are simple or .NET defined data types. They all belong to the same container called System. In C# these containers are called namespaces. In all the examples we have done so far, the namespace for the project was automatically created and named after the project name. For example, if the project was called **Person Details** then the namespace was called Person_Details. The class Program of these projects belongs to the Person_Details namespace, as shown in the following code example:

```
namespace Person_Details
{
  class Program
  {
    static void Main(string[] args)
    {

    }
  }
}
```

Person_Details is the default namespace of the project **Person Details.** Since the namespace name cannot have spaces, an underscore was automatically added.

NAMESPACE

The namespace is something where similar classes and types are all grouped together. That way we can refer to these classes and types later in the project by its namespace.

We have used the int and string data types by typing them as lower case C# keyword. These keywords are actually just shortcuts to classes built into .NET. The int keyword really belongs to the System.Int32 class. Int32 is a class located in the System namespace. So the int and string data types are from classes called System.Int32 and System.String. We have also used Console.WriteLine() many times which also belongs to the System namespace for the fully qualified name of System.Console.WriteLine().

In the applications we have built so far we have not needed to use the fully qualified name like System.Console.WriteLine(). Instead used the more simple Console.WriteLine() statement. The reason is that on the top of our Program.cs file we have specified the following namespace to be implied:

```
using System;
```

The statement `using System` is a directive that tells the compiler to look for the types referred to in this file under the `System` namespace. We can add more than one `using` statement to our code. If we remove the line `using System` then the more simple `Console.WriteLine()` statement will no longer work. We will then be required to use the fully qualify name `System.Console.WriteLine()`.

STRUCTURES

In Chapter 2 we created a Console Application called **Person Details** where we asked the user for a name, address and age to display to the console window. This application was done for one user and we were required to define three variables: one for the name, one for the address, and one for the age. If we have to extend the application for 5 users we have to define 5 x 3 = 15 variables. Ideally, each person's record should be one variable, which in itself should have a placeholder to store name, address, and age. What if there was a data type called Person in our program that held name, address, and age? It would be more complex by holding three pieces of information in one data type, but sadly it does not exist right now in .NET. The good news is we can achieve this functionality by creating our own data type that can contain these three fields to store the name, address, and age for a user.

Let's create a Console Application and call it **PersonRecord**. Looking at the Program.cs file we see the `PersonRecord` namespace is automatically created and inside it is a `class Program`,, as seen in this code example:

```
namespace PersonRecord
{
    class Program
    {
        static void Main(string[] args)
        {
        }
    }
}
```

Now let's create a new structure for a new complex data type called `Person` that will hold the name, address, and age. For this new `Person` structure we can have three attributes named `Name`, `Address`, and `Age`. In C# this type of container is called a structure or a `struct` for short. Just after the namespace statement define a structure (`struct`) and call it `Person`. The `struct` will be inside of our

PersonRecord namespace but will be outside of the Program class. The following code defines a struct called Person which contains fields for storing the person's information:

```
namespace PersonRecord
{
    struct Person
    {
        public string Name;
        public string Address;
        public byte Age;
    }
    class Program
    {
        static void Main(string[] args)
        {
        }
    }
}
```

We were able to group the person's information under one umbrella called Person. Another thing to note here is that every variable declared statement is prefixed with the word public. The keyword public is required to allow access to the structure's members. In this case the structure has three members (Name, Address, and Age). We will discuss more in depth about public and other access modifiers later in the book.

We know how to declare a variable of the data type int. To declare a Person variable we do the same thing. The following code is a side by side example of declaring an int named **i** and a Person variable named **p**:

```
int i;
Person p;
```

Setting the int i to a value is easy as it only needs one assignment, as seen in the following code:

```
i = 100;
```

The Person p variable can be assigned three values for name, address and age. We need to assign these one at a time. To assign values to the field members of the Person p object we can put a dot and then the field name which is seen in the following code:

```
p.Name = "John Doe";
```

Let's create a `Person` object as a variable called `personOne` inside our **Main** method and assign some values to its fields. The following code created the `personOne` variable and set the `Name`, `Address`, and `Age` fields with values:

```
static void Main(string[] args)
{
    Person personOne;

    personOne.Name = "John Doe";
    personOne.Address = "123 Tech Street, WA";
    personOne.Age = 23;
}
```

To access the field values we need to follow the same two-part naming rule for the object and field. We will use the structure variable name followed by a dot and then the field name. The three field members of our `Person` structure are using three basic data types.

Let's print the assigned values on the console by typing the following code, after the previous example, inside the **Main** method. The following code adds the last four lines to the **Main** method to display the values of the field members of `personOne` and pauses right before the end of the program with a `Console.ReadKey()` method.

```
static void Main(string[] args)
{
    Person personOne;

    personOne.Name = "John Doe";
    personOne.Address = "123 Tech Street, WA";
    personOne.Age = 23;

    Console.WriteLine("Name: {0}", personOne.Name);
    Console.WriteLine("Address: {0}", personOne.Address);
    Console.WriteLine("Age: {0}", personOne.Age);
    Console.ReadKey();
}
```

Build (F6 for VS Professional or F7 for VS Express) the project and if there are no errors then run (F5) the program. The output of the program should look like the one shown in **Figure 3.1**.

```
Name: John Doe
Address: 123 Tech Street, WA
Phone Number: 555-555
```

Figure 3.1 PersonRecord

The `struct` data type is a user-defined data type and is also known as a custom or complex data type. In a `struct` we are not limited to using `string` or `int` for its members. We are free to choose any data type inside the structure including custom data types. A few examples of valid `struct`s are seen in the following code:

```
struct Employee
{
    public System.String Name; // Same as string
    public System.Int32 EmployeeID; // Same as int
    public DateTime HireDate;
}
struct Company
{
    public string CompanyName;
    public Employee CEO; // Custom data type Employee
    public DateTime CreationDate;
    public bool IsPublic;
    public int NumberOfEmployees;
}
```

Lab 3.1: Structures

Skill Check 1: Create a Console Application and call it **Library**. Define a `struct` called **Book** with members: ID (`int`), Title (`string`), ISBN (`string`) and ReleaseDate (`DateTime`). Declare two variables of type `Book` and call them `book1` and `book2`. Assign the following values to the variables and display the information for the books.

Member	Type	book1 (Values)	book2 (Values)
ID	int	1	2
Title	string	C# Series 1	C# Series 2
ISBN	string	111	222
ReleaseDate	DateTime	DateTime.Now	DateTime.Now

Figure 3.2 This is the data for our Console Application.

`DateTime.Now` will assign the current time for the book's release date.

```
book1.ReleaseDate = DateTime.Now;
```

Once done, the output should look like the one shown in **Figure 3.3**.

```
ID: 1 Title: C# Series 1 ISBN: 111 Release Date 10/14/2012
5:39:58 PM
ID: 2 Title: C# Series 2 ISBN: 222 Release Date 10/14/2012
5:39:58 PM
```

Figure 3.3 Library Books.

Answer Code: The C# answer code for this lab is located in the downloadable files inside the Projects folder within the BeginningCS2012CompanionFiles.zip file.

Points to Ponder - Structures

1. Namespace lets us define the scope of a `class`, `struct,` etc.
2. Types defined in the same namespace can be used without specifying the full name.
3. The `using <NAMESPACE>;` directive increases the current file's scope. We can access the types and classes defined inside that namespace without providing the fully qualified names of the types.
4. The structures are used to group fields together as one unit.
5. Structures are value types like `int` and `double`. We will cover what value types means later in this book.

3.2 Enumerations

Pretend I am writing software for a paint company where each paint color has a numeric code. If I want I can store color codes in an integer data type. If I ask you what numbers can an integer variable store, you will say any number between −2147483648 and 2147483647. This new company only supports four colors: 1 (Red), 2 (Blue), 3 (Green), 4 (Yellow). If I use an integer variable somebody can accidently use 5, 10, or 30000 as a color code. These unused values can mess up the company system with orders that cannot be filled. What I need is an integer data type to store only a limited set of values and the user can choose from these limited values when assigning a color to a variable.

The enumeration (`enum`) type supports this kind of behavior where we can create an integer-like data type with a limited set of allowed values. The `enum` type also provides user friendly labels for the values like Red, Blue, Green, or Yellow.

Just like structures, the `enum` type should also be defined within a namespace. We can define an `enum` of color codes with the following code:

```
namespace Color_Codes
{
  enum ColorCode
  {
    Red = 1,
    Blue = 2,
    Green = 3,
    Yellow = 4
  }
```

Create a Console Application and call it **Color Codes**. Define an `enum` type called `ColorCode`, as shown in the previous code, before the class definition. Here `Red` has a value of `1`, `Blue 2`,, and so on.

To declare a variable of type `ColorCode` we can follow the same approach as any other variable declaration. Let's declare a variable of type `ColorCode` within the **Main** method and assign color code Green (3) to the variable.

```
static void Main(string[] args)
{
    ColorCode myColor = ColorCode.Green;
}
```

Now nobody has to memorize the codes because they can assign color codes with user friendly labels like Red, Green, Blue, and Yellow.

To print the value of the variable myColor. Use the following code:

```
static void Main(string[] args)
{
    ColorCode myColor = ColorCode.Green;
    Console.WriteLine("Selected Color: {0}", myColor);
}
```

Remember to add a `Console.ReadKey` statement at the end and run the program.

```
Selected Color: Green
```

Figure 3.4 Color Codes.

DEFAULT AND STARTING VALUES

In the previous example we have explicitly assigned values Red, Blue, Green and Yellow to be 1, 2, 3 and 4 respectively. If we had not provided any values but just the labels like Red, Blue, Green, and Yellow, we would have gotten the values 0, 1, 2, and 3, for Red, Blue, Green and Yellow.

```
namespace Color_Codes
{
  enum ColorCode
  {
    Red,
    Blue,
    Green,
    Yellow
  }
```

If we would have provided a value like `100` for `Red`, the code for `Blue` would have been `101`, and `102` for `Green`, and `103` for `Yellow`.

```
namespace Color_Codes
{
  enum ColorCode
  {
    Red = 100,
    Blue,
    Green,
    Yellow
  }
```

Now let's see what the values would be for the colors for the `enum` defined in this code.

```
namespace Color_Codes
{
  enum ColorCode
  {
    Red,
    Blue,
    Green = 300,
    Yellow
  }
```

Since the default `enum` value starts with zero, `Red` will have `0` and then `Blue` will have `1`. `Green` is explicitly defined to be `300,` so `Yellow` will be `301,` which is one more than its predecessor's value.

UNDERLYING TYPES

When we define an enumeration type, by default it becomes an integer type `enum`. Our ColorCode `enum` could also have been written the following way.

```
namespace Color_Codes
{
  enum ColorCode : int
  {
    Red = 1,
    Blue = 2,
    Green = 3,
    Yellow = 4
  }
```

Here we have explicitly mentioned the underlying data type for the `enum` is an `int`. We can also define different underlying types for our `enum`.

Since our `ColorCode enum` contains only 4 values, defining it with the underlying `int` type, which holds up to 2.1 billion, is a waste of our resources. We will never have more than 100 colors. A `byte` can hold 255 combinations. We should define our `ColorCode` with `byte` as the underlying type, as seen in this code:

```
namespace Color_Codes
{
  enum ColorCode : byte
  {
    Red = 1,
    Blue = 2,
    Green = 3,
    Yellow = 4
  }
```

Enumeration lists support the following underlying types.

- `byte`
- `sbyte`
- `short`
- `ushort`
- `int`
- `uint`
- `long`
- `ulong`

Notice the list of supporting data types belongs to the integer family. We cannot create an `enum` type of `double`, `string` or any other non-integer data type.

Enum Flags

Often we want to store more than one choice in an enum. For example, I am fine with taking a vacation on Tuesday or Thursday. Using what we have learned so far we can create two variables, one for choice 1 and one for choice 2, then assign two choices to these two variables.

To explain this let's create a Console Application and call it **VacationChoices**. Define an `enum` called `Days`, as shown in the following code:

```
enum Days : byte
{
  Sunday,
  Monday,
  Tuesday,
  Wednesday,
  Thursday,
  Friday,
  Saturday
}
```

In our code example, `Sunday` will have value `0`, `Monday 1`, and so on. Now create two variables of type `Days` inside the **Main** method and assign these choices. After assigning the values, display the choices on the console window.

```
static void Main(string[] args)
{
  Days choice1 = Days.Tuesday;
  Days choice2 = Days.Thursday;

  Console.WriteLine("{0}, {1}", choice1, choice2);

  Console.ReadKey();
}
```

The output of the program should look like the one shown in **Figure 3.5**.

```
Tuesday, Thursday
```

Figure 3.5 Vacation Choices.

There is a much better way to store these multiple choices by defining a special type of `enum`. Here we can have OR and AND choices built-in.

Create a Console Application and call it **EnumFlags**. Define the `Days enum, as seen in` the following code:

```
[Flags]
enum Days
{
  Sunday = 1,
  Monday = 2,
  Tuesday = 4,
  Wednesday = 8,
  Thursday = 16,
  Friday = 32,
  Saturday = 64
}
```

Here we have defined an `enum` with the attribute `Flags` which allows you to use bitwise operators like AND (&) and OR (`|`). Notice that each member of the `enum` is double that of the previous value.

To see how this works declare a variable called **choice** to capture the choices and then display the value(s) of the `choices` variable on the console window.

```
Days choices = Days.Tuesday | Days.Thursday;
Console.WriteLine(choices);
```

Here we declared only one variable for our choices and separated them with `|`, which is the OR operator. The output of the previous program will be the same, as shown in **Figure 3.5**. Choices are automatically separated by a comma.

Now if we want to specify 2 or more choices we don't have to declare 2 or more variables. It takes just one variable to hold our choices, as shown in the following code sample:

```
static void Main(string[] args)
{
  Days choices = Days.Tuesday | Days.Thursday |
  Days.Sunday; Console.ReadKey();
}
```

This kind of OR operation is also known as bitwise OR.

Lab 3.2: Enumerations

Skill Check 1: Create a Console Application and call it **Working Days**. Define an `enum` called `Weekdays` containing all weekdays from Monday to Friday. Make sure Monday has a value of 1 and Friday has a value of 5. Declare five variables, one for each weekday and display the variables, as shown in **Figure 3.6**.

```
Monday
Tuesday
Wednesday
Thursday
Friday
```

Figure 3.6 Working Days.

Skill Check 2: Create a Console Application and call it **CoffeeShop**. Define an `enum Coffee` to list coffee choices.

- Latte
- Mocha
- CaramelLatte
- VanillaLatte
- WhiteMocha.

Define the `enum` with the `Flags` attribute so that you can store multiple choices in one variable. Use one variable to store and display the coffee choices, as shown in **Figure 3.7**.

```
Choices: Latte, VanillaLatte, WhiteMocha
```

Figure 3.7 CoffeeShop.

Skill Check 3: Create a Console Application and call it **House**. Define an `enum` called `Color` to store `Red`, `Blue`, `Green`, `Pink` and `Yellow`. Make sure `Color` has an underlying type of `byte`. Define a structure called `Room` with the following fields:

`Name` (as a `string` type)
`RoomColor` (as a `Color` type)
`Windows` (as a `byte` type)
`Doors` (as a `byte` type)

Create three Room variables called `room1`, `room2`, and `room3` that contain the following fields and values:

	Type	room1	room2	room3
Name	`string`	Alpha	Beta	Gamma
RoomColor	`Color`	Red	Green	Yellow
Windows	`byte`	5	3	0
Doors	`byte`	2	2	1

Figure 3.8 Room variables to be created.

Display the House information, as shown in **Figure 3.9**.

```
Alpha room is Red with 5 windows and 2 doors
Beta room is Green with 3 windows and 2 doors
Gamma room is Yellow with 0 windows and 1 doors
```

Figure 3.9 House Information.

Answer Code: The C# answer code for this lab is located in the downloadable files inside the Projects folder within the BeginningCS2012CompanionFiles.zip file.

Points to Ponder - Enumerations

1. The enumeration type contains lists of named values.
2. An `enum` list is also known as a list of named constant values.
3. The default type of an `enum` list is `int` (`System.Int32`).
4. The default starting value of the first named constant is 0 and the value of the next named constant is 1,, and so on.
5. Default values of named constants in an `enum` can be overridden with the values of our choosing.
6. The underlying type of an `enum` can only be integer-like data types like such as `byte`, `int`, and `long`, etc.
7. Bitwise operations can be performed on an `enum` when you define the `enum` with the [Flags] attribute and each value is double the previous value.
8. The field member of a struct can be of any data type, including another struct

Review Quiz - Chapter Three

1.) Which access modifier is valid for fields of a struct?

O a) anywhere
O b) integer
O c) unique
O d) public

2.) Structures can only have system-defined data types as fields.

O a) TRUE
O b) FALSE

3.) The default starting value of an enum member is?

O a) -1
O b) 0
O c) 1
O d) 100

4.) Which underlying type is invalid for an enum?

O a) int
O b) long
O c) string
O d) byte

5.) Which attribute defines an enum to have an OR (multiple) behavior?

O a) [OR]
O b) [Multiple]
O c) [Flag]
O d) [AllowMultiple]

6.) Only an int data type is allowed for an enum's underlying type.

O a) TRUE
O b) FALSE

7.) Can structs have a user-defined type like another struct as a field variable?

O a) TRUE
O b) FALSE

ANSWER KEY

1.) Anywhere, integer, and unique are not access modifiers, making options (a), (b) and (c) invalid. The public keyword is a valid access modifier which allows access to field values defined in a struct. The correct answer is (d).

2.) A structure can have system-defined and user-defined types as field types making option (b) as the answer.

3.) When an enum is defined with no values assigned to the enum members, a value of 0 is assigned to the first member, making option (b) correct.

4.) An enum can only have integer-like data types as the underlying type. Option (c) is string and not a number, making it the correct answer.

5.) Attributes names [OR], [Multiple] and [AllowMultiple] are not valid. The [Flag] attribute enhances an enum to have the OR feature, making option (c) correct.

6.) An enum's underlying type can be of byte, long or any integer-like data type. So an int is not the only type, making (b) correct.

7.) A struct is a container to hold variables of various types as fields. Fields are not limited to system types like int or string, but to any type including user-defined types like structs and enums. Option (a) is correct, as it makes the statement true.

[NOTES]

Chapter 4 Data Type Casting and Parsing

When two people who speak different languages would like to talk to each other they need the help of a translator. Translators convert one language into another. A translator can be a human or a computer program. Similarly, computer programs can translate or convert one data type into another data type.

READER NOTE: *Before doing the steps in this section you need to have the following folder structure on your hard drive C:\Joes2Pros\C# 2012\Chapter 4. Within the Chapter 4 folder should be three more folders called Lab 4.1, Lab 4.2, and Lab 4.3. In order to follow along with the examples, you will need to have some version of Visual Studio 2012 installed.*

4.1 Casting Data Types

Implicit Casting

If you have a king size bed and put a queen size sheet on it, you will be left with space on the bed that is not covered. Similarly, if you have a byte type variable with a value of 200, and would like to store that number in an int you will be left with space in the int going to waste, but it is still possible.

In the next example an integer variable (called **integerValue**) is assigned as a byte type variable.

```
static void Main(string[] args)
{
    byte byteValue = 200;
    int integerValue = byteValue;
}
```

This conversion is called implicit casting. The int can store values from 0 to 255, but the integer type can store values from -2,147,483,648 to 2,147,483,647. Implicit casting is allowed at compile time because the maximum and minimum value of a byte can be easily stored as an int.

If we want to cast an int to a long, it can be done without any issues, as seen in this example:

```
int integerValue = 350000;
long longValue = integerValue;
```

Integer values can be stored in double or float data types without any errors.

```
int integerValue = 350000;
float floatValue = integerValue;

float floatValue = 10F;
double doubleValue = floatValue;
```

Implicit casting is always allowed when converting from a data type that is smaller than the converting “into” data type.

EXPLICIT CASTING

When working with external teams or partners we may be required to convert an integer data type to a `byte` (i.e. larger data type to smaller data type). We will get an error if we try to do that, as shown in **Figure 4.1**.

```
int integerValue = 200;
byte byteValue = integerValue;
```

(local variable) int integerValue

Error:
Cannot implicitly convert type 'int' to 'byte'. An explicit conversion exists (are you missing a cast?)

Figure 4.1 Implicit Casting Error.

Let say we are working on a project and we have gotten an agreement from an external team that data values will never be greater than 255 and there will be no negative numbers. So it is safe to do this conversion but the compiler is not allowing us to. In this case we can explicitly cast an `int` to a `byte`. Explicit casting is shown in the following code:

```
static void Main(string[] args)
{
    int integerValue = 200;
    byte byteValue = (byte)integerValue;
}
```

In the previous example the value 200 is stored in the `integerValue` variable and can be successfully stored inside the `byteValue` variable of `byte.` This is because 200 is less than 255 (the maximum of a `byte`). Here we have to tell the compiler that we know what we are doing, so please allow it.

When the source number is bigger than the destination number we are required to explicitly cast the variables, as shown in the following code:

```
long longValue = 250000;
int integerValue = (int)longValue;
```

In the previous code we are telling the compiler that the variable `integerValue` can handle the values from the `longValue` variable.

Explicit casting should be used with caution as it can lead to corrupt data or data loss.

```
int integerValue = 256;
byte byteValue = (byte)integerValue;
```

The previous example (where the integer variable contains a value of 256) is explicitly cast to a `byte` variable. So, can a byte variable store 256? The answer is no. It can only store values from 0 to 255. Will we see a runtime error, or just 255 or some other number?

The value of the `byte` variable will become 0 because it resets itself to the next number in a cyclic way. The following figure shows why the number 258 (when casted to a `byte`) becomes 2.

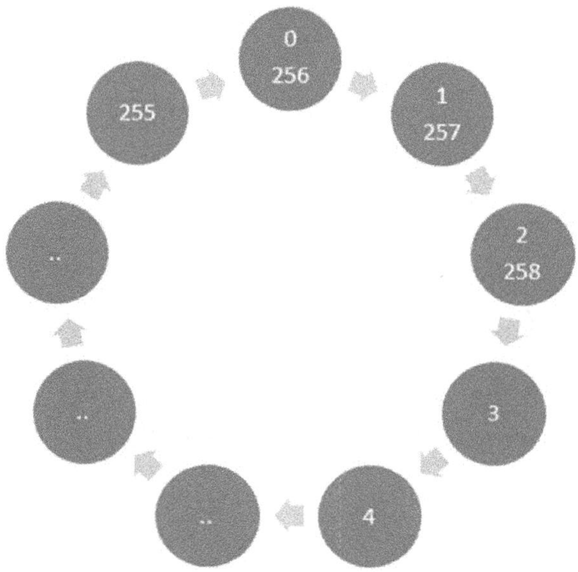

Figure 4.2 Byte Casting.

The same type of cyclic logic can be applied to a data type that supports both negative and positive numbers. For example, the `short` data type supports a range of numbers from −32768 to 32767. If we try to cast one value too high for the short with an `int` containing 32768 the value of the `short` variable will become −32768. If we subtract 1 from −32768 it will become 32767.

ENUMERATION CASTING

Enumeration types can be cast like any other variable. We know enumeration lists are nothing but integer or integer-like data types, such as `byte`, `short`, etc. We can cast any integer to `enum`.

Let's say we have an enum called ColorCode, as seen in the following example:

```
namespace EnumCast
{
  enum ColorCode : int
  {
    Red = 1,
    Blue = 2,
    Green = 3,
    Yellow = 4
  }
```

Our partner system only deals in integer color codes so we want to convert this integer color code to a more readable ColorCode enum.

```
static void Main(string[] args)
{
  int integerCode = 3;
  ColorCode myColor = (ColorCode)integerCode;
```

Here the value of the myColor variable will become Green since 3 is the value for Green.

If we want to store an enum value from an integer we can cast it using the following code:

```
ColorCode myColor = ColorCode.Red;
int integerColorCode = (int)myColor;
```

In the previous code, the enum variable myColor has to be explicitly cast to an integer type. Implicit casting will not work as it would generate a compile time error data type.

Boxing and Unboxing

We all know that water in a bottle can be stored in a big bucket, and water in a bucket can be stored in a bath tub, and water from any container can be dumped into an ocean. An ocean is considered the biggest container. The ocean could be considered the biggest water container.

Every data type in C# belongs to a parent object called `System.Object` which is also known as `object`. We can assign any value of any type to the `object` type, as shown in the following example:

```
static void Main(string[] args)
{
  object objInt = 30;
  object objDouble = 30.0;
  object objString = "Storing String in Object";
```

This type of conversion where we assign or store a value of any specific data type to an object type is known as boxing.

To consume the data stored in an `object` data type we need to convert an `object` type to the specific data type. We can do this conversion by casting the `object` type to a specific type, as shown in the following example:

```
int integerValue = (int)objInt;
double doubleValue = (double)objDouble;
string stringValue = (string)objString;
```

As mentioned before, converting a specific data type to an `object` type is called boxing. Casting an `object` type to a specific data type is called unboxing.

```
object objInt = 30; // Boxing
int intergerValue = (int)objInt; // Unboxing
```

Boxing and unboxing are costly operations and can slow the application. Boxing and unboxing should be avoided as much as possible.

When a specific data type is assigned to an `object` type it should use the exact same data type to cast it back to that original data type or else an error will occur while executing the program.

```
object objInteger = 100;
long longValue = (long)objInteger;
//int integerValue = (int)objInteger;

object objString = "100";
int integerValue = (int)objString;
//string stringValue = (string)objString;
```

The previous code samples will compile fine but will throw an error at runtime. The first example casts an integer value to `long`, and the second example casts numbers stored as a `string` to an `int`.

CASTING EXAMPLE

Let's create a Console Application and call it **Casting**.

Add the following lines of code inside the **Main** method:

```
static void Main(string[] args)
{
  byte byteValue1 = 200;
  int integerValue1 = byteValue1;

  Console.Write("Byte Value1: {0}", byteValue1);
  Console.WriteLine(" IntegerValue1: {0}", integerValue1);
  Console.ReadKey();
}
```

Here the code compiles and executes with the output shown in **Figure 4.3**.

```
Byte Value1: 200 IntegerValue1: 200
```

Figure 4.3 Casting Example 1.

Now add the following lines right above the `Console.ReadKey();` statement.

```
int integerValue2 = 250;
byte byteValue2 = integerValue2;
```

The previous example creates an error in Visual Studio since we were trying to convert the larger data type of integer to the smaller data type of `byte`. To fix the code we need to explicitly cast the `integerValue2` variable as `byte`.

```
int integerValue2 = 250;
byte byteValue2 = (byte)integerValue2;
```

Using `byte` casts the integer value to `byte` and the code compiles just fine. Add the following statements after these two previous statements to verify the values for both variables.

```
static void Main(string[] args)
{
  byte byteValue1 = 200;
  int integerValue1 = byteValue1;

  Console.Write("Byte Value1: {0}", byteValue1);
  Console.WriteLine(" IntegerValue1: {0}", integerValue1);

  int integerValue2 = 250;
  byte byteValue2 = (byte)integerValue2;

  Console.WriteLine();
  Console.Write("Byte Value2: {0}", byteValue2);
  Console.WriteLine(" IntegerValue2: {0}", integerValue2);

  Console.ReadKey();
}
```

Execute the program and the output should look like **Figure 4.4**.

```
Byte Value1: 200 IntegerValue1: 200

Byte Value2: 250 IntegerValue2: 250
```

Figure 4.4 Casting Example 2.

Define an `enum` named `ShirtSize` inside the namespace but outside the `Program` class.

```
namespace EnumCast
{
  enum ShirtSize
  {
    Small = 1,
    Medium = 2,
    Large = 3,
    ExtraLarge = 4,
    ExtraExtraLarge = 5,
  }
}
```

Create a variable of this `enum` type before the `Console.ReadKey()` statement and set the value to `Medium`. Create an integer variable and cast the `enum` variable to integer, as shown in the following example:

```
ShirtSize size = ShirtSize.Medium;
int integerSize = (int)size;
```

Add the following statements to display the output, as shown in **Figure 4.5**.

```
static void Main(string[] args)
{
  byte byteValue1 = 200;
  int integerValue1 = byteValue1;

  Console.Write("Byte Value1: {0}", byteValue1);
  Console.WriteLine(" IntegerValue1: {0}", integerValue1);

  int integerValue2 = 250;
  byte byteValue2 = (byte)integerValue2;

  Console.WriteLine();
  Console.Write("Byte Value2: {0}", byteValue2);
  Console.WriteLine(" IntegerValue2: {0}", integerValue2);

  ShirtSize size = ShirtSize.Medium;
  int integerSize = (int)size;

  Console.WriteLine();
  Console.Write("Integer Size: {0}", integerSize);
  Console.WriteLine(" Enum Size: {0}", size);

  Console.ReadKey();
}
```

```
Byte Value1: 200 IntegerValue1: 200

Byte Value2: 250 IntegerValue2: 250

Integer Size: 2 Enum Size: Medium
```

Figure 4.5 Casting Example 3.

Now let's try some boxing and unboxing. Add the following code to that in **Figure 4.5** just before the `ReadKey();`. Set an integer to be an `object` type and then cast it back to be an integer, as shown in the following example:

```
object objInteger = 100;
int integerValue = (int)objInteger;

Console.WriteLine();
Console.WriteLine("Casted Integer: {0}", integerValue);

Console.ReadKey();
```

Build and execute the program. **Figure 4.6** shows the output of the program on the console.

```
static void Main(string[] args)
{
  byte byteValue1 = 200;
  int integerValue1 = byteValue1;

  Console.Write("Byte Value1: {0}", byteValue1);
  Console.WriteLine(" IntegerValue1: {0}", integerValue1);

  int integerValue2 = 250;
  byte byteValue2 = (byte)integerValue2;

  Console.WriteLine();
  Console.Write("Byte Value2: {0}", byteValue2);
  Console.WriteLine(" IntegerValue2: {0}", integerValue2);

  ShirtSize size = ShirtSize.Medium;
  int integerSize = (int)size;

  Console.WriteLine();
  Console.Write("Integer Size: {0}", integerSize);
  Console.WriteLine(" Enum Size: {0}", size);

  object objInteger = 100;
  int integerValue = (int)objInteger;

  Console.WriteLine();
  Console.WriteLine("Casted Integer: {0}", integerValue);

  Console.ReadKey();
  }
```

```
Byte Value1: 200 IntegerValue1: 200

Byte Value2: 250 IntegerValue2: 250

Integer Size: 2 Enum Size: Medium

Casted Integer: 100
```

Figure 4.6 Casting Example 4.

Boxing and unboxing are not limited to simple data types like `int`, or `long`, `string`. they can also be used for user-defined data types as well.

Create a `struct` named `Person`, outside the `Program` class along with the `enum`, as seen in the following code sample:

```
namespace EnumCast
{
  enum ShirtSize
  {
    Small = 1,
    Medium = 2,
    Large = 3,
    ExtraLarge = 4,
    ExtraExtraLarge = 5,
  }
  struct Person
  {
    public string Name;
    public string Address;
     public byte Age;
}
  class Program
  {
```

Now create an instance of the `Person` type and assign values to the fields, as shown in the following code sample:

```
Person person;
person.Name = "John Doe";
person.Address = "123 Tech St, WA";
person.Age = 23;
```

Now assign the `person` variable to an `object` type variable and then cast it back to a `newPerson` variable.

```
object objPerson = person;
Person newPerson = (Person)objPerson;
```

The previous code will compile and execute. To verify the field values are copied let's display the field values of the `newPerson` variable on the console, as shown in **Figure 4.7**.

```
byte byteValue1 = 200;
int integerValue1 = byteValue1;

Console.Write("Byte Value1: {0}", byteValue1);
Console.WriteLine(" IntegerValue1: {0}", integerValue1);

int integerValue2 = 250;
byte byteValue2 = (byte)integerValue2;

Console.WriteLine();
Console.WriteLine(" IntegerValue2: {0}", integerValue2);

ShirtSize size = ShirtSize.Medium;
int integerSize = (int)size;

Console.WriteLine();
Console.Write("Integer Size: {0}", integerSize);
Console.WriteLine(" Enum Size: {0}", size);

object objInteger = 100;
int integerValue = (int)objInteger;

Console.WriteLine();
Console.WriteLine("Casted Integer: {0}", integerValue);

Person person;
person.Name = "John Doe";
person.Address = "123 Tech St, WA";
person.Age = 23;

object objPerson = person;
Person newPerson = (Person)objPerson;

Console.WriteLine();
Console.WriteLine("{0} {1} {2}", newPerson.Name,
newPerson.Address, newPerson.Age);

Console.ReadKey();
```

```
Byte Value1: 200 IntegerValue1: 200
Byte Value2: 250 IntegerValue2: 250
Integer Size: 2 Enum Size: Medium
Casted Integer: 100
John Doe 123 Tech St, WA 23
```

Figure 4.7 Casting Example 5.

Lab 4.1: Casting Data Types

Skill Check 1: Create a Console Application and call it **Numbers**. Declare and initialize three `int` variables called **integer1**, **integer2**, and **integer3**. Set them equal to the values 100, 200 and 257. Cast these `int` variables to `byte` variables called **byte1**, **byte2**, and **byte3**. Display the `int` and `byte` value of these variables on the console, as shown in **Figure 4.8**.

```
Integer Value:100 Byte Value: 100
Integer Value:200 Byte Value: 200
Integer Value:257 Byte Value: 1
```

Figure 4.8 Numbers.

Skill Check 2: Create a Console Application named **EnumCasting**. Define an `enum` called Status as show in this code:

```
enum Status
{
    Unknown = 0,
    Active = 1,
    Inactive = 2
}
```

Declare two variables of `Status` type `enum` called **statusUnknown** and **statusActive**. Assign Active and Unknown values, respectively, to the variables. Display the `enum` name and integer value of these variables on the console, as shown in **Figure 4.9**.

```
Unknown:0
Active:1
```

Figure 4.9 Enum Casting.

Skill Check 3: Create a Console Application called **Boxing**. Declare a variable of `object` type called `obj`. Assign the current date and time to the variable using `DateTime.Now`. Cast this `object` variable to the `DateTime` data type variable and display the `DateTime` variable on the console, as shown in **Figure 4.10**.

```
10/20/2012 9:35:47 AM
```

Figure 4.10 Boxing.

Answer Code: The C# answer code for this lab is located in the downloadable files inside the Projects folder within the BeginningCS2012CompanionFiles.zip file.

Points to Ponder - Casting Data Types

1. When a value of a smaller data type, like a `byte` , is assigned to a larger data type like an `int`, explicit casting is not required. Smaller data types can be assigned to larger data types. This is known as implicit casting.
2. Explicit casting is required when converting an `object` variable to any specific data type.
3. Assigning a specific data type to an `object` type is called boxing. Casting an `object` type to a specific data type is called unboxing.
4. `Enum` types can be explicitly cast to their underlying numeric data type.
5. Explicitly casting a larger numeric data type to a smaller data type can cause data loss, such as assigning 256 to a `byte` (the value will become 0).
6. Casting is not limited to simple data types.

4.2 Data Type Parsing

So far we know we can store water in different sized water containers. We can also store different sized number in different data types. For example, the integer value can be stored in integer-like data types such as `long` and `byte`. But what is a string is stored a “5” and we want to turn that into an integer 5 (without the quotes). Sometimes an integer value is stored in a `string` data type. We know we cannot cast a `string` data type to an integer data type. The following code will not compile and will throw an error.

```
static void Main(string[] args)
{
    string stringAge = "23";
    int integerAge = (int)stringAge;
}
```

There are scenarios where values that are stored in string data types are required to be converted to other data types. For example, we want to find out how many years we have until retirement from our current age. In the previous code, age is stored in a `string` data type and there is no way to do math on `string` data types. To do addition or subtraction, this string should be converted into a numeric data type. This type of conversion is called parsing.

Data Parsing

As mentioned before, we need to convert the `stringAge` variable’s number to an integer data type. We can convert the integer value stored in the string to the integer type by parsing, which is shown as follows in the following code:

```
string stringAge = "23";
int integerAge = int.Parse(stringAge);
```

In the previous example, we are using the `Parse` method of `int` (also known as `Int32`) to do the conversion. If we try to parse a non-integer value stored in a `string` variable to an integer value we will get a runtime error. The following code will throw an error at runtime:

```
string stringAge = “Twenty Three";
int integerAge = int.Parse(stringAge);
```

A lot of data types provide the `Parse` method. A few examples are shown here:

```
Double.Parse(..);
DateTime.Parse(..);
Decimal.Parse(..);
Boolean.Parse(..);
```

A `string` variable containing a `DateTime` value can be parsed to a `DateTime` data type using the `Parse` method of `DateTime, as shown` in the following code:

```
string stringDate = "01-01-2013";
DateTime dateTime = DateTime.Parse(stringDate);
```

Parsing is also used when we get input from a user using `Console.ReadLine` and would like to store the values in proper data types other than in `string` data types. The `ReadLine()` method of `Console` returns a string.

Let's create a Console Application and call it **DataParsing**. Here we will get input from the user starting with their name.

```
Console.Write("Please enter your name: ");
string name = Console.ReadLine();
```

No conversion is required since `name` is a string and it will remain a string. Now let's ask their age, which is shown as in this code:

```
Console.Write("Please enter your age: ");
string stringAge = Console.ReadLine();
```

We need to convert the `stringAge` variable to a `byte` and then we can do any math calculation for the age.

```
Byte byteAge = Byte.Parse(stringAge);
```

The previous code is parsing the age (integer) that is stored as a string to be a specific `byte` value. Finally, we want to ask the user if they are married. Since the answer can be yes (true) or no (false) we can store the answer as a `bool` type. Because `ReadLine` only returns a string we need to parse the string to the `bool` type as with the following code:

```
Console.Write("Are you married (True/False): ");
bool married = Boolean.Parse(Console.ReadLine());
```

Here we directly parsed the value returned from `ReadLine` to a `bool` data type. It is no different than our previous approach of storing a string value from `ReadLine` to a string variable and then converting the variable to a specific type.

Finally, add the following statements to display the output on the console, as shown in **Figure 4.11**.

```
Console.Write("Please enter your name: ");
string name = Console.ReadLine();

Console.Write("Please enter your age: ");
string stringAge = Console.ReadLine();
Byte byteAge = Byte.Parse(stringAge);

Console.Write("Are you married (True/False): ");
bool married = Boolean.Parse(Console.ReadLine());

Console.WriteLine();
Console.WriteLine("{0} {1} {2}", name, byteAge, married);

Console.ReadKey();
```

```
Please enter your name: John
Please enter your age: 25
Are you married (True/False): false

John 25 False
```

Figure 4.11 Parsing Data.

STRUCT PARSING

Let's create another Console Application called **Sales**. Here we will be asking the user to input product order details and we will be storing them in a user-defined data type.

Start by creating a `struct` called `Order` inside the namespace but outside the `Program` class.

```
struct Order
{
    public string CustomerName;
    public string ProductName;
    public double RetailPrice;
    public int Quantity;
}
```

Our goal is to ask the user for input from the console for customer name, product name, retail price, and quantity, then calculate the total order price and display it on the console.

Start by creating an `object` of type `Order` and then take input from the console using the `ReadLine` method. `CustomerName` and `ProductName` are `string` types and `ReadLine` returns a string, so no parsing is required. The code sample is shown here:

```
Order custOrder;

Console.Write("Customer Name: ");
custOrder.CustomerName = Console.ReadLine();
Console.Write("Product Name: ");
custOrder.ProductName = Console.ReadLine();
```

`RetailPrice` and `Quantity` are `double` and `int` data types, so we need to parse them before assigning them to the fields of `custOrder`, as shown in the following code:

```
Console.Write("Retail Price: ");
custOrder.RetailPrice = double.Parse(Console.ReadLine());
Console.Write("Quantity: ");
custOrder.Quantity = int.Parse(Console.ReadLine());
```

Create a variable of type `double` to store the total order price and then use the variable to display the total on the console.

```
double orderTotal = custOrder.RetailPrice *
    custOrder.Quantity;

Console.WriteLine();
Console.WriteLine("Total: {0}", orderTotal);

Console.ReadKey();
```

The output is shown in **Figure 4.12**.

```
Order custOrder;

Console.Write("Customer Name: ");
custOrder.CustomerName = Console.ReadLine();

Console.Write("Product Name: ");
custOrder.ProductName = Console.ReadLine();
```

```
Console.Write("Retail Price: ");
custOrder.RetailPrice = double.Parse(Console.ReadLine());

Console.Write("Quantity: ");
custOrder.Quantity = int.Parse(Console.ReadLine());

double orderTotal = custOrder.RetailPrice
    *custOrder.Quantity;
Console.WriteLine();
Console.WriteLine("Total: {0}", orderTotal);

Console.ReadKey();
```

```
Customer Name: John Doe
Product Name: Headphone
Retail Price: 49.99
Quantity: 4

Total: 199.96
```

Figure 4.12 Sales Order.

ENUM PARSING

As discussed in the previous section we know we can change `enum` types to their underlying types by casting. We can see this code example for the `Status enum` as in the following code:

```
namespace EnumStatus
{
  enum Status
  {
      Unknown = 0,
      Active = 1,
      Inactive = 2
  }
```

`Active` is `1`, so we can get that out by casting it as an `int`. The example of this code is shown in the **Main** method:

```
Status activeStatus = Status.Active;
int intStatus = (int)activeStatus;
```

```
Console.WriteLine(intStatus);
Console.ReadKey();
```

We can also cast an integer value to an `enum` which is shown in the following code:

```
Status inactiveStatus = (Status)2;

Console.WriteLine(inactiveStatus);
Console.ReadKey();
```

Now the question is how can we convert the string label (like Active) stored in the `string` variable to the type `Status`? Remember how we parsed the `string` "100" to an `int` of 100? The `Parse` method of `int` did this for us. The `Parse` method is also available for the `enum` class. There could be many enumerations in your project of all different types and that's the reason the `Parse` method of `enum` takes two arguments, one for type `enum` (which is `Status`) and another for the `string` value (which is `"Active"`) that needs to be parsed.

```
object objStatus = Enum.Parse(typeof(Status), "Active");
```

The `Parse` method can be used for any type of `enum`. It returns an `object` type. To get the specific `enum` type (like `Status`) we need to cast it to the `Status` type.

```
Status status = (Status)objStatus;
```

We can replace these two statements with the following single statement:

```
Status status = (Status)Enum.Parse(typeof(Status),
    "Active");
```

Lab 4.2: Data Type Parsing

Skill Check 1: Create a Console Application and call it **AddTwoIntegers**. Ask the user to input two numbers one after the other and then display the sum on the console, as shown in **Figure 4.13**. Make sure to store the sum in a `long` (`Int64`) type variable before displaying the total on the console.

```
Please enter the first number: 45
Please enter the second number: 55

Sum of 45 and 55 is 100
```

Figure 4.13 AddTwoIntegers.

Skill Check 2: Create a Console Application and call it **CSharp**. Declare `int` and `bool` data types to store the values of the questions shown in **Figure 4.14**. You will be required to `Parse` the `string` values to `int` and `bool` types respectively.

```
In which year C# 4.0 was released: 2010
Is C# object oriented (true/false): true

C# 4.0 Release Year: 2010
Is C# object oriented: True
```

Figure 4.14 CSharp.

Skill Check 3: Create a Console Application and call it **VacationDays**. Create an `enum` called "Days" containing all the days of the week from Sunday to Saturday. Ask the user to enter two days as vacation days, one after the other and `Parse` the user input into the `Days enum`. Display the label and value of the selected vacation days, as shown in **Figure 4.15**.

```
Please enter your first choice for vacation: Sunday
Please enter your second choice for vacation: Wednesday

You selected Sunday:0 and Wednesday:3
```

Figure 4.15 VacationDays.

Answer Code: The C# answer code for this lab is located in the downloadable files inside the Projects folder within the BeginningCS2012CompanionFiles.zip file.

Points to Ponder - Data Type Parsing

1. Converting string values to specific data types can be done using the `Parse` method of simple data types.
2. Parsing is not the same as casting, as parsing usually uses the `Parse` method whereas casting is done by prefixing a variable or value with the casted data type using brackets.
3. `enum` parsing requires casting a value returned from the `Parse` method to a specific type of `enum`.
4. `enum` parsing is case-sensitive unless the third parameter `ignoreCase` is passed to the `Parse` method as `true`.
5. Data type conversion can also be done using the `Convert` class, which provides a lot of methods like `ToInt32`, `ToDecimal`, `ToBoolean`, etc.

4.3 Nullable Types

We may come across a question when filling out an application where the answer is N/A (Not Applicable) or if we don't want to answer that question we can leave it blank. In most programming languages when we don't want to assign a value to a variable, or if it is unknown, we call it `null`.

Basic Types

Ideally, the age of a person should be stored as a `byte` type as it is a number. Many users leave their age field empty on their social networks profile page. How will we store a `null` value for an age when the user has not answered the question or left it blank? The `byte` type can only be assigned with numbers. One way to do this can be to store a default value, which nobody can put as an age, like -1. Now when the profile web page sees the age field is empty it will assign -1 to the `age` variable.

There is a much better way to handle this scenario, use a nullable type. The null value of a variable means the value is unknown or no value has been assigned to the variable.

We cannot assign a null value to basic value types, like `int`, `bool`, and `long`, etc. The following code will throw a compiler error:

```
int age = null;
```

We can create a nullable version of these basic types. To declare an integer as nullable we can declare it like this:

```
int? nullableInteger;
```

OR

```
Nullable<int> nullableInteger;
```

The first notation to declare a nullable type is preferable. This variable works just like any other integer variable with an additional `null` support (i.e. `null` value can be assigned to it).

```
nullableInteger = 10;
nullableInteger = null;
```

Let's create a Console Application and call it **WorkingWithNulls** and create two nullable `byte` variables.

```
byte? byteOne;
byte? byteTwo;
```

Assign the `byteOne` variable a value of 30 and the `byteTwo` variable a value of `null`. Display the variable value on the console, as shown in **Figure 4.16**.

```
byteOne = 30;
byteTwo = null;
Console.WriteLine("Byte One: {0}", byteOne);
Console.WriteLine("Byte Two: {0}", byteTwo);
Console.ReadKey();
```

```
Byte One: 30
Byte Two:
```

Figure 4.16 WorkingWithNulls.

In **Figure 4.16** the `null` value is shown as empty. Nullable types provide an extra property to the variable called `HasValue`, which tells us if the value is `null` or if it is a legitimate value. The `HasValue` property is a `bool` type and returns `true/false` depending on whether the variable has any value assigned to it.

Write the following code before the `Console.ReadKey();` statement to show if the `HasValue` property of the `byteOne` and `byteTwo` variables is `true` or `false`, as shown in **Figure 4.17**.

```
Console.WriteLine("Byte One: {0}", byteOne.HasValue);
Console.WriteLine("Byte Two: {0}", byteTwo.HasValue);
```

```
Byte One: 30
Byte Two:
Byte One: True
Byte Two: False
```

Figure 4.17 HasValue.

NULLABLE CASTING

One thing to note here is that we cannot assign a nullable type or an expression involving a nullable type to any non-nullable type. The following code will not compile since the variable `y` can only store integers even though the variable `x` has a possibility of storing a `null` value.

```
int? x = 10;
int y = x;
```

To fix the previous code cast `y` as a non-nullable type integer.

```
int? x = 10;
int y = (int)y;
```

Lab 4.3: Nullable Types

Skill Check 1: Create a Console Application called **NullableTypes**. Declare two `DateTime` variables, the first one as nullable and the second as non-nullable. Assign the current date and time to the first variable using `DateTime.Now`. Assign the value stored in the nullable variable to the non-nullable variable by casting it. The output should match what is shown in **Figure 4.18**.

```
Nullable Date:10/21/2012 6:18:46 PM
Non-Nullable Date:10/21/2012 6:18:46 PM
```

Figure 4.18 Nullable Types.

Answer Code: The C# answer code for this lab is located in the downloadable files inside the Projects folder within the BeginningCS2012CompanionFiles.zip file.

Points to Ponder - Nullable Types

1. Data types like `int`, and `long` can be made nullable for storing a `null` value.
2. Non-nullable basic types can be assigned to nullable basic types.
3. Nullable basic types can be assigned non-nullable basic types by explicitly casting the nullable type to a non-nullable type.
4. Even though the `string` type is a basic type, it is nullable by default.

Review Quiz - Chapter Four

1.) Implicit casting can be used to assign a long type variable to an int type variable.

O a) TRUE
O b) FALSE

2.) Which is the correct way to assign the int variable x to the byte variable y?

O a) y = x;
O b) y = (byte)x;
O c) y = (int)x;
O d) y = x(byte);

3.) In which statement is boxing happening?

O a) string obj = "100";
O b) int obj = 100;
O c) long obj = 100;
O d) object obj = 100;

4.) Parsing and casting are the same.

O a) TRUE
O b) FALSE

5.) To unbox an actual variable type stored in an object type, one can use parsing.

O a) TRUE
O b) FALSE

6.) A string variable holding a number can be converted to an int type using parsing.

O a) TRUE
O b) FALSE

7.) An integer variable can store a null value.

O a) TRUE
O b) FALSE

8.) A value type int variable can be made nullable using:

O a) Nullable(int) x = 100;
O b) int? x = 100;
O c) int x = nullable;

ANSWER KEY

1.) Implicit casting is used when a smaller size variable like byte is assigned to a bigger size variable like int. In this case, the long is getting assigned to an int. The long type is larger than an int type. To assign a long type to an int you have to use explicit casting, so the correct answer is (b).

2.) An int type is bigger than a byte type so you need to use explicit casting, making option (b) the correct answer.

3.) Boxing is used when a specific data type value is stored in an object type. In the case of option (a), (b) and (c) the variable is assigned a value that is equal to its data type. In option (d), we are putting an integer of 100 into an unspecified object, which is "boxing" so, (d) is correct.

4.) Parsing and casting are not the same, making option (b) correct. Parsing is used to convert a string type data into a specific data type, whereas casting is used to convert similar data types (long to int) or to unbox a specific data type from an object type.

5.) Unboxing converts data stored in an object type to a specific type using casting and not using parsing, so the correct answer is (b).

6.) A number stored as a string type can be converted into an int type using parsing, making option (a) the correct answer.

7.) An integer type cannot store a null value unless it is made nullable using int, or Nullable<int>. The correct answer is (b).

8.) There are two ways to make value types like an int a nullable type. One way is int? and another way is Nullable<int>. Option (b) here is using the first way, making option (b) the correct answer.

[NOTES]

Chapter 5 Decisions

We all encounter situations where we tell ourselves "if this happens then I will do this or else I will do that". We make decisions and choose different plans of action based on current conditions. In Figure 5.1 we are making a decision to do yard work or watch TV based on the current weather conditions. These types of decisions and various plans of action are also possible in a computer program.

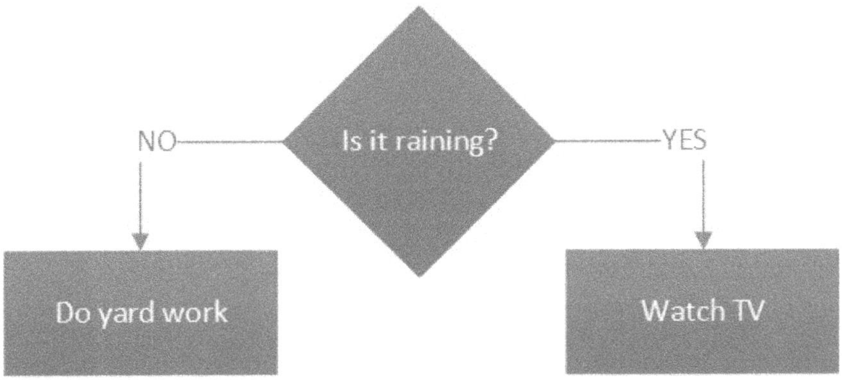

Figure 5.1 Decisions.

READER NOTE: *Before doing the steps in this section you need to have the following folder structure on your hard drive C:\Joes2Pros\C# 2012\Chapter 5. Within the Chapter 5 folder there should be two more folders called Lab 5.1 and Lab 5.2.. In order to follow along with the examples, you will need to have some version of Visual Studio 2012 installed.*

5.1 If-Else

All of our applications in this book ran every statement from the beginning of the **Main** method to the end. Every statement was run one after the other until the program completed. We have done some examples where we took user input from the console. We never made decisions to skip any statement, or provided different code paths, based on user input. In this section we will be making decisions on what statement to run based on certain conditions.

IF

Let's say we are writing an age warning system for a gaming company. This system will show a warning message if a person's age is less than 17. After that check it will continue with the normal execution of the program. Our workflow can look something like **Figure 5.2**.

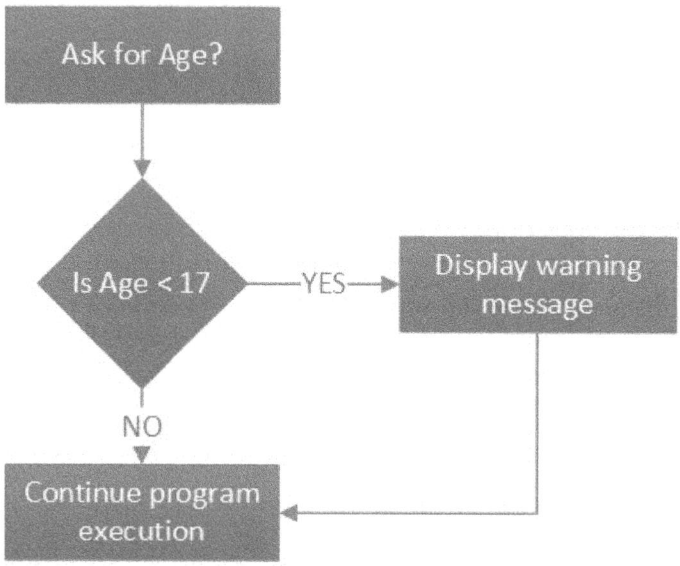

Figure 5.2 Warning Message.

Create a Console Application called **Age Warning** and add the following code inside the **Main** method:

```
Console.Write("Please enter your age: ");
byte age = Byte.Parse(Console.ReadLine());
```

This code will take user input and parse the age as a `byte` type. We want to check if the user's age is less than 17 and if that is true a warning message should be displayed. For checking conditions or expressions we can use an `if` statement, as shown in the following code:

```
if (age < 17)
{
    Console.WriteLine("Recommended age is 17!");
}
```

The expression inside the brackets `(age < 17)` is evaluated and if the answer is yes (`true`) the code inside the curly braces is executed.

Add the following statements to complete the program and to halt the execution:

```
Console.WriteLine("Enjoy your game");
Console.ReadKey();
```

Build and execute the program and use 15 as the input age. Notice the warning message is displayed on the console, as shown in **Figure 5.3**.

```
Console.Write("Please enter your age: ");
byte age = Byte.Parse(Console.ReadLine());

if (age < 17)
{
    Console.WriteLine("Recommended age is 17!");
}

Console.WriteLine("Enjoy your game");
Console.ReadKey();
```

```
Please enter your age: 15
Recommended age is 17!
Enjoy your game
```

Figure 5.3 Age Warning Displayed.

Now rerun the program with the input age as 21 and notice the warning message is not displayed (**Figure 5.4**).

```
Please enter your age: 21
Enjoy your game
```

Figure 5.4 Age Warning Not Displayed.

The expressions or conditions for an `if` statement can only have two answers, yes (`true`) or no (`false`). The expressions for an `if` statement are of the Boolean (`bool`) type.

Is 10 greater than 50? In programming we form that question to become `(10 > 50)`. In plain English the answer would be no, in programming languages the answer becomes `false`.

```
bool result = 10 > 50;
```

This code assigns the result to a `bool` type variable, which is `false`.

Greater than and less than operators are > and < respectively. For evaluating equality use == (two equal signs). Using two equal signs is different than using a single equal sign since one equal sign is for assigning values to a variable. The following code sample assigns `true` to the result variable:

```
bool result = 10 == 10;
// OR
bool result = (10 == 10);
```

If something is not equal to something we use the != operator. For example, it is true that 5 is not equal to 10. The following code will have a `bool` result of `true`:

```
bool result = (5 != 10);
```

Any expression that can be evaluated as Boolean can be used as a condition for an `if` statement. Here are a few Boolean examples which are evaluated and shown on the console (**Figure 5.5**).

```
Console.WriteLine("10>15: {0}", 10 > 15);
Console.WriteLine("10<15: {0}", 10 < 15);
Console.WriteLine("15<=15: {0}", 15 <= 15);
Console.WriteLine("20>=15: {0}", 20 >= 15);
Console.WriteLine("20==15: {0}", 20 == 15);
```

```
Console.WriteLine("40==40: {0}", 40 == 40);
Console.WriteLine("20!=40: {0}", 20 != 40);

Console.ReadKey();
```

```
10>15: False
10<15: True
15<=15: True
20>=15: True
20==15: False
40==40: True
20!=40: True
```

Figure 5.5 Boolean Expressions.

ELSE

We know how to execute a piece of code if a condition is met. What if we want to execute a different piece of code if a condition is not met (if Plan-A is not true we run plan-B)? We can write the Plan-B code inside an `else` block.

```
if (true)
{          IF Block          }
else
{          ELSE Block        }
```

Figure 5.6 If Else Blocks

The following code snippet expresses an example of the pseudo code from the scenario shown in **Figure 5.6**:

```
if (age < 17)
{
    Console.WriteLine("Sorry minimum age is 17!");
}
else
{
    Console.WriteLine("Enjoy your game");
}
```

The preceding code doesn't allow the user to play the game if their age is less than 17, but the `else` block allows it otherwise.

Create a Console Application called **AdditionChecker**. The user will enter two numbers along with the total of those two numbers. If the user provides the correct total then display "You are correct!" or else display "Sorry the correct total is: [*Actual Total*]".

Add the following code inside the **Main** method to ask for two numbers and a total:

```
Console.Write("Please enter first number : ");
int firstNumber = Int32.Parse(Console.ReadLine());

Console.Write("Please enter second number : ");
int secondNumber = Int32.Parse(Console.ReadLine());

Console.Write("Please enter sum of {0} and {1} : ",
    firstNumber, secondNumber);
int userTotal = Int32.Parse(Console.ReadLine());
```

The previous code takes input from the user and parses the string input to an integer data type for calculations.

Now we will check to see if the user provided the correct total. Add the following statements to the code to check if the user entered a correct total:

```
int actualtotal = firstNumber + secondNumber;

if (actualtotal == userTotal)
{
    Console.WriteLine("You are correct!");
}
```

```
else
{
    Console.WriteLine("Sorry the correct total is: {0}",
    actualtotal);
}
Console.ReadKey();
```

Here the expression `(actualtotal == userTotal)` is used to check the actual total with the user provided total. If the user total and the actual total matches, code execution enters the following `if` block.

```
{
    Console.WriteLine("You are correct!");
}
```

If the expression `(actualtotal == userTotal)` result turns out to be `false`, execution enters the following `else` block.

```
Else
{
    Console.WriteLine("Sorry the correct total is: {0}",
    actualtotal);
}
```

Let's try out the program with 10 and 20 as the two numbers and 30 as the sum. We provided the correct total so the expression should evaluate as `true` and enter the `if` block. The output of the execution is shown in **Figure 5.7**.

```
Console.Write("Please enter first number : ");
int firstNumber = Int32.Parse(Console.ReadLine());

Console.Write("Please enter second number : ");
int secondNumber = Int32.Parse(Console.ReadLine());

Console.Write("Please enter sum of {0} and {1} : ",
    firstNumber, secondNumber);
int userTotal = Int32.Parse(Console.ReadLine());

int actualtotal = firstNumber + secondNumber;

if (actualtotal == userTotal)
{
    Console.WriteLine("You are correct!");
}
```

```
else
{
    Console.WriteLine("Sorry the correct total is: {0}",
    actualtotal);
}
Console.ReadKey();
```

```
Please enter first number : 10
Please enter second number : 20
Please enter sum of 10 and 20 : 30
You are correct!
```

Figure 5.7 The if Block.

With 10 and 20 for the numbers and the incorrect sum of 40, the `else` block will be executed. The output is shown in **Figure 5.8**.

```
Please enter first number : 10
Please enter second number : 20
Please enter sum of 10 and 20 : 40
Sorry the correct total is: 30
```

Figure 5.8 The else Block.

IF-ELSE

We know if we have to choose two different paths based on a condition we can use the `if` and `else` statements. Sometimes decisions are not a simple Plan-A and Plan-B style. We may need to choose our code path after checking many conditions one after another. It is like having many plans for the same problem. If condition **X** is `true` take Plan-A or else check condition **Y**, and if `true` take Plan-B or else check the condition **Z** and if `true` take Plan **C**, and so on. **Figure 5.9** shows multiple plans with multiple condition checks.

```
if (value > 500)      // Condition X
    {     Plan A      }
else if (value > 400) // Condition Y
    {     Plan B      }
else if (value > 300) // Condition Z
    {     Plan C      }
else
    {  Fallback Plan  }
```

Figure 5.9 The if else block.

We start by checking a condition `(value > 500)`. If the value is greater than 500, code block Plan-A is executed. If the value is not greater than 500, then the next condition is checked `(value > 400)`. If the value is greater than 400, then the code block Plan-B is executed. If the value is not greater than 400 then the next condition `(value > 300)` is checked. If the value is 250 (i.e. not greater than 300) then the last `else` block is executed. The last `else` statement is optional, but when present, it works like a fallback plan. When none of the conditions are `true` this last `else` block is executed. This means none of the `if` blocks ran.

Create a Console Application called **Fruits**. The user should be able to choose a fruit from various options. Based on the user selection a different message should be displayed on the console. The possibilities for this program are show in the following figure:

Fruit	Message
Apple	Apple a day
Banana	George loves banana
Grape	Wines are made from grapes
Mango	Mangoes are yummy

Figure 5.10 This lists the possibilities for the program.

Add the following statements to display the fruit options to the user and then ask the user to provide their choice:

```
Console.WriteLine("Fruit Choices!");
Console.WriteLine("");
Console.WriteLine("Apple");
Console.WriteLine("Banana");
Console.WriteLine("Grape");
Console.WriteLine("Mango");
Console.WriteLine("");
Console.Write("Please enter your choice: ");
string fruit = Console.ReadLine();
```

The previous code will show the user's fruit choices and then ask for a fruit name. Based on the selection, it will show a different message. Since there are many possible conditions, we need to use an `if` statement followed by many `if else` statements. Add the following statements to show different messages for the different selections:

```
if (fruit == "Apple")
{
    Console.WriteLine("Apple a day ");
}
else if (fruit == "Banana")
{
    Console.WriteLine("George loves banana");
}
else if (fruit == "Grape")
{
    Console.WriteLine("Wines are made from grapes");
}
else if (fruit == "Mango")
{
    Console.WriteLine("Mangoes are yummy");
}
Console.ReadKey();
```

We start by comparing the contents on the variable **fruit** with the string literal "Apple". If the user didn't choose "Apple" then we check if the user selected "Banana",, and so on. **Figure 5.11** and **Figure 5.12** show two sample outputs after executing the program.

```
Console.WriteLine("Fruit Choices!");
Console.WriteLine("");
Console.WriteLine("Apple");
Console.WriteLine("Banana");
Console.WriteLine("Grape");
Console.WriteLine("Mango");
Console.WriteLine("");
Console.Write("Please enter your choice: ");
string fruit = Console.ReadLine();
if (fruit == "Apple")
{
    Console.WriteLine("Apple a day ");
}
else if (fruit == "Banana")
{
    Console.WriteLine("George loves banana");
}
else if (fruit == "Grape")
{
    Console.WriteLine("Wines are made from grapes");
}
else if (fruit == "Mango")
{
    Console.WriteLine("Mangoes are yummy");
}
Console.ReadKey();
```

```
Fruit Choices!

Apple
Banana
Grape
Mango

Please enter your choice: Banana
George loves banana
```

Figure 5.11 Banana Fruit.

```
Fruit Choices!

Apple
Banana
Grape
Mango

Please enter your choice: Apple
Apple a day
```

Figure 5.12 Apple Fruit.

If the user selects "mango" (all lower case) then no message is displayed (**Figure 5.13**). The expression for checking the fruit name is case-sensitive and it is looking for "Mango".

```
Fruit Choices!

Apple
Banana
Grape
Mango

Please enter your choice: mango
```

Figure 5.13 Mango Fruit.

Ternary Operator

Let's say you are a manager who decides the bonus money for your employees. If an employee has done all tasks then the employee gets 1,000 dollars. If not (`else`) they get 100 dollars. To set the bonus money, write the following code:

```
int bonus=0;
// allTasksDone is bool type
if (allTasksDone)
{
    bonus = 1000;
}
else
{
    bonus = 100;
}
```

The code is checking for a Boolean condition and if the condition is `true`, the bonus becomes 1000 or else it becomes 100. We can replace the code with a ternary operator where a value is returned based on a condition.

```
int bonus = allTasksDone ? 1000 : 100;
```

We just replaced multiple statements with one statement. So what happened? The first part of the ternary operator is a Boolean condition which can be `true` or `false`. If the condition is `true` then the first value (1000) is returned or else the second value (100) is returned.

Let's express the ternary operator in pseudo code. The following code is a more generic way to express the previous code:

Condition ? First Expression (`true`) : Second Expression (`false`);

We can either display the value returned from this expression or assign it to some variable just like in the bonus example. The pseudo code would look like the following:

Variable xyz = Condition ? First Expression (`true`) : Second Expression (`false`);

Why does the pseudo code show *First Expression* and *Second Expression* and not *First Value* and *Second Value*? They are expressions because they are not limited to hard-coded values like 1000 or 100. It can be a variable or a literal calculation, as shown in the following examples:

```
// If x is greater, return x-y or else return y-x
int x = 100;
int y = 300;
int positiveValue = (x >= y) ? x - y : y - x;
```

```
// Return type can be any .NET Type

int m = 5;
string text = m == 5 ? "May" : "Not May";
```

MORE DECISIONS

So far we have checked one condition to decide which code path should execute, but sometimes more than one condition is required to be checked. For example, if it is not raining, and I don't have any afternoon appointments, then I will do yard work, or else no yard work.

If ("Not raining" AND "No appointment")
  Do yard work
Else
  No yard work

We need both the conditions to be `true` to do the yard work. In C# we can separate multiple AND conditions with **&&**, as shown in the following code:

```
bool notRaining = true;
bool noAppointment = true;

if (notRaining && noAppointment)
{
    Console.WriteLine("Not raining and I am free");
    Console.WriteLine("Let me do yard work");
}
else
{
    Console.WriteLine("Sorry no yard work today");
}
```

The previous code has hard-coded `bool` variables and since both conditions are `true` the code will enter the `if` block. The following code will enter the `else` block since both conditions are not `true`.

```
bool notRaining = true;
bool noCommitment = false;
```

```
if (notRaining && noCommitment)
{
    Console.WriteLine("Not raining and I am free");
    Console.WriteLine("Let me do yard work");
}
else
{
    Console.WriteLine("Sorry no yard work today");
}
```

For our next example we want to execute a code path if any one condition is `true`. For example, I can go to work if "I have a car" OR "Public transit is working" OR "Taxi service is available". In this case I don't need both conditions to be `true` since any single one would take me to work. In C# OR is expressed as `||` (two pipes). The following example shows multiple OR conditions together.

```
bool haveCar = false;
bool publicTransitWorking = true;
bool taxiInService = false;
if (haveCar || publicTransitWorking || taxiInService)
{
    Console.WriteLine("I can go to work");
}
else
{
    Console.WriteLine("Will work from home");
}
```

In the previous example only one condition is `true` (publicTransitWorking). Having just one condition `true` is enough to execute the `if` block. The only way the `else` would have run is if all the conditions did not evaluate to `true`.

Lab 5.1: If-Else

Skill Check 1: Create a Console Application called **NumberToWord**. Ask the user to input a number from 1 to 5. If the user enters a 1, display **One**, if 2, then display **Two**, and so on. Use an `if else` statement. Try out the program with the following example:

```
Please enter a number (1-5): 3
Three
```

Figure 5.14 NumberToWord.

Skill Check 2: Modify Skill Check 1, if the user inputs a number other than 1 to 5 display "Invalid number choice!" on the console.

```
Please enter a number (1-5): 7
Invalid number choice!
```

Figure 5.15 Invalid number choice.

Skill Check 3: Create a Console Application called **MyCalculator**. Ask the user to input two numbers and an operator (+, -, *, /). Capture the operator using the following statement:

```
char mathOperator = Console.ReadKey().KeyChar;
```

Based on the user selected operator, display the computed value on the console, as shown in **Figure 5.16**. The part of the code with the `if` block should look like the following:

```
char mathOperator = Console.ReadKey().KeyChar;
int result = 0;
if (mathOperator == '+')
{
    result = firstNum + secondNum;
}
else if (mathOperator == '-')
```

```
Please enter the first number : 100
Please enter the second number : 5
Please enter the operator : /
100 / 5 = 20
```

Figure 5.16 MyCalculator.

Answer Code: The C# answer code for this lab is located in the downloadable files inside the Projects folder within the BeginningCS2012CompanionFiles.zip file.

Points to Ponder - If-Else

1. `if else` statements provide a way to make decisions in our code and help us choose different code paths for execution.
2. Whenever we have many plans for the same situation we can use `if else` statements.
3. An `else` statement is optional and works as a fallback code path for when any of the `if` or `if else` statements do not evaluate to `true`.
4. In simple variable assignment situations, the variable value depends on a condition use a ternary operator.
5. We are not limited to use one or two conditions to decide the `if` logic, we can use as many as we want.
6. Multiple Boolean expressions can be ANDed together using **&&**.
7. Multiple Boolean expressions can be ORed together using **||**.
8. We can use a combination of ANDs and ORs to formulate the final Boolean expression.

5.2 Switches

Let's say you have to write a program where a user can select one option from various options. Based on the user selection the program will display a different message to the console. This example is similar to the **Fruits** example from the previous section where the user selects a fruit. Based on the fruit selection a message is displayed on the console. The code for displaying different messages in the **Fruits** example is shown in the following code:

```
if (fruit == "Apple")
{
    Console.WriteLine("Apple a day");
}
else if (fruit == "Banana")
{
    Console.WriteLine("George loves banana");
}
else if (fruit == "Grape")
{
    Console.WriteLine("Wines are made from grapes");
}
else if (fruit == "Mango")
{
    Console.WriteLine("Mangoes are yummy");
}
```

In this code we start the comparison with `Apple`, then `Banana`, until we find a match or we run out of options. We used one `if` statement and three `else if` statements. What if we need to provide 10 fruits? The code will look cumbersome with one initial `if` statement and nine `else if` statements. We want to see the previous code in a workflow to look somewhat like **Figure 5.17**.

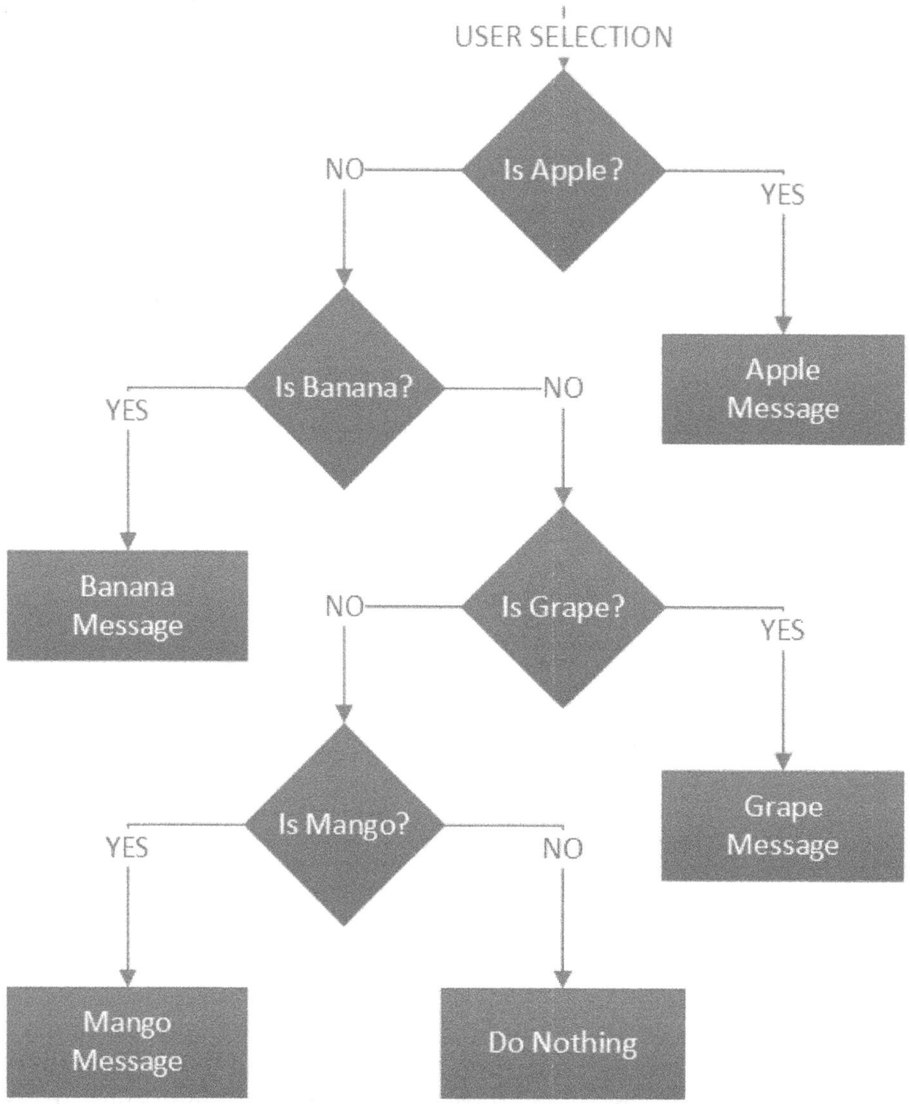

Figure 5.17 Multiple Else If Options.

From this workflow we see that when the user chooses "Mango" it goes through a series of checks saying no to Apple, Banana, and Grape. If it is "Mango" we might be better off jumping directly to that option.

Switch Case

Figure 5.17 shows we have to check each and every condition one-by-one until we either find one or we run out of options. With two or three options `if else` works fine, but if you have 10 cases to check then using this hierarchy would make the code look bulky and run slower.

There is a better way to list the various options, or cases. If a match is found, that block of code is executed directly. **Figure 5.18** shows what we want and what the `switch` statement supports.

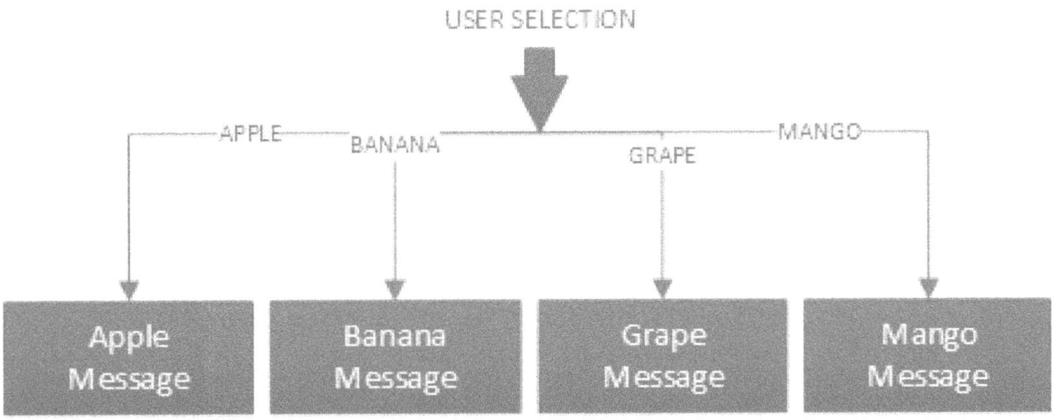

Figure 5.18 Multiple Switch Case Options.

The flow diagram of **Figure 5.18** using a `switch` statement would look like the following code syntax:

```
switch (userSelection)
{
  case "Apple":
    Display Message;
    break;

  case "Banana":
    Display Message;
    break;

  case "Grape":
    Display Message;
    break;

  case "Mango":
    Display Message;
    break;
}
```

Here the `switch` statement is on a variable, `userSelection,` and is based on its value. Control of the execution will move to that particular case block. Every case block is ending with a `break` statement which tells the compiler that this particular `case` block ends here.

Code for the **Fruit** example using a `switch` statement would look like this:

```
switch (fruit)
{
  case "Apple":
    Console.WriteLine("Apple a day");
    break;

  case "Banana":
    Console.WriteLine("George loves banana");
    break;

  case "Grape":
    Console.WriteLine("Wines are made from grapes");
    break;

  case "Mango ":
    Console.WriteLine("Mangoes are yummy");
    break;
}
```

In the previous code sample we are using a **fruit** variable as the input to the `switch` and then the defined four cases for each of the different selections. Each `case` block can have any number of statements with `break` as the last statement.

As mentioned before, the `if` statement has an unconditional `else` block which works like a fallback option. The `else` block is great when none of the conditions inside the `else if` conditions are `true`. The `switch` statement has a default `case` block which works the same way. We will want to display a message, “Sorry invalid fruit selection”, when the user does not select one of our fruits. To do this we can add the `default` case. The next code sample shows all these cases:

```
switch (fruit)
{
  case "Apple":
    Console.WriteLine("Apple a day");
    break;
```

```
  case "Banana":
    Console.WriteLine("George loves banana");
    break;
  case "Grape":
    Console.WriteLine("Wines are made from grapes");
    break;
  case "Mango ":
    Console.WriteLine("Mangoes are yummy");
    break;
  default:
    Console.WriteLine("Sorry invalid fruit selection");
    break;
}
```

The `default` case is optional but when present it works as a fallback.

Create a Console Application called **ABC**. In this example the user will be asked to enter a character in upper case and the console will display two words starting with that letter. Only three characters, A, B, and C, will be allowed. If the user enters some other character then a warning message will display. The warning should say "Sorry choices are A, B and C".

The following code will display the options and assign the user input to a `char` variable:

```
Console.Write("Please select a character (A B C): ");
char userSelection = Console.ReadKey().KeyChar;
```

Use a `switch` statement with the three cases for each letter (A, B, C) and also add the `default` case for the warning message.

```
switch (userSelection)
{
  case "A":
    Console.WriteLine("Aeroplane");
    Console.WriteLine("Apple");
    break;
  case "B":
    Console.WriteLine("Bread");
    Console.WriteLine("Bear");
    break;
```

```
  case "C":
    Console.WriteLine("Cat");
    Console.WriteLine("Car");
    break;

  default:
    Console.WriteLine("Sorry choices are A, B and C");
    break;
}
Console.ReadKey();
```

Execute the program with the letter **B** as input and the output will look like **Figure 5.19**. If there is invalid input the output will look like **Figure 5.20**.

```
Please select a character (A B C): B
Bread
Bear
```

Figure 5.19 ABC Valid Input.

```
Please select a character (A B C): F
Sorry choices are A, B and C
```

Figure 5.20 ABC Invalid Input.

MULTIPLE CASES

In the previous example the user was forced to use upper case letters, but we want to give the user flexibility to enter a matching character irrespective of the case of the letter. In other words, '**a**' or '**A**' will get **Aeroplane** and **Apple**. There are many ways to solve this problem, but we will use features provided by the `switch` statement to focus on how it works.

We can add three more cases for each lower case letter with the same corresponding message as shown in this code:

```
switch (userSelection)}
{
  case "A":
    Console.WriteLine("Aeroplane");
    Console.WriteLine("Apple");
    break;

  case "a":
    Console.WriteLine("Aeroplane");
    Console.WriteLine("Apple");
    break;

    case "B":
        Console.WriteLine("Bread");
        Console.WriteLine("Bear");
        break;

  case "b":
    Console.WriteLine("Bread");
    Console.WriteLine("Bear");
    break;

  case "C":
    Console.WriteLine("Cat");
    Console.WriteLine("Car");
    break;

  case "c":
    Console.WriteLine("Cat");
    Console.WriteLine("Car");
    break;

  default:
    Console.WriteLine("Sorry choices are A, B and C");
    break;
}
```

That previous example would be very bad practice since we are repeating the code twice for each `case` block. What we can do instead is bundle cases together with one `break` statement, as seen in the following example:

```
switch (userSelection)
{
  case "A":
  case "a":
    Console.WriteLine("Aeroplane");
    Console.WriteLine("Apple");
    break;

  case "B":
  case "b":
    Console.WriteLine("Bread");
    Console.WriteLine("Bear");
    break;

  case "C":
  case "c":
    Console.WriteLine("Cat");
    Console.WriteLine("Car");
    break;

  default:
    Console.WriteLine("Sorry choices are A, B and C");
    break;
}
```

This approach is much cleaner and the same code is not repeated.

Lab 5.2: Switches

Skill Check 1: Create a Console Application called **Drinks**. Ask the user to input a drink choice as a number. Use a `switch` statement to decide which message to display on the screen based on their choice. The choices are shown in Figure 5.21:

User Input	Message
1	Thank you for ordering Apple Juice
2	Thank you for ordering Orange Juice
3	Thank you for ordering Tea
4	Thank you for ordering Milk
5	Thank you for ordering Coffee

Figure 5.21 This shows the expected user inputs and associated message to be displayed.

The sample output of the program should look like **Figure 5.22** for selection 3.

```
Please select your drink (1-5): 3

Thank you for ordering Tea
```

Figure 5.22 Drinks.

Skill Check 2: Modify Skill Check 1 so that if the user inputs a number other than 1- 5, the message "Invalid Choice!!!" is displayed on the console.

```
Please select your drink (1-5): 9

Invalid Choice!!!
```

Figure 5.23 Drinks Default Message.

Skill Check 3: Create a Console Application called **Materials**. The user should be allowed to enter a material choice either in all upper case letters or all lower case letters. Based on that selection, display a message on the console based on **Figure 5.24**

User Input	Message
CLOTH/cloth	You can make clothes
PLASTIC/plastic	Plastic toys are common
GLASS/glass	Be careful with glass
PAPER/paper	Use recycled paper

Figure 5.24 This shows the expected user inputs and associated message to be displayed.

Sample outputs are shown in **Figure 5.25** and **Figure 5.26**.

```
Material choices are:
Cloth
Plastic
Glass
Paper
Your Choice (UPPER/lower Characters) : PLASTIC

Plastic toys are common
```

Figure 5.25 Materials Sample 1.

```
Material choices are:
Cloth
Plastic
Glass
Paper
Your Choice (UPPER/lower Characters) : plastic

Plastic toys are common
```

Figure 5.26 Materials Sample 2.

Answer Code: The C# answer code for this lab is located in the downloadable files inside the Projects folder within the BeginningCS2012CompanionFiles.zip file.

Points to Ponder - Switches

1. Each `case` block is separated by a `break` statement.
2. Multiple cases can be combined as one when `case` blocks are the same for both cases.
3. Use the `default` case as the fallback case when no particular case match is found.
4. The `default` case is not a required case.
5. We can combine multiple cases for one block. For example, if we want 'A' and 'a' to match we can use the following code:

```
switch (userSelection)
{
    case "A":
    case "a":
```

Review Quiz - Chapter Five

1.) Which of the following can be used to make decisions?

O a) namespace
O b) choice
O c) decision
O d) switch

2.) Which of the following helps in cascading conditions?

O a) if
O b) switch
O c) cascade
O d) else if

3.) The expression of an if statement allows only one condition to be checked.

O a) TRUE
O b) FALSE

4.) Will the following code compile?

```
switch ("RED")
{
  case "BLACK":
  Console.WriteLine("Hello");
  break;
}
```

O a) Yes
O b) No

5.) Which keyword is good at handling complex conditions that would normally require cascaded `if` statements?

O a) else if
O b) switch
O c) goto

6.) A break is always required between each case of switch statements.

O a) TRUE
O b) FALSE

ANSWER KEY

1.) The option (a) namespace is used for grouping objects in containers called namespace. Option (b) and (c) are invalid keywords. Option (d) is used to control the flow of execution based on the value of the switch expression. Decisions are made using switch, making option (d) the correct answer.

2.) Cascading conditions are made using multiple “else if” statements, making option (d) correct.

3.) The expression of an `if` statement can contain many sub expressions (i.e. many conditions can be checked). Therefore, option (b) is the correct answer.

4.) Here the switch expression is hard-coded to “RED” rather than a variable. The code will compile but will generate a warning “Unreachable code detected” since case “BLACK” will never be true. But since the code compiles the correct answer is option (a).

5.) A switch statement can replace many “else if” blocks with simple case blocks, making option (b) the correct answer.

6.) This is tricky, but the correct answer is (b).
If we comment the break after the “Red” case block, the code will not compile.

```
switch (color)
{
  case "Red":
    Console.WriteLine("Red Color");
  //break;  case "White":
    Console.WriteLine("White Color");
    break;
  case "Blue":
    Console.WriteLine("Blue Color");
    break;
}
```

But in the case of the following, where case “Red” has no code to execute, the code compiles fine.

```
switch (color)
{
  case "Red":
  case "White":
    Console.WriteLine("Red or White Color");
    break;
  case "Blue":
    Console.WriteLine("Blue Color");
    break;
}
```

[NOTES]

Chapter 6 Looping

How does a child learn to recite the alphabet? Through repetition, repetition and more repetition. When I start playing a new video game I have to play it again and again to get better at it. Similarly, in programming we might have to do the same task again and again. When we have to do repetitive tasks in real life we get bored. In C# we can automate these repetitive tasks with machines or computer programs. In the programming world we can achieve these repetitive tasks through loops.

READER NOTE: *Before doing the steps in this section you need to have the following folder structure on your hard drive C:\Joes2Pros\C# 2012\Chapter 6. Within the Chapter 6 folder there should be two more folders called Lab 6.1, Lab 6.2, and Lab 6.3.. In order to follow along with the examples, you will need to have some version of Visual Studio 2012 installed.*

6.1 Do-While Loops

Let's say you are a little kid just learning how to write. You are given an assignment to write "A for Apple" 10 times on a sheet of paper. You will write this once and then get to the next line and write it again. As you get close to being done you might check to see if you have written it 10 times. If you are not at 10 yet you will write another line and then check again until you are done. To do this assignment you will keep repeating each line until you have written it 10 times. Maybe you are counting as you go and know how many times you have written "A for Apple". Every time you write it you will increase your count by one and check until it is 10. You will keep increasing this count and will keep checking the count until you stop at 10. **Figure 6.1** is the flowchart to write "A for Apple" 10 times.

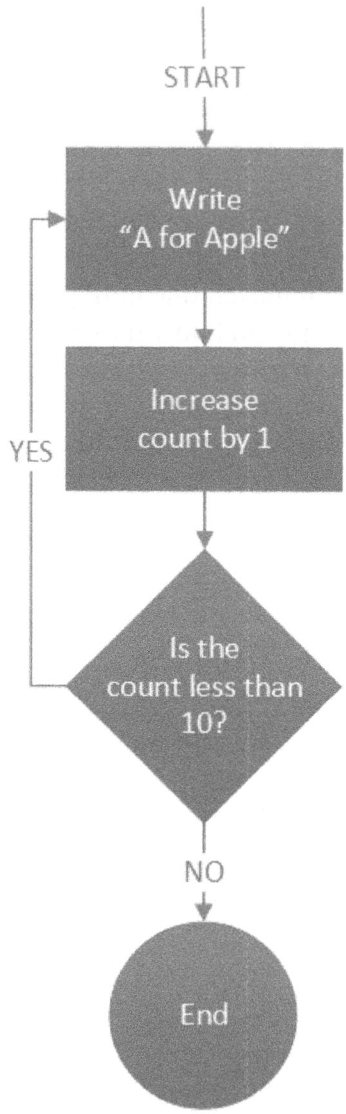

Figure 6.1 A for Apple.

TOUGH WAY

Let's see how we will solve this problem with the skills we've learned so far in this book. Our goal is to display "A for Apple" 10 times on the console. Create a Console Application called **A for Apple**. To display "A for Apple" on the console one time we would write the following statement inside the **Main** method:

```
Console.WriteLine("A for Apple");
```

Our goal is to display the message 10 times. We can copy this statement and paste it 9 times so we have 10 `WriteLine` statements.

```
Console.WriteLine("A for Apple");
Console.WriteLine("A for Apple");
Console.WriteLine("A for Apple");
Console.WriteLine("A for Apple");
Console.WriteLine("A for Apple");
Console.WriteLine("A for Apple");
Console.WriteLine("A for Apple");
Console.WriteLine("A for Apple");
Console.WriteLine("A for Apple");
Console.WriteLine("A for Apple");
```

The copy and paste idea was not that bad and it worked. It took a couple of seconds to code. When we execute the program the output looks like the one shown in **Figure 6.2**.

```
A for Apple
A for Apple
A for Apple
A for Apple
A for Apple
A for Apple
A for Apple
A for Apple
A for Apple
A for Apple
```

Figure 6.2 A for Apple Tough Way.

If we need to display "A for Apple" 100 times or 1,000 times or even 1,000,000 times then the cut and paste method is no longer practical. The next section will show a smarter way to repeat the execution of code statements.

SMART WAY

In the previous example we learned that if we do something again and again it might take us forever to write that code. So what we need is a smart way to do a task again and again until the completion of the condition is reached. In the previous case our task was to display “A for Apple” on the console 10 times. In other words, keep doing this task until the completion condition of 10 is met.

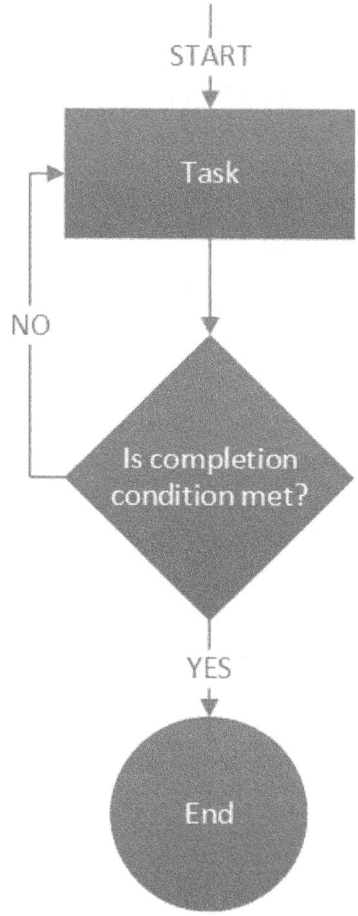

Figure 6.3 Smart Way.

As shown in **Figure 6.3**, we keep repeating the task until the completion condition is met. To achieve the same functionality in C# we can use a `do-while` loop. The following pseudo code of the `do-while` loop shows similar functionality.

```
Do
{
  // Task
} while (condition);
```

Here the task will be repeated as long as the condition remains `true`.

Create a Console Application called **A for Apple Smart Way**. Here we will solve the same problem of displaying "A for Apple" 10 times on the console. We will use a count variable to remember how many times we have displayed the message on the console. It is the same approach we saw in **Figure 6.1**.

Declare and initialize the count variable and create a `do-while` loop, as shown in the following code:

```
int count = 0;
do
{
  Console.WriteLine("A for Apple");
  count = count + 1;
} while (count != 10);
```

In this code the count starts with a value of 0. Then the execution enters the `do` block. After displaying the message, the count variable is incremented by 1, then the `while` statement checks if the value of the count is not equal to 10. Since the count is now 1, it is `true` that the count is not equal to 10. So `count != 10` returns `true` and the loop will run again. Next time the count value becomes 2, then 3,, and so on until the count value reaches 10. Once the count variable reaches 10 the condition of `count != 10` returns a `false` value and the loop finishes.

Another way to look at this is that the loop will remain active until the condition is `true` for the `while` condition. There is another more common way to write the previous code. In the following code example the condition `count < 10` will remain `true` until the count reaches 10:

```
int count = 0;
do
{
  Console.WriteLine("A for Apple");
  count = count + 1;
} while (count < 10);
```

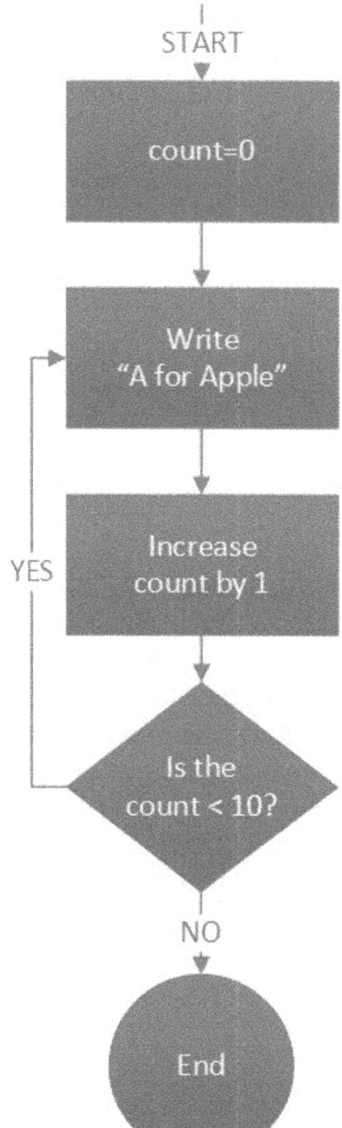

Figure 6.4 Do-While Execution.

INFINITE LOOPS

An infinite loop is one that will run forever. To run an infinite loop hard code the value to `true` as the condition for the `do-while` loop,, as seen in the following example:

```
Do
{
  // Statements in this block will run forever
} while (true);
```

LOOP CONDITIONS

In the first `do-while` loop example we defined the condition of the `while` loop with a hard-coded value of 10. Sometimes the user might want to go to 12 or 15. Can we change this value of 10 to any value which the user inputs at runtime? Yes, we can replace this hard-coded value of 10 with a variable.

Let's start by creating a Console Application called **MathTables**. Our goal is to display the mathematical table for any user selected number. For example, if the user entered 5 and 10, the output should look something like **Figure 6.5**.

```
5 * 1 = 5
5 * 2 = 10
5 * 3 = 15
5 * 4 = 20
5 * 5 = 25
5 * 6 = 30
5 * 7 = 35
5 * 8 = 40
5 * 9 = 45
5 * 10 = 50
```

Figure 6.5 Table of 5.

Looking at this figure we see that the user input value stays fixed or constant at 5 while the second number starts at 1 and goes until 10 in increments of 1. This problem looks like a good candidate to use loops since we are doing a similar task repeatedly.

The following statements will ask the user to input a number and then a loop count number.

```
Console.Write("Please enter a number: ");
int number = int.Parse(Console.ReadLine());

Console.Write("Please enter a loop number: ");
int loopNumer = int.Parse(Console.ReadLine());
```

Start the loop with a count value of 1 and then increment the count value by 1 for each iteration until the count value is less than or equal to the `loopNumber` variable.

The following statements will declare and initialize the count variable and complete the task using a `do-while` loop:

```
int count = 1;
do
{
  Console.WriteLine("{0} * {1} = {2}", number,
  count, number * count);
  count++;
} while (count <= loopNumer);
```

If the user inputs 9 as a `number` and 11 as a `loopNumber`, the loop will start with a `count` value of 1 and then display the computation. Then `count++` will increment the `count` value by 1 making it 2. The condition of `while (count <= loopNumber)` returns `true` since `2<=11`. After the loop has printed 10 times the `count` value becomes 11 making `11<=11` which still returns a `true` value. This causes the loop to iterate again. In this next iteration the `count` will become 12 making `12<=11` to return `false`, causing the loop to end. Execute the program with the `number` as 10 and the `loopNumber` as 12. The output will look like **Figure 6.6**.

```
Please enter a number: 10
Please enter a loop number: 12
10 * 1 = 10
10 * 2 = 20
10 * 3 = 30
10 * 4 = 40
10 * 5 = 50
10 * 6 = 60
10 * 7 = 70
10 * 8 = 80
10 * 9 = 90
10 * 10 = 100
10 * 11 = 110
10 * 12 = 120
```

Figure 6.6 Math Tables.

Lab 6.1: Do-While Loops

Skill Check 1: Create a Console Application called **Numbers** to print numbers on the console from 1 to 7 using a `do-while` loop. The output should look like **Figure 6.7**.

```
1
2
3
4
5
6
7
```

Figure 6.7 Numbers.

Skill Check 2: Create a Console Application called **Number Gaps** to print the numbers on the console, as shown in **Figure 6.8**. The starting number will be 100 and the increment number will be 5. Use a `do-while` loop.

```
100
105
110
115
120
125
130
```

Figure 6.8 Number Gaps.

Answer Code: The C# answer code for this lab is located in the downloadable files inside the Projects folder within the BeginningCS2012CompanionFiles.zip file.

Points to Ponder - Do-While Loops

1. Loops allow us to do repetitive tasks.
2. The `do-while` loop's first task is executed without checking the loop condition.
3. A semicolon is required after the `while` statement when using the `do-while` loop.
4. A loop will remain active until the condition of `while` stays `true`.

6.2 While Loops

A `do-while` loop's first task is executed and then it checks the condition. This means irrespective of the loop condition the `do-while` loop will iterate at least one time. Sometimes we don't want to execute any loop task until the condition is `true`. To achieve condition checking before entering the loop we can use a `while` loop.

The following figure shows the difference between the `while` and `do-while` loops.

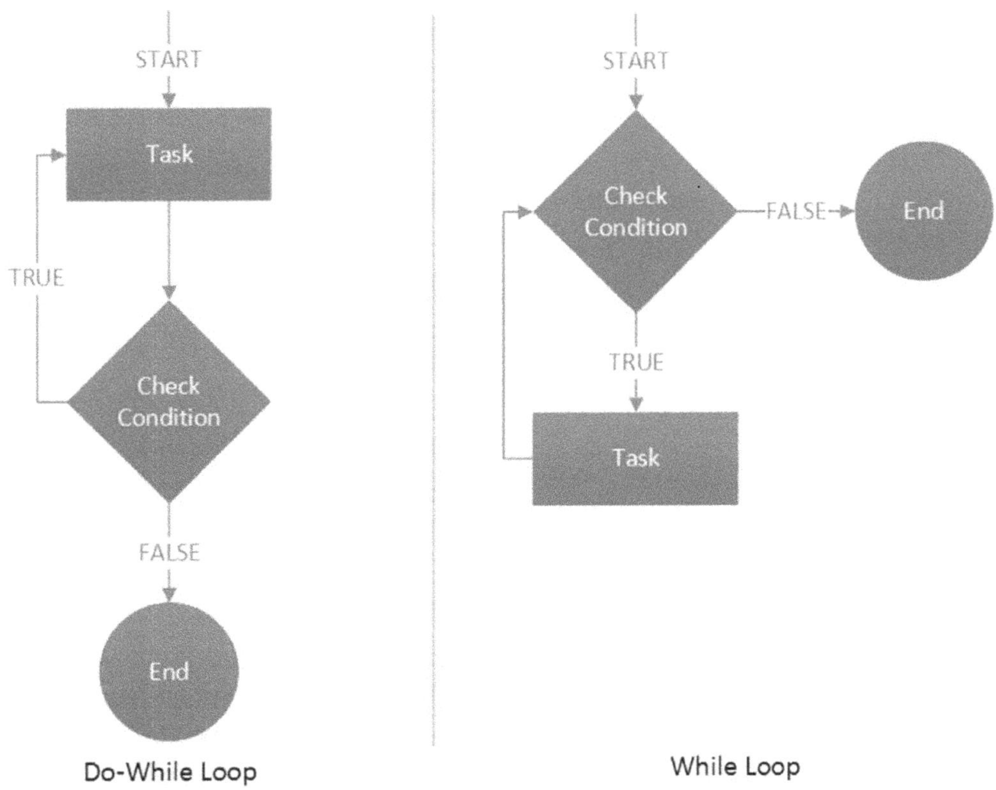

Figure 6.9 While and Do-While.

In the case of a `while` loop, condition checking is first; whereas task execution is first for the `do-while` loop.

The following is the pseudo code for a `while` loop, where the loop executes until the condition is `true`.

```
while (condition)
{
  // Task
}
```

WHILE EXAMPLE

Create a Console Application called **MessageBoard**. The goal is to display a message to the console N number of times. For our example, N is the number provided by the user. If the user enters the number 3, the message will be displayed 3 times. If the user enters 0 or any negative number then no message should be displayed.

We can achieve this functionality using a `do-while` loop, as shown in the following code:

```
Console.Write("Please enter a number: ");
int number = Int32.Parse(Console.ReadLine());

if (number > 0)
{
  int counter = 1;
  do
  {
    Console.WriteLine("Message");
    counter++;
  } while (counter<=number);
}
```

This code takes a number from the user. Then the `if` statement checks if the number is greater than zero. We have to use an `if` statement here since the `do-while` loop will execute the loop first and then check the condition to see if the loop needs to repeat.

We can avoid the `if` statement check when we use a `while` loop, since the condition check happens before executing the loop, as shown in **Figure 6.9**.

Write the following code inside the **Main** method of the **MessageBoard** program:

```
Console.Write("Please enter a number: ");
int number = Int32.Parse(Console.ReadLine());

int counter = 1;
while (counter <= number)
{
  Console.WriteLine("Message");
  counter++;
}
```

Start the counter with a 1 and then check the condition to see if the counter is less than or equal to the user's number. In case of a zero or a negative number the condition will return `false` and the execution will never enter the loop. For a positive number such as 5, the loop will start since the counter is 1 and the number is 5. Every time the message is displayed on the console the counter is incremented by 1. When the message has been displayed five times, the counter will become 6 and the loop condition will return `false`. This is because 6 is not less than or equal to 5.

The execution of the program should look like **Figure 6.10**.

```
Please enter a number: 5
Message
Message
Message
Message
Message
```

Figure 6.10 MessageBoard.

Break

Sometimes we want to execute a loop forever until something bad happens or some condition changes inside the loop. Assume you are responsible for creating an electronic billboard to show advertisements. The billboard should always show the advertisements as long as it can connect to the main server. An internet connection can break between the billboard and the main server. When the connection breaks, the billboard should no longer display any message.

Another way to look at it is that inside the loop we are performing a bunch of tasks which are complicated and error prone. If something goes wrong with any of the tasks, we want to exit the loop.

Figure 6.11 shows the previous scenario where a `while` loop is performing three tasks. If something goes wrong in any of the tasks (anywhere in the loop), the `while` loop breaks and ends the loop.

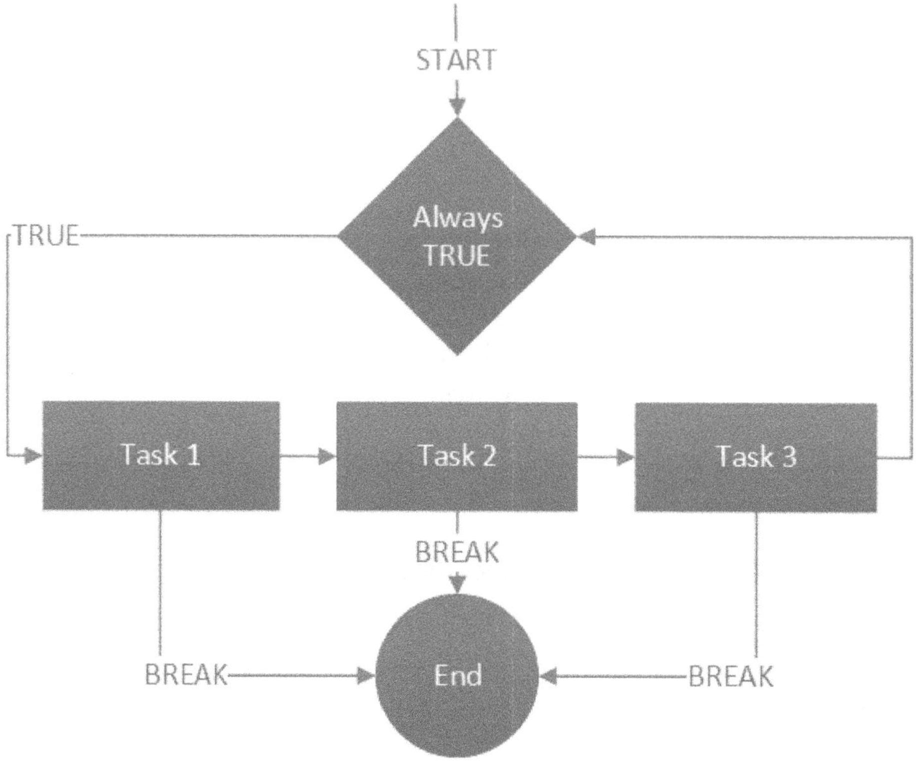

Figure 6.11 Breaking a Loop.

Stopping or breaking the loop functionality is provided by the `break` statement. Whenever we use the `break` statement inside a loop (irrespective of any condition) the loop terminates. The following example shows that an infinite loop terminates after displaying a message on the console five times:

```
int counter = 1;
while (true)
{
  Console.WriteLine("Message Break");
```

```
  if (counter == 5)
  {
    break;
  }
  counter++;
}
```

Lab 6.2: While Loops

Skill Check 1: Create a Console Application called **Numbers**. Ask the user to input a number, display all numbers between the user entered number and 10 using a `while` loop. If the user enters 6, numbers 7, 8 and 9 are displayed on the console.

Try the program with the following example:

```
Please enter a number: -2
-1
0
1
2
3
4
5
6
7
8
9
```

Figure 6.12 Numbers.

Skill Check 2: Create a Console Application called **Billboard**. Continuously display the message "I will run forever" on the console using a `while` loop. **Figure 6.13** shows the output of the program where three dots are shown to emulate that the program is running forever.

```
I will run forever
I will run forever
...
...
I will run forever
I will run forever
I will run forever
I will run forever
I will run forever
I will run forever
...
```

Figure 6.13 Billboard.

Skill Check 3: Modify the program for Skill Check 2 to break out of the loop after displaying the message three times, as shown in **Figure 6.14**. Do not change the loop condition, but add a `break` statement with the appropriate condition.

```
I will run forever
I will run forever
I will run forever
```

Figure 6.14 Billboard Break.

Answer Code: The C# answer code for this lab is located in the downloadable files inside the Projects folder within the BeginningCS2012CompanionFiles.zip file.

Points to Ponder - While Loops

1. A `while` loop executes when the condition is `true`.
2. Having a hard-coded `true` as a condition for a loop makes it an infinite loop.
3. The difference between a `do-while` and a `while` loop is that the `do-while` loop executes once and then checks the condition.
4. To terminate a `while` loop anywhere in the loop use a `break` statement.
5. The `break` statement can be used inside the `while` and `do-while` loops. It can also be used in a `for` loop which is explained in the next section.

6.3 For Loops

We know loops are for performing repetitive tasks. When we create a `while` or `do-while` loop we often create a counter variable to keep track of how many times we have executed the loop. We use the counter variable when we know how many times to execute the loop. The `while` and `do-while` loops only care about the Boolean condition, as shown in the following code:

```
while (<Boolean Condition>)
{    // Task
}

do
{    // Task
} while (<Boolean Condition>);
```

To get the `while` loop to run 10 times we initialized a counter to 1 and checked the Boolean until it was greater than 10 to exit the loop. To make sure the loop did not run forever we incremented the counter for the next iteration. The sample and pseudo code for making the `while` loop run 10 times is shown here:

```
// Sample code
int iteration = 1;
while (iteration <= 10)
{
  Console.WriteLine(iteration);
  iteration++;
}
// Pseudo code
<Initialize>
while (<Boolean Condition>)
{
  Console.WriteLine(iteration);
  <iteration>
}
```

Looping Iterations

In the previous example the `while` loop takes a condition so we set up the initialization and iteration for the variable outside the loop. Having a starting and ending point is a common goal. There is another kind of loop called the `for` loop which can combine the counter and the Boolean logic together. The pseudo code of a `for` loop is as follows:

```
for (<Initialize>; <Boolean Condition>; <Iteration>)
{
  // Task
}
```

<Initialize> is for initializing a counter. For example, to start a counter at 1 we can write it as the following code:

```
for (int counter = 1; <Boolean Condition>; <iterator>)
{
// Task
}
```

The variable can be named anything; here we named it `counter`. The *<Boolean Condition>* is similar to the condition in a `while` loop. The *<iterator>* `is` used to tell how to increment the `counter` (every time the loop executes it increments the counter by 1, 2, 5,, etc.).

If we want a loop to run 10 times, then the condition and iterator should be something like the following code:

```
for (int counter = 1; counter <= 10; counter = counter + 1)
{
  // Task
}
```

Another common modification is to use a unary operator for the iterator.

```
for (int counter = 1; counter <= 10; counter++)
{
  // Task
}
```

Replace the comment `// Task` with a `Console.WriteLine` statement, as seen in the following code:

```
for (int counter = 1; counter <= 10; counter++)
{
  Console.WriteLine(counter); // Task
}
```

In every iteration we will display the `counter` value on the console, as shown in **Figure 6.15**.

```
1
2
3
4
5
6
7
8
9
10
```

Figure 6.15 For Loop.

In a previous section we created an **A for Apple** application that used a `while` loop. Now we are going to use a `for` loop. Let's create a Console Application called **A for Loop Apple** to practice the skills of the `for` loop. We will get exactly the same output as we did before.

We will display the message, "A for Apple" on the console 10 times, along with its `counter` value. Write the following code inside the **Main** method:

```
for (int counter = 1; counter <= 10; counter++)
{
  Console.WriteLine("{0} : A for Apple", counter);
}
Console.ReadKey();
```

Execute the program and the output will look like the one shown in **Figure 6.16**.

```
1 : A for Apple
2 : A for Apple
3 : A for Apple
4 : A for Apple
5 : A for Apple
6 : A for Apple
7 : A for Apple
8 : A for Apple
9 : A for Apple
10 : A for Apple
```

Figure 6.16 For A for Loop Apple.

If the counter increments by one it hits every number from 1 to 2 to 3... If we incremented by 2 then we would go 1, 3, 5 for our count. Modify the iterator to display only the odd numbers on the console. In the following code we are incrementing the counter variable for each iteration by 2:

```
for (int counter = 1; counter <= 10; counter = counter + 2)
```

When we execute the program, the `counter` values 1, 3, 5, 7 and 9 are displayed, as shown in **Figure 6.17**. As soon as the counter reaches 11 the condition `counter <= 10` is no longer `true` and the loop finishes execution. We now know how to change the iterator of a `for` loop to make it run at different increments.

```
1 : A for Apple
3 : A for Apple
5 : A for Apple
7 : A for Apple
9 : A for Apple
```

Figure 6.17 For Odd Numbers.

CONTINUE

Have you heard the term "Next please"? This term is not much fun if you are a job applicant and realize you did not qualify for a job. The company will have more people to keep looping through until they find who they want. If a company says we are going to interview 10 people they are probably not going to hire all 10 people. If the first person does not qualify then they will say "Next please" and loop to the next applicant. If the first person does not qualify the company doesn't quit looking, they just stop that iteration (or interview) and start the next one.

We learned from earlier in this chapter that if we want to terminate a loop at any time we can use a `break` statement. Assume we have a scenario where a loop executes three tasks. We would like to execute all tasks for all iterations. If **Task 1** didn't meet the requirements then we don't want **Task 2** and **Task 3** to run for that iteration. In other words, this iteration should not run but we should start the next one and keep the loop going. If we use a `break` statement for checking **Task 1** it will just end the loop and no more iterations will run. We want a more subtle approach where we don't want to run **Task 2** and **Task 3** for the current iteration, but we would like to continue executing the other iterations.

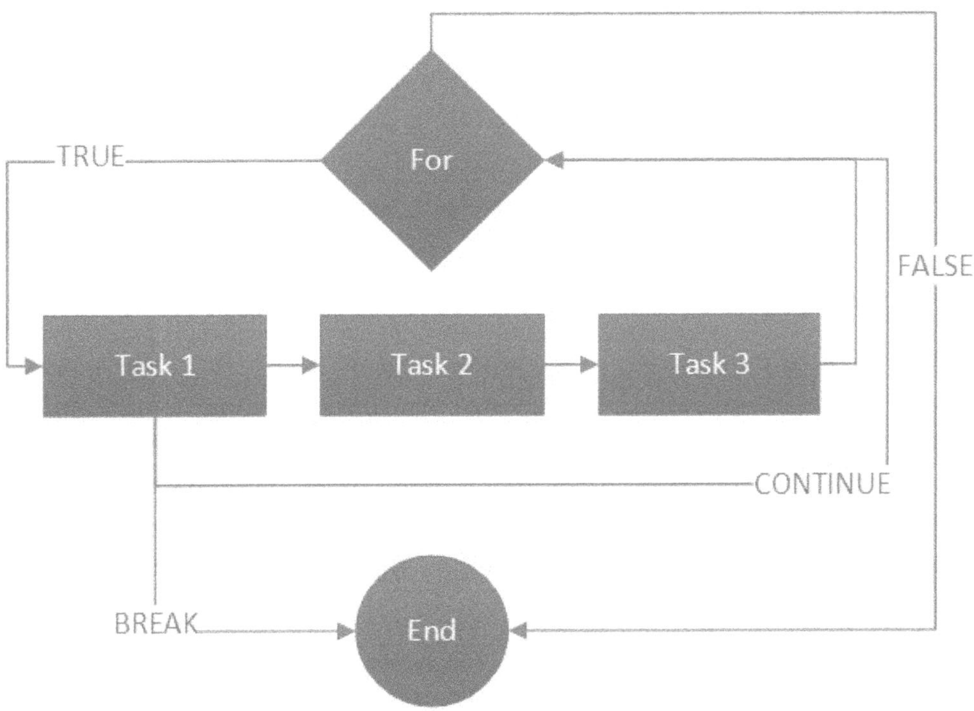

Figure 6.18 Continue.

Figure 6.18 shows the loop is executing 3 tasks. In the case of a `break` statement, the loop terminates, but because there is a `continue` statement, the current iteration ignores all remaining tasks or statements and starts a new iteration. The `continue` statement can also be used in other types of loops.

Let's look at the goal of the next Console Application. The program will talk to three applicants. To interview with our company an applicant must have valid ID. If they bring ID then we start the interview off with asking their name. If they did not bring their ID then we finish the iteration by saying "Next please".

```
Applicant #1: Have ID? (y/n): y
What is your name: Joe
Hello Joe

Applicant #2: Have ID? (y/n): n (Next Please!)
Applicant #3: Have ID? (y/n): y
What is your name: Mary
Hello Mary
```

Figure 6.19 The continue keyword skips to the next iteration.

Let's create a Console Application called **Applicant**. In the **Main** method create a `for` loop that runs 3 times (initializing as 1) and pause the program at the end, as seen in the following code:

```
for (int ct = 1; ct <= 3; ct++)
{
}
Console.ReadKey();
```

Start off by asking the user if they have ID. If the answer is 'N' or 'n' then continue on to the next applicant, as seen in the following code:

```
for (int ct = 1; ct <= 3; ct++)
{
  Console.Write("Applicant #{0}: Have ID (y/n)? ", ct);
  char answer = Console.ReadKey().KeyChar;
  if (answer == 'n' || answer == 'N')
  {
    Console.WriteLine(" (Next Please!)");
    continue;
  }
}
Console.ReadKey();
```

If they have ID then the `if` block will be skipped. The remaining part of the loop will ask for the applicant's name and show the name on the console, as seen in the following code:

```
for (int ct = 1; ct <= 3; ct++)
{
  Console.Write("Applicant #{0}: Have ID (y/n)? ", ct);
  char answer = Console.ReadKey().KeyChar;
  if (answer == 'n' || answer == 'N')
  {
    Console.WriteLine(" (Next Please!)");
    continue;
  }
  Console.WriteLine();
  Console.Write("What is your name: ");
  string userName = Console.ReadLine();
  Console.WriteLine("Hello {0} ", userName);
  Console.WriteLine();
}
Console.ReadKey();
```

Run and test the code where Applicant #1 and Applicant #3 have their ID but Applicant #2 doesn't. The results will resemble **Figure 6.19**.

NESTED LOOPS

Many people have played the Minesweeper game where hidden mines are placed on a grid. The grid is nothing but a set of rows and columns, and mines are placed in a few of the cells, as shown in **Figure 6.20**.

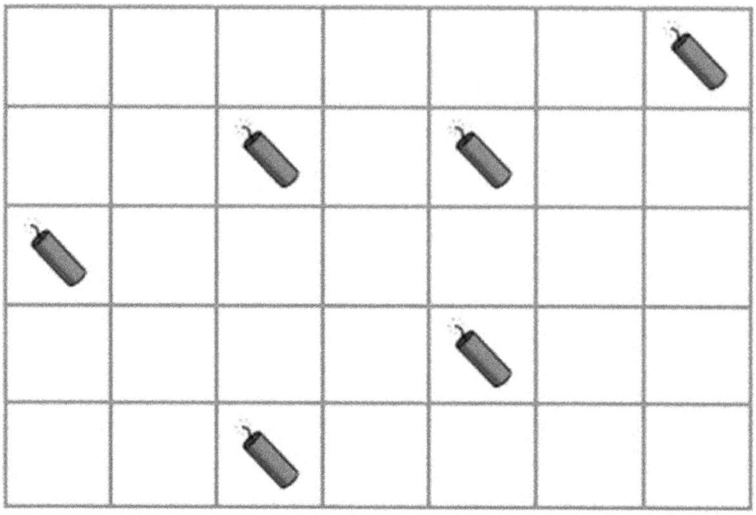

Figure 6.20 Minesweeper.

Here we will see how to build a grid of * with 5 rows and 7 columns. The output will look like the one shown in **Figure 6.21**.We can achieve this functionality by using the following code:

```
Console.WriteLine("* * * * * * *");
Console.WriteLine("* * * * * * *");
Console.WriteLine("* * * * * * *");
Console.WriteLine("* * * * * * *");
Console.WriteLine("* * * * * * *");
```

```
* * * * * * *
* * * * * * *
* * * * * * *
* * * * * * *
* * * * * * *
```

Figure 6.21 Grid.

To make 100 writing lines on the console is tedious. If we built a grid with 100 rows and 7 columns, we can use a `for` loop. The `for` loop to do this is shown in the following code:

```
for (int rowIndex = 0; rowIndex < 100; rowIndex++)
{
  Console.WriteLine("* * * * * * *");
}
Console.ReadKey();
```

In the previous code example the loop starts at `rowIndex` 0 and runs until `rowIndex` 99. 0-99 is therefore, making a total of 100 iterations, or 100 rows, on the console.

How about having a grid with 100 rows and 20 columns? Having 20 * inside `Console.WriteLine` will work but might not be a good solution. Typing 20 of anything means we need to count them which is very manual and error prone. We can use another loop to display * 20 times on the console inside the existing loop, as shown in the following code:

```
for (int rowIndex = 0; rowIndex < 100; rowIndex ++)
{
  for (int colIndex = 0; colIndex < 20; colIndex++)
  {
    Console.Write("* ");
  }
  Console.WriteLine();
}
Console.ReadKey();
```

We created a loop inside another loop making them nested loops. The inner loop is using `Console.Write` to print * 20 times on the same line. The outside loop is repeating this whole action 100 times. In other words, the inner loop defines the number of columns and the outer loop defines the number of rows.

```
* * * * * * * * * * * * * * * * * * * *
* * * * * * * * * * * * * * * * * * * *
* * * * * * * * * * * * * * * * * * * *
* * * * * * * * * * * * * * * * * * * *
* * * * * * * * * * * * * * * * * * * *
* * * * * * * * * * * * * * * * * * * *
* * * * * * * * * * * * * * * * * * * *
* * * * * * * * * * * * * * * * * * * *
* * * * * * * * * * * * * * * * * * * *
* * * * * * * * * * * * * * * * * * * *
* * * * * * * * * * * * * * * * * * * *
* * * * * * * * * * * * * * * * * * * *
* * * * * * * * * * * * * * * * * * * *
* * * * * * * * * * * * * * * * * * * *
* * * * * * * * * * * * * * * * * * * *
```

Figure 6.22 This shows the output of a for loop inside a for loop.

Lab 6.3: For Loops

Skill Check 1: Create a Console Application called **Grid**. Ask the user to input the number of times (columns) to display $ on the console. Use a `for` loop to code this program. The output of the program is shown in **Figure 6.23**.

```
Please enter the number of columns: 9
$ $ $ $ $ $ $ $ $
```

Figure 6.23 Grid Column.

Skill Check 2: Modify the code of Skill Check 1 to ask the user to input the number of rows to repeat the pattern. Test the program with 3 rows, as shown in **Figure 6.24**.

```
Please enter the number of columns: 9
Please enter the number of rows: 3
$ $ $ $ $ $ $ $ $
$ $ $ $ $ $ $ $ $
$ $ $ $ $ $ $ $ $
```

Figure 6.24 Grid Rows.

Answer Code: The C# answer code for this lab is located in the downloadable files inside the Projects folder within the BeginningCS2012CompanionFiles.zip file.

Points to Ponder - For Loops

1. The `for` loop combines the counter and the condition logic together.
2. The loop counter increment is defined by the user at loop creation time and is not limited to just adding 1 to the previous counter.
3. The `for` loop is not limited to executing a counter loop but it can take any condition. The following is an example of an infinite `for` loop:

   ```
   for (; true ; )
   {
     // Task
   }
   ```
4. Loops which have another loop inside them are called nested loops.
5. To skip the remaining statements inside a loop use a `continue` statement.

Review Quiz - Chapter Six

1.) Which of the following can be used to do repetitive tasks?

O a) while
O b) repeat
O c) decision
O d) switch

2.) In case of a do-while loop, the condition needs to be true to execute the loop code.

O a) TRUE
O b) FALSE

3.) A semicolon is required at the end of a do-while loop.

O a) TRUE
O b) FALSE

4.) Which statement can end a loop?

O a) stop
O b) end
O c) break
O d) loop

5.) Only a for loop can have nested loops.

O a) TRUE
O b) FALSE

6.) Which statement can be used to skip remaining statements inside a loop without ending the loop itself?

O a) skip
O b) skip_remaining
O c) break
O d) continue

7.) Which cannot be used for doing repetitive tasks?

O a) for
O b) repeat
O c) do-while
O d) while

ANSWER KEY

1.) A while loop can repeat a set of statements until the condition is true, making option (a) is the correct answer.

2.) In case of a while loop, the condition needs to be true to execute the loop code. In the case of a do-while loop, the loop statements are executed for the first time irrespective of the condition being true or false. The condition of the do-while loop is checked after the loop executes for the first time, making the correct answer as (b).

3.) Option (a) is the correct answer.

```
do
{
} while (x < 10);
```

4.) A break statement is used to end a loop, making option (c) the correct answer.

5.) Any type of loop for, while or do-while, can be used for nesting. Therefore option (b) is the correct answer.

6.) Options (a) and (b) are invalid, and option (c) will end the loop. A continue statement is used for skipping remaining loop statements to take the control of execution back to the loop condition checking. So option (d) is the correct answer.

7.) Options (a) for, (c) do-while and (d) while can be used for repetitive tasks. Therefore option (b) "repeat" is invalid and the correct answer.

[NOTES]

Chapter 7 Arrays

How many values can be stored in a single variable? Using what we have learned that answer would be one. An integer variable number can be assigned one and only one integer value. In this chapter we will learn how to store more than one value in one variable name.

READER NOTE: *Before doing the steps in this section you need to have the following folder structure on your hard drive C:\Joes2Pros\C# 2012\Chapter 7. Within the Chapter 7 folder there should be two more folders called Lab 7.1 and Lab 7.2.. In order to follow along with the examples, you will need to have some version of Visual Studio 2012 installed.*

7.1 Simple Arrays

To store one number we can declare one integer variable and to store four numbers we can declare four integer variables, as seen in the following code:

```
int a = 10;
int b = 20;
int c = 30;
int d = 40;
```

Here we have declared and initialized four different variables with four different names. In the computer's memory four different spaces are storing the variables, as shown in **Figure 7.1**.

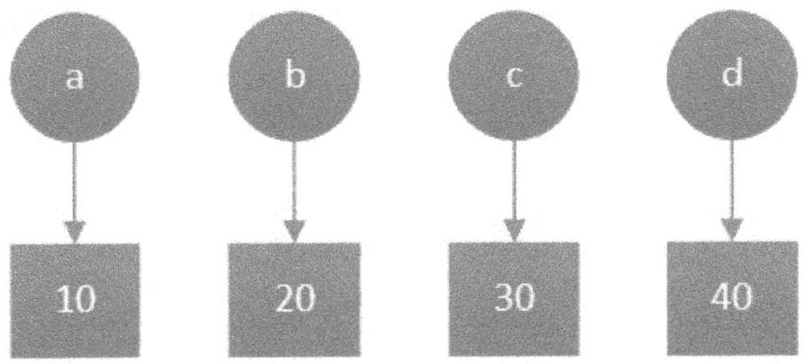

Figure 7.1 Four Variables.

What if we have to store 100 or 1,000 numbers? Creating 1,000 variables and keeping track of variable names would be a nightmare. What we want here is some way to store 1,000 values under one variable name. We can store a series of numbers in one named variable if the variable is an array type. **Figure 7.2** shows an array type variable called **numbers** storing four values.

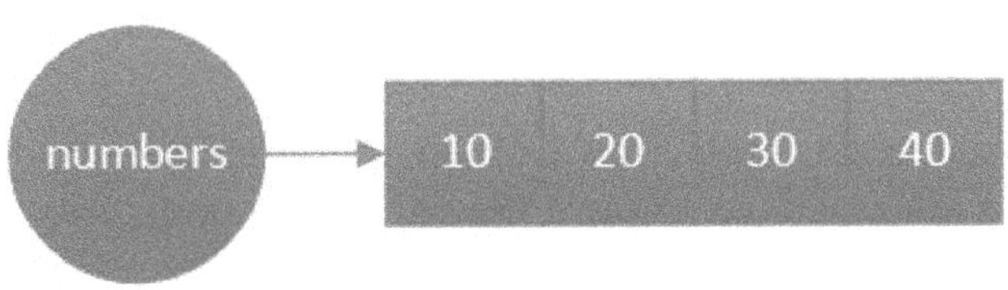

Figure 7.2 Numbers Array.

Now we have one variable called **numbers** that is storing four values. In an array the values are referred to by position. The value of 10 is at position 0, the value of 20 is at position 1, and so on.

Now the question is how can one variable store four different numbers? Internally the **numbers** variable is comprised of four different variables but for ease of the developer these different variables are wrapped as one variable name. Different values are accessed based on their position in an array. In other words, each value is accessed by its index. Index 0 contains the value of 10, index 1 contains the value of 20, and so on.

DECLARATION

To declare any variable we provide the data type followed by the variable name. A `string` variable can be declared as follows:

```
string name;
```

An array of `string` types can be declared in a similar way with additional square brackets. The following code declares an array of strings:

```
string[] names;
```

The previous example is a declaration that just says the `names` variable is of array type. It does not tell us how many values can be stored in the array. To declare an array type with the size of 5 we can use the following code:

```
string[] names = new string[5];
```

Now we know the `names` variable can store five values. The five values are at the 0, 1, 2, 3 and 4 index positions. To refer to a particular array item we have to provide the array name along with the array index.

```
names[0] = "John";
names[1] = "Roger";
```

The previous statements assigned John and Roger at index 0 and 1 respectively. If we want to print these values we can use the following code:

```
Console.WriteLine(names[0]);
Console.WriteLine(names[1]);
```

So far we have seen how to declare the array and size and then fill the array with values based on the positions. We can declare and initialize array variables at the same time. To declare an `int[]` array and a `string[]` array and how to initialize each is shown in the following code samples:

```
int[] numbers = new int[3] { 100, 200, 300 };
string[] names = new string[2] { "John", "Roger" };
```

In the previous declaration the `int[]` array has a size of 3 and the `string[]` array has a size of 2. During initialization we have to make sure the size provided and number of values provided match. The following code will throw an error since we are trying to put 3 values into an array that has a size of 2:

```
int[] numbers = new int[2] { 100, 200, 300 };
```

Another way to declare and initialize arrays is to just provide the values and not the size. Array size is automatically selected based on the number of values provided during the initialization. The following code creates a `string` array and automatically sets the correct size:

```
string[] names = { "John", "Roger" };
```

In the previous example the `names` array is of size 2.

Let's create a Console Application called **Numbers**. Here we will declare and initialize an array of type `double` and find the sum and the average:

```
double[] numbers =
  new double[5] { 100.5, 300.4, 500.5, 700.6, 900 };
```

Let's display these numbers to the user via the console. We can have five `Console.WriteLine` statements to display the five values, as seen in the following code:

```
Console.WriteLine(numbers[0]);
Console.WriteLine(numbers[1]);
Console.WriteLine(numbers[2]);
Console.WriteLine(numbers[3]);
Console.WriteLine(numbers[4]);
```

We have a repeating task of printing values on screen with the array index starting from 0 and going to 4. We could have achieved the same result using a `for` loop using the following code:

```
for (int index = 0; index < 5; index++)
{
```

```
    Console.WriteLine(numbers[index]);
}
```

The loop idea is the more common approach when dealing with iterating through array types. Here the loop starts with index 0 to print the value on the screen. In the next iteration the index 1 is used, and so on. The execution output of the program would look like the one shown in **Figure 7.3**.

```
static void Main(string[] args)
{
    double[] numbers =
    new double[5] { 100.5, 300.4, 500.5, 700.6, 900 };

    Console.WriteLine(numbers[0]);
    Console.WriteLine(numbers[1]);
    Console.WriteLine(numbers[2]);
    Console.WriteLine(numbers[3]);
    Console.WriteLine(numbers[4]);

    Console.ReadKey();
}
```

```
100.5
300.4
500.5
700.6
900
```

Figure 7.3 Numbers Using For Loop.

Our next goal is find out the sum and average of values defined in the `numbers` array. Declare two `double` variables. One will store the sum and the other will store the average. These will be below the previously declared `numbers` array, as seen in the following code:

```
double[] numbers =
    new double[5] { 100.5, 300.4, 500.5, 700.6, 900 };
double sum = 0;
double average = 0;
```

To find the sum we have to add every number to the sum variable. We have already written a `for` loop to go through all the array values. We can insert another statement to add the number for each iteration to the sum variable. The code for this is as follows:

```
for (int index = 0; index < 5; index++)
{
  Console.WriteLine(numbers[index]);
  sum = sum + numbers[index];
}
```

In the previous example the `for` loop is doing two things. First, it is printing the value on the console and second, it is adding the current number to the sum variable. The following table in **Figure 7.4** shows the execution of the `for` loop with the value of the `sum` variable after each iteration.

Iteration	Array Index	Sum
1	0	100.5
2	1	400.9
3	2	901.4
4	3	1602
5	4	2502

Figure 7.4 This shows the value of the `sum` variable after each iteration.

Now we have the `sum` as 2502. To find the average we can divide the sum variable by 5 and assign the result to the `average` variable.

```
average = sum / 5;
```

Write the following statements to display the `sum` and `average` to the console.

```
Console.WriteLine("Sum: {0}", sum);
Console.WriteLine("Avg: {0}", average);
```

The output should look like the one shown in Figure 7.5.

```
static void Main(string[] args)
{
  double[] numbers =
  new double[5] { 100.5, 300.4, 500.5, 700.6, 900 };
  double sum = 0;
  double average = 0;
```

```
  for (int index = 0; index < 5; index++)
  {
    Console.WriteLine(numbers[index]);
    sum = sum + numbers[index];
  }

  Console.ReadKey();
}
```

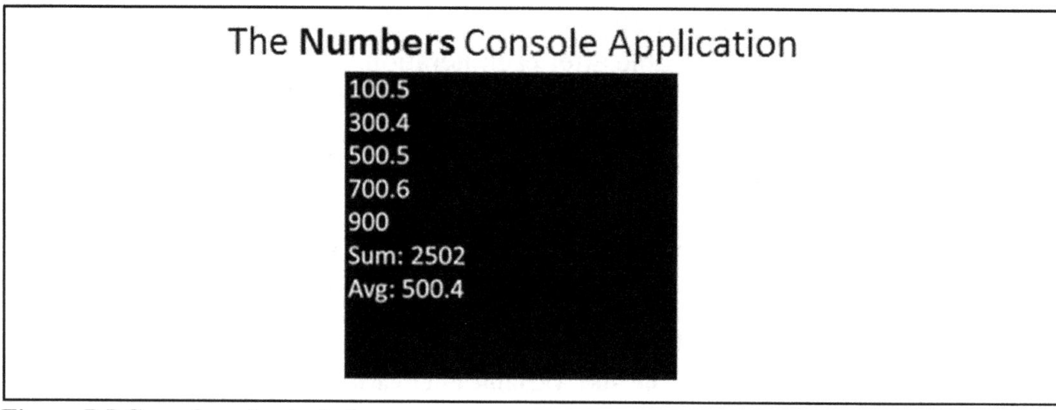

Figure 7.5 Console output window.

COMPLEX TYPES

When dealing with arrays, we are not limited to using simple data types. Arrays can also be of user-defined types.

Let's create a Console Application called **PersonArray**. We will define a `struct` called `Person` outside the `Program` class but inside namespace `PersonArray`, as seen in the following example:

```
struct Person
{
  public string Name;
  public int Age;
}

class Program
{
  static void Main(string[] args)
  {
  }
}
```

Declaring a `struct` array is similar to declaring any other array. Declare an array of type `Person` of size 3 inside the **Main** method.

```
Person[] persons = new Person[3];
```

Now we can take each person one-by-one and assign some values as seen here:

```
persons[0].Name = "John";
persons[0].Age = 23;

persons[1].Name = "Roger";
persons[1].Age = 34;

persons[2].Name = "Smith";
persons[2].Age = 45;
```

The only difference when dealing with an array `struct` and a regular `struct` is that in an array `struct` we have to provide an array index. Now we have all the values assigned to the array variable. To display the values of the array we can use a `for` loop with index values from 0 to 2.

```
for (int index = 0; index < 3; index++)
{
  Console.WriteLine("{0} : {1}",
    persons[index].Name, persons[index].Age);
}
```

To iterate through the values on an array we could have also used another type of loop called `foreach`. With a `foreach` loop it is not required to know the size of the array. The `foreach` loop iterates through all the values of an array one-by-one. The following code uses a `foreach` loop with the `Persons` array:

```
foreach (Person person in persons)
{
  Console.WriteLine("{0} : {1}", person.Name, person.Age);
}
```

In each iteration of the loop the `person` variable of the loop is assigned a value from the `persons` array. In the first iteration, the `person` variable gets `persons`[0], in the second iteration the `person` variable becomes `persons`[1] and `persons`[2] in the third iteration.

Build and execute your program to verify that the output looks like the one shown in **Figure 7.6**.

```
static void Main(string[] args)
{
  Person[] persons = new Person[3];
    persons[0].Name = "John";
    persons[0].Age = 23;
    persons[1].Name = "Roger";
    persons[1].Age = 34;
    persons[2].Name = "Smith";
    persons[2].Age = 45;
  foreach (Person person in persons)
  {
    Console.WriteLine("{0} : {1}", person.Name, person.Age);
  }
  Console.ReadKey();
}
```

```
John : 23
Roger : 34
Smith : 45
```

Figure 7.6 Person Array.

Lab 7.1: Simple Arrays

Skill Check 1: Create a Console Application called **ArrayNumbers**. Assign the following numbers to a `byte` array and display the numbers on the console, as shown in **Figure 7.7**. Use a `for` loop to display the numbers.

Byte Numbers
10
20
30
40
50
60
70
80

```
10 20 30 40 50 60 70 80
```

Figure 7.7 Array Numbers.

Skill Check 2: Modify Skill Check 1 to use a `foreach` loop.

Skill Check 3: Modify Skill Check 2 to display the sum and average of the numbers in the `byte` array. Use a `double` variable to store the sum and average.

```
10 20 30 40 50 60 70 80
Sum: 360 Average: 45
```

Figure 7.8 Array Numbers Sum & Average.

Answer Code: The C# answer code for this lab is located in the downloadable files inside the Projects folder within the BeginningCS2012CompanionFiles.zip file.

Points to Ponder - Simple Arrays

1. Array types are used to declare more than one variable of the same type.
2. The size of an array remains fixed after declaration.
3. Arrays can be initialized at declaration time.
4. Indexes of an array of size N goes from 0 to N - 1. For example, an array the size of 10 will go from 0 to 9.
5. To access a particular value of an array use square brackets along with an index of the item.
6. To iterate through all the values of an array you can use a `foreach` loop.

7.2 Two-dimensional Arrays

In Chapter 6 we discussed how the Minesweeper games are comprised of a grid (as shown in **Figure 6.20**). The grid is nothing but rectangular blocks of repeating rows and columns. In this section we will mostly talk about grid situations where data is stored in rows and columns.

GRID

The following is what a one row grid of numbers would look like:

500	200	400	100

Figure 7.9 This is a one row grid.

The previous example looks like an array of four numbers. If we want to create an array variable to represent the previous one row grid it would look like the following code sample:

```
int[] oneRowGrid = { 500, 200, 400, 100 };
```

The arrays we have used so far hold one row of N numbers. An array like the previous example is called a one-dimensional array. If we have to represent more than one row we can create many one-dimensional arrays, as seen in the following example:

500	200	400	100
600	340	510	830
120	900	750	300

Figure 7.10 This shows three one-dimensional arrays.

```
int[] row0 = { 500, 200, 400, 100 };
int[] row1 = { 600, 340, 510, 830 };
int[] row2 = { 120, 900, 750, 300 };
```

Here we created three separate arrays to represent three rows to make up the grid. Now if we want to access number 510 we can use row1[2] since the number 510 is in the second row and third column. In other words, it is at row index 1 and column index 2. **Figure 7.11** shows row and column indexes of all the blocks in the grid.

0,0	0,1	0,2	0,3
1,0	1,1	1,2	1,3
2,0	2,1	2,2	2,3

Figure 7.11 This shows three row array with coordinates.

We can combine these three array variables as one two-dimensional array which can contain both the row and column information. The code sample to create the array from **Figure 7.12** is shown as follows:

```
int[,] grid = new int[3, 4];
```

The previous statement created a two-dimensional array of 3 rows and 4 columns or in other words, it is a 3x4 (read as 3 by 4) array. Adding a comma inside square brackets when declaring an array makes it a two-dimensional array.

We can declare and initialize a two-dimensional array in one statement. The following code creates the array from **Figure 7.12**:

```
int[,] grid =
{
  { 500, 200, 400, 100 },
  { 600, 340, 510, 830 },
  { 120, 900, 750, 300 }
};
```

In the previous statement each row is defined in its own set of curly braces separated by commas. To access any value of the array we need to provide the row and column index with the variable name.

```
int row0col0 = grid[0, 0]; // Value 500
int row1col2 = grid[1, 2]; // Value 510
int row2col3 = grid[2, 3]; // Value 300
```

To display all the values of the grid we can use a nested `for` loop. The inner loop will be moving the column and the outer loop will be moving the row one after the other.

```
for (int rowIndex = 0; rowIndex < 3; rowIndex++)
{
  for (int colIndex = 0; colIndex < 4; colIndex++)
  {
    Console.Write("{0} ", grid[rowIndex, colIndex]);
  }
```

```
  Console.WriteLine();
}
```

In the previous example, the outer loop starts with a rowIndex at 0 and then enters the inner loop with a colIndex at 0. The inner loop will execute completely with colIndex values as 0, 1, 2 and 3, and the following pair of indexes will be displayed on the console.

[0,0] [0,1] [0,2] [0,3]

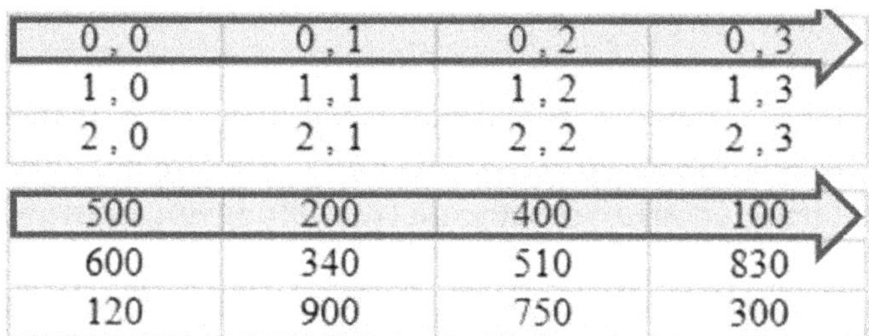

Figure 7.12 This shows the pair of indexes that will be displayed on the console.

The inner loop is using `Console.Write` to display the values on the same line. When the inner loop finishes, `Console.WriteLine` moves the cursor to the next line. In the next iteration, rowIndex becomes 1 and the inner loop again starts at the left with colIndex 0. The inner loop executes with the following pair of indexes.

[1,0] [1,1] [1,2] [1,3]

This process goes on until the outer loop is finished with all the iterations. Output of the execution is shown in **Figure 7.13**.

```
500 200 400 100
600 340 510 830
120 900 750 300
```

Figure 7.13 Two-dimensional Array.

GRID PATTERN

Let's create a Console Application called **GridPattern**. Here we will create a 10x10 grid using a two-dimensional array and create a pattern on the console, as shown in **Figure 7.14**.

```
# # * * * * * * # #
# # * * * * * * # #
# # * * * * * * # #
# # * * * * * * # #
# # * * * * * * # #
# # * * * * * * # #
# # * * * * * * # #
# # * * * * * * # #
# # * * * * * * # #
# # * * * * * * # #
```

Figure 7.14 Grid Pattern.

We can visualize the table shown in Figure 7.15. This table has row and column indexes from 0 to 9 (i.e. 10 values). Column indexes 0, 1, 8 and 9 have a value of # signs whereas column indexes 2, 3, 4, 5, 6 and 7 have a value of * signs.

	0	1	2	3	4	5	6	7	8	9
0	#	#	*	*	*	*	*	*	#	#
1	#	#	*	*	*	*	*	*	#	#
2	#	#	*	*	*	*	*	*	#	#
3	#	#	*	*	*	*	*	*	#	#
4	#	#	*	*	*	*	*	*	#	#
5	#	#	*	*	*	*	*	*	#	#
6	#	#	*	*	*	*	*	*	#	#
7	#	#	*	*	*	*	*	*	#	#
8	#	#	*	*	*	*	*	*	#	#
9	#	#	*	*	*	*	*	*	#	#

Figure 7.15 Grid Table.

We need to store 10 characters at each row and 10 such rows. Creating a two-dimensional `char` array of 10 rows and 10 columns would be a good start.

```
char[,] grid = new char[10, 10];
```

The array is empty right now and we need to populate the rows and columns with # and * at the appropriate row and column indexes. As discussed earlier we can use nested `for` loops to go through rows in the outer loop and then go through the columns in the inner loop.

The following code will populate * for all rows and column indexes 2, 3, 4, 5, 6 and 7:

```
for (int rowIndex = 0; rowIndex < 10; rowIndex+=1)
{
  for (int colIndex = 2; colIndex <= 7; colIndex+=1)
  {
    grid[rowIndex, colIndex] = '*';
  }
}
```

The outer row loop will start at row index 0 and then the inner column loop will start at column index 2 and finish at column index 7. So after the first iteration of the outer loop, the first row of the array contains * at column indexes from 2 to 7. After all 10 iterations of the outer row loop, all rows will be populated with * at column indexes 2 to 7.

Our next step would be to populate the array with # at column indexes 0, 1, 8 and 9. We can achieve this in many ways. Let's do this by modifying the outer loop. The following modified nested loop code will populate all the rows and columns of the array:

```
for (int rowIndex = 0; rowIndex < 10; rowIndex+=1)
{
  grid[rowIndex, 0] = '#';
  grid[rowIndex, 1] = '#';

  for (int colIndex = 2; colIndex <= 7; colIndex+=1)
  {
    grid[rowIndex, colIndex] = '*';
  }

  grid[rowIndex, 8] = '#';
  grid[rowIndex, 9] = '#';
}
```

Here we hard-coded the column indexes 0 and 1 to populate #, then used the inner loop for column indexes 2 to 7 to populate the * in them. Finally we used hard-coded column indexes 8 and 9 to populate #.

At this point the grid array is fully assigned with values. To display the array we can use another nested loop which is seen in the following code:

```
for (int rowIndex = 0; rowIndex < 10; rowIndex++)
{
  for (int colIndex = 0; colIndex < 10; colIndex++)
  {
    Console.Write(grid[rowIndex, colIndex] + " ");
  }
  Console.WriteLine();
}
```

After every row has written out all its column values, the cursor is moved to the next line using a `Console.WriteLine` statement. Then the outer loop continues on and iterates again. Executing the previous program will display the pattern on the console, as shown in **Figure 7.16**.

```
# # * * * * * * # #
# # * * * * * * # #
# # * * * * * * # #
# # * * * * * * # #
# # * * * * * * # #
# # * * * * * * # #
# # * * * * * * # #
# # * * * * * * # #
# # * * * * * * # #
# # * * * * * * # #
```

Figure 7.16 Grid Pattern Output.

ARRAY SIZE

So far whenever we wanted to iterate through the values in an array we started from index 0 to the size of the array less one (i.e. if an array is of size 10 we would iterate from 0 to 9). Size minus one covers all the members (in our case that is 10 minus 1). We can either set our condition to `index < 9` or `index < 10`. Luckily we knew the size of the array so we hard-coded 10, as seen in the following code:

```
int[] numbers = new int[10];
```

```
for (int index = 0; index < 10; index++)
{
  numbers[index] = 100 + index;
}
```

There is a better way to handle this scenario without hard-coding the array size in our code. We can use the `Length` property of an array which returns the size of an array, as shown in this code sample:

```
int[] numbers = new int[10];
for (int index = 0; index < numbers.Length; index++)
{
  numbers[index] = 100 + index;
}
```

The `Length` property works well for a one-dimensional array. In the case of two-dimensional arrays the `Length` property returns the total size of an array. This means an array of type `[10, 5]` would return 50 and an array of type `[10, 10]` would return 100.

What we want is the number of rows and columns listed separately. We can use the `GetLength()` method of two-dimensional arrays to get the size for each dimension of an array. Dimension 0 is for rows and dimension 1 is for columns. The following code uses the `GetLength()` method to iterate through all rows and columns to display the contents of the grid (a two-dimensional array).

```
for (int ri = 0; ri < grid.GetLength(0); ri++)
{
  for (int ci = 0; ci < grid.GetLength(1); ci++)
  {
    Console.Write(grid[ri, ci] + " ");
  }
  Console.WriteLine();
}
```

The row loop (or the outer loop) is providing dimension 0 whereas the column loop is providing dimension 1 as the input parameter to the `GetLength()` method. We will learn even more about properties and methods as this book progresses.

SORTING

Sometimes when we create a report we sort, or order, the values before displaying them. We can use sorting to display lists of people sorted by their last name, city, or age. The C# language supports sorting items of an array using the `Array.Sort()` method in your statement.

The following code sorts the numbers:

```
int[] values = new int[5] { 200, 400, 500, 100, 300 };
Array.Sort(values);
```

After the second statement executes, numbers in the `values` array are sorted as 100, 200, 300, 400 and 500. A similar approach to sorting can be applied to other data types.

Lab 7.2: Two-dimensional Arrays

Skill Check 1: Create a Console Application called **NumberGrid** to display numbers on the console, as shown in **Figure 7.17**. Make sure to populate a two-dimensional array of size 5x5 before displaying the numbers.

```
0 0 0 0 0
1 1 1 1 1
2 2 2 2 2
3 3 3 3 3
4 4 4 4 4
```

Figure 7.17 NumberGrid.

Skill Check 2: Modify Skill Check 1 to use the `GetLength()`method in the `for` loops to get the size of the array at each dimension.

Skill Check 3: Create a Console Application called **SortedWords**. Declare the `words` array as follows:

```
string[] words = {"Rod", "Pen", "Fruit", "Bed", "Ape" };
```

Display each word on a separate line on the console in sorted order, as shown in **Figure 7.18**. When iterating through the array in a `for` loop use the `Length` property to get the size of the array.

```
Ape
Bed
Fruit
Pen
Rod
```

Figure 7.18 SortedWords.

Answer Code: The C# answer code for this lab is located in the downloadable files inside the Projects folder within the BeginningCS2012CompanionFiles.zip file.

Points to Ponder - Two-dimensional Arrays

1. Two-dimensional arrays are nothing but multiple one-dimensional arrays.
2. To initialize a two-dimensional array each row values are stored in curly brackets with each value and each row separated by a comma.
3. Use the `Length` property to get the size of a one-dimensional array.
4. Use the `GetLength` method to get the size of each dimension of a two-dimensional array.
5. Total number of values stored in a two-dimensional array is the product of row and column count.

Review Quiz - Chapter Seven

1.) How many maximum items can the following array hold?

```
int[] items = { 0, 2, 3, 8, 1 };
```

O a) 6
O b) 1
O c) 5
O d) Unlimited

2.) Will the following code compile?

```
string[] names = new string[5] { "John", "Roger" };
```

O a) Yes
O b) No

3.) Will the following code compile?

```
double[] numbers = new double[3] { 10.1, 10.2, 10.3 };
Console.WriteLine(numbers[3]);
```

O c) Yes
O d) No

4.) Can the size of an array change after declaration?

O a) Yes
O b) No

5.) What will be the output of the following code?

```
int[,] numbers = new int[2, 3];
Console.WriteLine(numbers.Length);
```

O a) 2
O b) 3
O c) 5
O d) 6

ANSWER KEY

1.) There are 5 values initialized during array declaration so the maximum value an array can hold is 5, making option (c) the correct answer.

2.) The names array tells the compiler its length to be 5 but the values supplied during initialization are only 2. When the size defined and number of values provided are different, compiler throws an error, making option (b) the correct answer.

3.) The numbers array has a length of 3 and can hold 3 values at index 0, 1 and 2. Even though Console.WriteLine is accessing index 3 which is greater than 2, the compiler at compile time doesn't check that. From compiler perspective, the syntax of statements are correct and will not issue any error. The correct answer is (a) (However the code will result in a runtime error).

4.) The size of an array cannot be changed after declaration, making option (b) the correct answer.

5.) The Length property is generally used in the case of one dimensional arrays. Two-dimensional arrays generally use GetLength(INDEX) where INDEX parameter is either 0 or 1. The GetLength(0) will return 2 and GetLength(1) will return 3. When we use the Length property in the case of two-dimensional arrays it tells the total length (i.e. total number of items that can be stored in the array). In this case the array can hold 2 x 3 = 6 items, making option (d) as correct answer.

[NOTES]

Chapter 8 Methods and Functions

Some big tasks (like remodeling a home) are ones that more than one person should be doing. A big task can be broken down into many smaller tasks. Out of these smaller tasks, I would do some on my own, and get some help by delegating the rest of the tasks for others to complete. In programming languages when we have a big task we divide it into small tasks called methods or functions. Calling these tasks as individual methods is more common in C#. The term "function" is more common in languages like C++. Methods and functions are just two words for the same thing but we will use the term "method" since this book is about C#.

READER NOTE: *Before doing the steps in this section you need to have the following folder structure on your hard drive C:\Joes2Pros\C# 2012\Chapter 8. Within the Chapter 8 folder there should be two more folders called Lab 8.1 and Lab 8.2. In order to follow along with the examples, you will need to have some version of Visual Studio 2012 installed.*

8.1 Simple Methods

Let's say I need to do the following tasks:

- Paint the room
- Buy groceries
- Mow the lawn

Since I will be the only one doing these tasks I have to do them one-by-one. Painting the room is not one action by itself. The paint needs to be mixed, areas need to be taped off, and a roller and brush are needed. These tasks of painting, buying groceries, and mowing the lawn have a bunch of steps to complete them. The following table shows the steps (For simplicity each task has 5 steps):

Step #	Paint Room	Buy Groceries	Mow Lawn
1	Buy paints	Prepare list	Put gas in the mower
2	Buy brushes	Drive to store	Mow lawn
3	Mix paints	Fill the cart	Pull the weeds
4	Prepare the room	Pay for groceries	Blow the leaves
5	Paint the room	Drive back	Water the lawn

Figure 8.1 This shows the steps for three tasks.

To convert this table into C# code let's display the steps to the console after it gets done. Each task has 5 steps. Create a Console Application called **MyTasks** and add the following statements in the **Main** method.

```
// Paint Room
Console.WriteLine("Buy paints");
Console.WriteLine("Buy brushes");
Console.WriteLine("Mix paints");
Console.WriteLine("Prepare the room");
Console.WriteLine("Paint the room");

// Buy Groceries
Console.WriteLine("Prepare list");
Console.WriteLine("Drive to store");
Console.WriteLine("Fill the cart");
Console.WriteLine("Pay for Groceries");
Console.WriteLine("Drive back");
```

```
// Mow Lawn
Console.WriteLine("Put gas in the mower");
Console.WriteLine("Mow Lawn");
Console.WriteLine("Pull the weeds");
Console.WriteLine("Blow the leaves");
Console.WriteLine("Water the lawn");
```

Looking at the code, each step is a `Console.WriteLine` statement and the tasks are separated by a comment line. What if we have 50 steps for each task? Then it would be messy to have all the tasks in one **Main** method. We need to do more than separate these tasks with comment lines. One of these tasks might be run by someone else so we get done faster. What we want is complete separation of the tasks.

DIVIDE AND CONQUER

In the previous example all the tasks and steps are done together in one **Main** method. We want to treat each task as an individual unit and not all together as one unit, as shown in **Figure 8.2**.

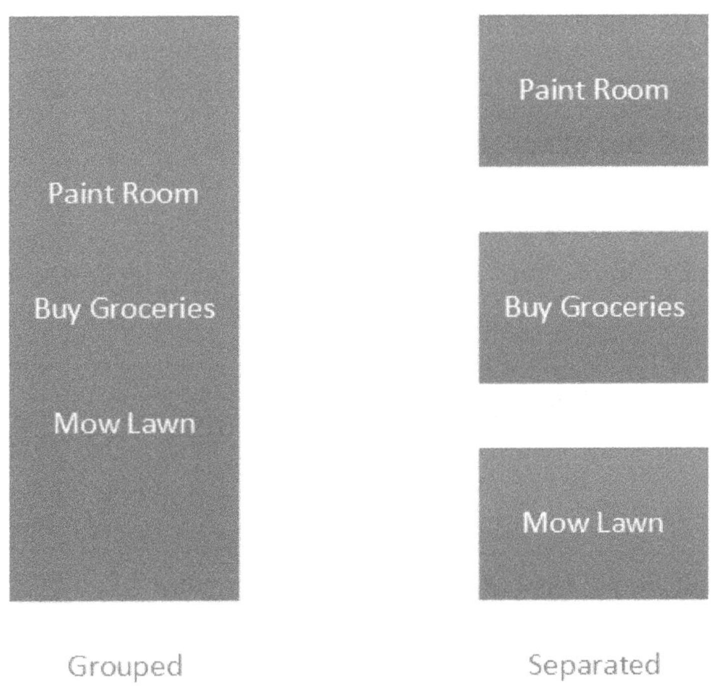

Figure 8.2 Separate work into smaller pieces.

As shown in the previous figure we separate each task to be its own individual unit. We can achieve this in C# by using methods. When we do this, each task will be a separate method.

Create a Console Application called **MyTasksMethod**. When we create a new Console Application we get an empty **Main** method already written for us to put code there. The **Main** method is the entry point of the application and looks like the one shown in this code.

```
class Program
{
  static void Main(string[] args)
  {
  }
}
```

We can create more methods similar to the **Main** method which is seen in the following code:

```
class Program
{
  static void Main(string[] args)
  {
  }
  static void PaintRoom()
  {
  }
  static void BuyGroceries()
  {
  }
  static void MowLawn()
  {
  }
}
```

In the previous code we have created three methods named PaintRoom, BuyGroceries and MowLawn. Before we write more code let's get to know some of the keywords used to create these methods.

The keyword `void` means that a method doesn't return anything. What is meant by "returns" is that there can be methods which do some processing and give us back a value. For example, if we have a method to give back the current temperature, the method would not have `void` but may be `double` which is seen as follows:

```
static double GetCurrentTemperature()
{
}
```

Another thing to note here is that the **Main** method's parentheses contains `(string[] args)` whereas the new methods do not. Whenever we specify anything in the method's parentheses it means that method takes in some parameter. For example, the `GetCurrentTemperature` method can take a parameter called `zipCode` which is seen as follows:

```
static double GetCurrentTemperature(int zipCode)
```

The methods we will be using will have no inputs so they will have no parameters. We will cover parameters in detail in the next section. Now that we have some idea of what methods are let's add the steps to each method. Each method will have five steps which are seen in the following:

```
static void PaintRoom()
{
  // Paint Room
  Console.WriteLine("Buy paints");
  Console.WriteLine("Buy brushes");
  Console.WriteLine("Mix paints");
  Console.WriteLine("Prepare the room");
  Console.WriteLine("Paint the room");
}
static void BuyGroceries()
{

  // Buy Groceries
  Console.WriteLine("Prepare list");
  Console.WriteLine("Drive to store");
  Console.WriteLine("Fill the cart");
  Console.WriteLine("Pay for Groceries");
  Console.WriteLine("Drive back");
}
static void MowLawn()
{
```

```
  // Mow Lawn
  Console.WriteLine("Put gas in the mower");
  Console.WriteLine("Mow Lawn");
  Console.WriteLine("Pull the weeds");
  Console.WriteLine("Blow the leaves");
  Console.WriteLine("Water the lawn");
}
```

Now the methods are ready but they will not run unless we call on them. As mentioned before, the **Main** method is the entry point of the program. The **Main** method is called when we run the application. Currently the **Main** method contains no code and would show nothing when it is executed. We want the **Main** method to execute the other three methods. After adding the method calls for the three methods our **Main** method would look like the following:

```
static void Main(string[] args)
{
  PaintRoom();
  BuyGroceries();
  MowLawn();
  Console.ReadKey();
}
```

To call the methods we created we just use the method name with the parentheses and end the statement with a semicolon. This code looks much cleaner and if we want to distribute the code to different developers we can do it easily. This way a developer can be responsible for writing a method, and many developers can work on separate parts of the project at one time and be more productive.

Build and execute the code. The output will look similar to what is shown in **Figure 8.3**.

```
static void Main(string[] args)
{
  PaintRoom();
  BuyGroceries();
  MowLawn();
  Console.ReadKey();
}
```

```
static void PaintRoom()
{
  // Paint Room
  Console.WriteLine("Buy paints");
  Console.WriteLine("Buy brushes");
  Console.WriteLine("Mix paints");
  Console.WriteLine("Prepare the room");
  Console.WriteLine("Paint the room");
}
static void BuyGroceries()
{
  // Buy Groceries
  Console.WriteLine("Prepare list");
  Console.WriteLine("Drive to store");
  Console.WriteLine("Fill the cart");
  Console.WriteLine("Pay for Groceries");
  Console.WriteLine("Drive back");
}
static void MowLawn()
{
  // Mow Lawn
  Console.WriteLine("Put gas in the mower");
  Console.WriteLine("Mow Lawn");
  Console.WriteLine("Pull the weeds");
  Console.WriteLine("Blow the leaves");
  Console.WriteLine("Water the lawn");
}
```

```
Buy paints
Buy brushes
Mix paints
Prepare the room
Paint the room
Prepare list
Drive to store
Fill the cart
Pay for Groceries
Drive back
Put gas in the mower
Mow Lawn
Pull the weeds
Blow the leaves
Water the lawn
```

Figure 8.3 MyTasks Method.

METHOD INPUTS AND RETURNS

Now our goal is to write a calculator application that takes two numbers from a user. With those two numbers it will perform an operation like addition, subtraction, multiplication or division and return the result. We can start by creating a Console Application called **Calculator**.

In the **Main** method add the following statements to take input from the user:

```
Console.Write("Enter 1st number: ");
double number1 = double.Parse(Console.ReadLine());
Console.Write("Enter 2nd number: ");
double number2 = double.Parse(Console.ReadLine());
```

Now we have two variables (`number1` and `number2`) assigned for the user inputs. To add the numbers we can create a third variable to store the result of `number1` and `number2` which is seen as follows:

```
double result = number1 + number2;
Console.WriteLine(result);

Console.ReadKey();
```

Adding two numbers is simple, so the previous code would work just fine. This method should take two numbers as input and should return the sum of the input numbers. We can write a method called AddTwoNumbers to meet our requirements, as seen in the following:

```
static double AddTwoNumbers(double num1, double num2)
{
  double sum = num1 + num2;
  return sum;
}
static void Main(string[] args)
{
  Console.Write("Enter 1st number: ");
  double number1 = double.Parse(Console.ReadLine());
  Console.Write("Enter 2nd number: ");
  double number2 = double.Parse(Console.ReadLine());

  double result = number1 + number2;
  Console.ReadKey();
}
```

The AddTwoNumbers method takes two parameters called num1 and num2, and assigns the sum of num1 and num2 to the sum variable. The final step of the method returns the value of the sum variable to the caller of this method.

Don't do this yet but we can invoke (or call) this method using the following code sample:

```
double result = AddTwoNumbers(10, 20);
```

When the previous statement executes, the execution of the code enters the method. Here, the values 10 and 20 are assigned to the num1 and num2 parameters respectively. Inside the method the sum variable gets assigned to 10+20 which is 30 and then the method returns 30 to get assigned to the total variable.

We don't want to use the same numbers each time we run this application. The goal is to let the user pick the numbers. We can now use the method in the **Calculator** project, as shown on the last line of the following code:

```
Console.Write("Enter 1st number: ");
double number1 = double.Parse(Console.ReadLine());
Console.Write("Enter 2nd number: ");
double number2 = double.Parse(Console.ReadLine());
double result = AddTwoNumbers(number1, number2);
```

It would be a good idea to take these results and display it to the console. The following statement will show the user the output they are wanting:

```
Console.WriteLine("{0}+{1}={2}", number1, number2, result);
```

Run and test the code by entering 100 and 200 then 15 and 25. The console will resemble the results, as shown in **Figure 8.4** and **Figure 8.5** respectively.

```
static void Main(string[] args)
{
  Console.Write("Enter 1st number: ");
  double number1 = double.Parse(Console.ReadLine());

  Console.Write("Enter 2nd number: ");
  double number2 = double.Parse(Console.ReadLine());

  double result = AddTwoNumbers(number1, number2);

  Console.WriteLine("{0}+{1}={2}", number1, number2,
    result);

  Console.ReadKey();
}

static double AddTwoNumbers(double num1, double num2)
{
  double sum = num1 + num2;
  return sum;
}
```

```
Enter 1st number: 100
Enter 2nd number: 200
100+200=300
```

Figure 8.4 Calculator 1.

```
Enter 1st number: 15
Enter 2nd number: 25
15+25=40
```

Figure 8.5 Calculator 2.

OVERLOADING

It makes sense to call a method that adds two numbers together with the name Add. What would be a good name to call a method that adds three numbers together? We can use the same name if we like. There are times when methods can have the same name but a different set of parameters.

Create a new Console Application named **ManyAdder**. In the Program class below the Main method we will be creating two more methods. We can have a method called Add which takes two parameters and adds two numbers. There can also be a method called Add which takes three parameters to add three numbers which is seen as follows:

```
class Program
{
  static void Main(string[] args)
  {
  }
  static double Add(double x, double y)
  {
    return x + y;
  }
  static double Add(double x, double y, double z)
  {
    return x + y + z;
  }
}
```

Here the method name is Add for both the methods. When we try to invoke the Add method then the IntelliSense shows two options for the method. The options are shown in **Figure 8.6** and **Figure 8.7**.

Figure 8.6 Overload two parameters.

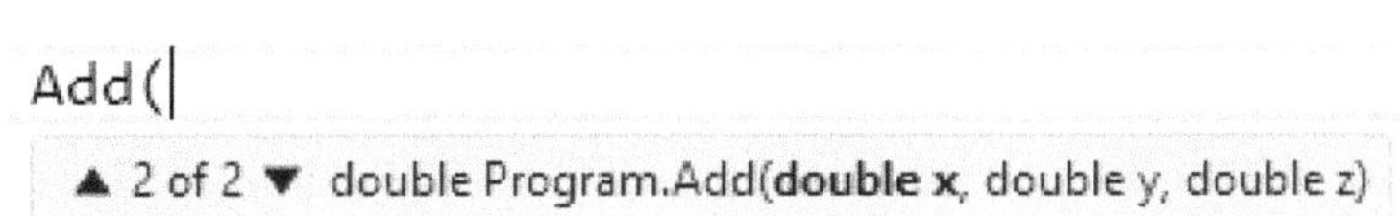

Figure 8.7 Overload three parameters.

If we provide two parameters to the `Add` method, the first `Add` method we created (with two parameters) will be called. If we call and provide three parameters then the second `Add` method we created will be called. This technique of methods having the same name with a different parameter list is called method overloading.

```
static void Main(string[] args)
{
  double total1 = Add(5, 8);
  Console.WriteLine(total1);

  double total2 = Add(5, 8, 10);
  Console.WriteLine(total2);

  Console.ReadKey();
}
```

Another example of method overloading would be to show a message on the console, or several messages. Create a new Console Application named **ManyAdder**. In the Program class below the Main method we will be creating two more methods. The following code overloads the `DisplayMessage` method:

```
class Program{
static void Main(string[] args)
{
}
  static void DisplayMessage(string message)
  {
    Console.WriteLine(message);
  }
  static void DisplayMessage(string[] messages)
  {
    foreach (string message in messages)
    {
       Console.WriteLine(message);
     }
  }
}
```

In the previous example both methods take one parameter but of different types. The first one takes a `string` parameter and the other takes a `string[]` array as it's parameter. Even though both `DisplayMessage` methods take one parameter it is a perfectly fine example of overloading a method. We can invoke the `DisplayMessage` method both ways by using the following code:

```
static void Main(string[] args)
{
  DisplayMessage("Hello!");
  DisplayMessage(new string[]{"Hello!", "Hi!"});

    Console.ReadKey();
}
```

Lab 8.1: Simple Methods

Skill Check 1: Create a Console Application called **HelloMethod**. Create a method called `Hello` which (upon invoking it) displays a message "Hello There!" to the console, as shown in **Figure 8.8**.

```
static void Main(string[] args)
{
  Hello();
  Console.ReadKey();
}
```

```
Hello There!
```

Figure 8.8 HelloMethod.

Skill Check 2: Create a Console Application called **SimpleCalculator**. Implement the following 4 methods.

```
static double Add(double x, double y) {}
static double Subtract(double x, double y) {}
static double Multiply(double x, double y) {}
static double Divide(double x, double y) {}
```

Verify these methods with the following code in the **Main** method:

```
double a = 500,b = 100;
Console.WriteLine("{0}+{1}={2}", a, b, Add(a, b));
Console.WriteLine("{0}-{1}={2}", a, b, Subtract(a, b));
Console.WriteLine("{0}*{1}={2}", a, b, Multiply(a, b));
Console.WriteLine("{0}/{1}={2}", a, b, Divide(a, b));
```

Make sure the output is the same as what is shown in **Figure 8.9**.

```
500+100=600
500-100=400
500*100=50000
500/100=5
```

Figure 8.9 SimpleCalculator.

Skill Check 3: Create a Console Application called **Adder**. Create two Add methods with the following parameter signatures:

```
static long Add(int number1, int number2) {}
static long Add(int[] numbers) {}
```

Both the Add methods should return the sum of the numbers supplied. Verify the output of the program with the following code in the **Main** method:

```
int number1 = 500, number2 = 700;
int[] numbers =
{
  100,
  200,
  300,
  400
};

Console.WriteLine(Add(number1, number2));
Console.WriteLine(Add(numbers));
```

The output of the program should look like the one shown in **Figure 8.10**.

```
1200
1000
```

Figure 8.10 Adder.

Answer Code: The C# answer code for this lab is located in the downloadable files inside the Projects folder within the BeginningCS2012CompanionFiles.zip file.

Points to Ponder - Simple Methods

1. Methods are used to separate out a big piece of code into smaller code modules.
2. Methods make the code more reusable. For example, the `Add` and `Subtract` methods can be used by one program or multiple programs.
3. The method name should start with a capital letter and each subsequent word's first letter should be capitalized (Pascal case).
4. Methods that don't return any value have a `void` return type in the method definition.
5. Methods can take parameters or have no parameters.
6. To invoke (or call) a method, use the method name and supply the parameter values in the method's parentheses.
7. Methods that have the same name but different parameters are called overloaded methods.
8. Changing the return type of a method to create an overload will cause a compile time error. We can overload a different parameter list but not use a different return type.

8.2 Parameters

In the previous section we learned that some methods have parameters and some methods have none. In this section we are going to learn about method parameters in detail.

INPUT

When a chef is putting ingredients into a recipe they expect to get back a tasty meal. The do not expect to get back the salt, potatoes, or carrots. Those items are the input to getting the meal cooked. When you run a calculator and put in 8 + 5 you aren't expecting your input numbers back but you would like to get back 13.

Input parameters are inputs to the methods to take some action based on the values provided, or process the values provided, or do both. For a method to have input parameters we must define the method to expect them. To create a method with input parameters defined, use the following pseudo code:

```
<ReturnType> Name(DataType1 p1, DataType2 p2,… DataTypeN pN)
```

Every method needs to have a return type. If you don't need a return type you still must specify this with a return type of `void`. Parameters also should have data types (like `int`, `string`, `double`, etc.) and names like p1, p2, or p3. Parameter data types can also be user-defined types like `enum` and `struct`.

Create a Console Application called **PersonMethod**. Here we will create two user-defined data types (`enum` and `struct`) to be used as an input to a method.

Define an `enum` called `Color` inside the namespace and output the `Program` class. Also, define a `struct` called `Person` which has `Name`, `Age` and `FavoriteColor` as the fields. The code should appear as follows:

```
enum Color
{
  Red,
  Blue,
  Green
}
```

```
struct Person
{
  public string Name;
  public int Age;
  public Color FavoriteColor;
}
```

In our next step we will create a method which takes three inputs. These inputs will be `Name`, `Age` and `FavoriteColor`. This method returns the `Person` object. Make sure to create the `GetPerson` method inside the `Program` class right below the **Main** method as follows:

```
static Person GetPerson(string name, int age, Color
favoriteColor)
{
  Person person;
  person.Name = name;
  person.Age = age;
  person.FavoriteColor = favoriteColor;
  return person;
}
```

The `GetPerson` method takes the `string`, `int`, and `Color` data types with parameter names as `Name`, `Age` and `FavoriteColor` respectively. In this method the parameter values are assigned to the fields of the object `Person`. Then that `Person` object is returned. Here we were able to return an object of type `Person` since the method defines the return type as `Person`.

Now we have an `enum`, a `struct` and a method to create the `Person` object. Let's create two `Person` objects, as shown in the following code using the `GetPerson` method inside the **Main** method.

```
static void Main(string[] args)
{
  Person p1 = GetPerson("John", 23, Color.Red);
  Person p2 = GetPerson("Sally", 34, Color.Green);
}
```

Variables `p1` and `p2` are of the `Person` type and were created using a method which took three parameters. To display the contents of each `Person` object we can write a couple of `Console.WriteLine` statements or we can create a method which takes a `Person` object as input and displays that person's detail. Write a method called `ShowPersonDetails` in the `Program` class as follows:

```
static void ShowPersonDetails(Person person)
{
  Console.WriteLine("================");
  Console.WriteLine("Name : {0}", person.Name);
  Console.WriteLine("Age : {0}", person.Age);
  Console.WriteLine("Color: {0}", person.FavoriteColor);
}
```

To display the `p1` and `p2` details we can invoke the `ShowPersonDetails` method one-by-one with `p1` and `p2` as parameters, as seen in the following example:

```
ShowPersonDetails(p1);
ShowPersonDetails(p2);
```

The complete code inside the **Main** method would look like this:

```
static void Main(string[] args)
{
  Person p1 = GetPerson("John", 23, Color.Red);
  Person p2 = GetPerson("Sally", 34, Color.Green);

  ShowPersonDetails(p1);
  ShowPersonDetails(p2);

  Console.ReadKey();
}
```

Here we see that the method makes our code in **Main** more readable and manageable. It only takes one statement inside of **Main** to show all the details. The important thing to note is that we are using some special formatting to display the person's details, which we don't have to worry about when we add more `Person` objects. This is because we are going to use the `ShowPersonDetails` method to display the person's details and not clutter the **Main** method with many custom `Console.WriteLine` statements.

Build and execute the program. The output should look like the one shown in **Figure 8.11**.

```
static void Main(string[] args)
{
  Person p1 = GetPerson("John", 23, Color.Red);
  Person p2 = GetPerson("Sally", 34, Color.Green);

  ShowPersonDetails(p1);
  ShowPersonDetails(p2);
  Console.ReadKey();
}

static Person GetPerson(string name, int age, Color
favoriteColor)
{
  Person person;
  person.Name = name;
  person.Age = age;
  person.FavoriteColor = favoriteColor;

  return person;
}

static void ShowPersonDetails(Person person)
{
  Console.WriteLine("================");
  Console.WriteLine("Name : {0}", person.Name);
  Console.WriteLine("Age : {0}", person.Age);
  Console.WriteLine("Color: {0}", person.FavoriteColor);
}
```

```
================
Name : John
Age : 23
Color: Red
================
Name : Sally
Age : 34
Color: Green
```

Figure 8.11 PersonMethod.

OUTPUT

From the previous sections we know that methods can return values to the method caller. For example, a method to return the sum of two numbers can look like the following code:

```
static double SumOfTwoNumbers(double num1, double num2)
{
  return num1 + num2;
}
```

If we want to get the average of two numbers the code to create such a method is seen as follows:

```
static double AvgOfTwoNumbers(double num1, double num2)
{
  return (num1 + num2)/2;
}
```

We can invoke both of these methods in the **Main** method using the following code:

```
double x = 300, y = 500, sum, avg;
sum = SumOfTwoNumbers(x, y);
avg = AvgOfTwoNumbers(x, y);
```

Here we declared four `double` variables and initialized two of the variables `x` and `y` for inputs to the methods. Later we invoked the two methods, one after the other, to set the values for the sum and average of `x` and `y`. If our business case is to get the sum and average one after the other all the time, we would like to optimize our code. How about one method (which we will call `SumAvgOfTwoNumbers`) that returns two values? But a method can return only one value at a time, so there has to be another solution.

Methods can return only one value but they can output many more values. This will become clear as we do the upcoming examples. When we are defining a method we can define some of the parameters as an output type. So far we have only talked about input parameters, where we provide values to the method to process or take any action. To change the parameter to output we can use the `out` keyword when defining parameters for a method.

```
static void SumAvgOfTwoNumbers(double num1, double num2,
  out double sum, out double avg)
```

This new method has two input parameters and two output parameters. The only difference between output and input parameters at the definition time is the use of the keyword `out` before the data type of the parameter.

Also, when invoking the method we need to specify that a parameter is of the output type by using the `out` keyword.

```
double x = 300, y = 500, sum, avg;
SumAvgOfTwoNumbers(x, y, out sum, out avg);
```

As shown in the previous code, we declared two variables, `sum` and `avg`, to be passed into the method `SumAvgOfTwoNumbers` as output parameters. Inside the `SumAvgOfTwoNumbers` method, the only requirement is that these output parameters are assigned some value before the method finishes execution.

The following code of the method will result in a compile time error since the output parameters are not assigned any value throughout the method execution:

```
static void SumAvgOfTwoNumbers(double num1, double num2, out
double sum, out double avg)
{
//There is no code yet so the sum and avg are not assigned
}
```

To fix this we need to assign a value to the output parameters because that is a requirement when we define a parameter as output type. The following code fixes the compile time error:

```
static void SumAvgOfTwoNumbers(double num1, double num2, out
double sum, out double avg)
{
  sum = 0;
  avg = 0;
}
```

We know setting 0 to the `sum` and `avg` variables is not the correct value but this will help get rid of the compiler issues while you keep writing more code. To set the correct values use the following assignment statements:

```
static void SumAvgOfTwoNumbers(double num1, double num2, out
double sum, out double avg)
{
  sum = num1 + num2;
  avg = (num1 + num2) / 2;
}
```

Create a Console Application and call it **SumAvg**. Create the method, `SumAvg`, with two parameters in the `Program` class, as seen in the following example:

```
static void SumAvg(double num1, double num2, out double sum,
out double avg)
{
  sum = num1 + num2;
  avg = (num1 + num2) / 2;
}
```

Add the following statements in the **Main** method to invoke the `SumAvg` method and display the result on the console.

```
static void Main(string[] args)
{
  double x = 300, y = 500, sum, avg;
  SumAvg(x, y, out sum, out avg);

  Console.WriteLine("Sum of {0} & {1} is {2}", x, y, sum);
  Console.WriteLine("Avg of {0} & {1} is {2}", x, y, avg);
  Console.ReadKey();
}
```

Build and execute the program. The output of the program should look like the one shown in **Figure 8.12**.

```
Sum of 300 & 500 is 800
Avg of 300 & 500 is 400
```

Figure 8.12 SumAvg.

REFERENCE

Assume you are working for an advertising company and you are responsible for writing a method which takes in an advertising message and a counter. The counter tells us how many times the message was displayed previously and the method adds one to the counter each time the advertisement message is displayed.

Create a Console Application **Advertisement**. Add a method called `Advertise` to display the advertisement message to the console. This method should also increase the counter value each time the message is displayed. The following code increases the counter by two since the message is displayed twice:

```
static void Advertise(string message, int displayCount)
{
  Console.WriteLine("Online: {0}", message);
  displayCount++;
  Console.WriteLine("Print: {0}", message);
  displayCount++;
}
```

Invoking the method with a message "Sale Today!" and the counter starting at value 5 will display the message twice and increase the counter value to 6 and then 7. Add the following statements in the **Main** method to invoke the `Advertise` method:

```
string adMessage = "Sale Today!";
int counter = 5;
Advertise(adMessage, counter);

Console.WriteLine("Current Counter: {0}", counter);

Console.ReadKey();
```

After invoking the `Advertise` method, we are displaying the current counter value to the console. Since we are starting with a counter value of 5, our assumption would be that after the method executes the counter value should become 7. Build and execute your program. The output should look like the one shown in **Figure 8.13**.

```
Online: Sale Today!
Print: Sale Today!
Current Counter: 5
```

Figure 8.13 Advertisement counter 5.

Looking at **Figure 8.13** it looks like the counter value didn't change to 7 as expected. It stayed at the initial value of 5.

When basic data types (like `int`, `double`, `string`, etc.) are passed to the method as parameters, only the value is passed, not the actual variable. So any value changes to the parameter inside the method will not impact the variable value.

The default behavior (of passing only the value of the parameters) can be changed. Adding the `ref` keyword to the parameter declaration will pass the variable as a reference and not just a copy of the value. Any changes to the parameters passed as a reference will change the value of the passed variable.

Change the `Advertise` method, where the parameter counter is passed as a reference. The following code shows the `ref` keyword was added right before the `int displayCount` of the second parameter.

```
static void Advertise(string message, ref int displayCount)
{
  Console.WriteLine("Online: {0}", message);
  displayCount++;
  Console.WriteLine("Print: {0}", message);
  displayCount++;
}
```

Invoking a method with the `ref` parameter also requires the `ref` keyword. Change your code in the **Main** method as follows:

```
Advertise(adMessage, ref counter);
```

After the previous changes, execute your program and the output will look like the one shown in **Figure 8.14**.

```
Online: Sale Today!
Print: Sale Today!
Current Counter: 7
```

Figure 8.14 Advertisement.

As shown in **Figure 8.14**, the value of the variable counter in the **Main** method changed to 7.

What is meant by passing a variable as a reference and passing a variable as a value? Objects in a computer's memory have addresses just like we have addresses for our houses, or apartments.

A simplified representation of variables in memory is shown in **Figure 8.15**:

Address	Variable Name	Value
1000	adMessage	Sale Today!
2000	counter	5
3000		
4000		
5000		

Figure 8.15 This shows a graphical representation of variable address vs value.

Here, addresses are numbers like 1000, 2000, etc. When a variable gets created it knows the address and not the value. In our simplified representation when we created the variables `adMessage` and `counter`, the computer's memory blocked some space at address 1000 and 2000 respectively. Now the variable `adMessage` knows its value is at address 1000 and the variable `counter` knows its value can be found at address 2000.

In the case of the non-reference method parameter `adMessage`, the value of "Sale Today!" is passed to the method. The method would have no knowledge about the address of `adMessage` in memory. That means a new variable declared as a message is created with the value "Sale Today!". Any changes to this new variable will only change this new variable at its own address in memory. For our example the memory table can look like the following figure:

Address	Variable Name	Value
1000	adMessage	Sale Today!
2000	counter	5
3000	memory	Sale Today!
4000		
5000		

Figure 8.16 Variable adMessage and memory pointing to different addresses.

Now we see address 1000 and 3000 contain the value "Sale Today!". If we change the memory variable inside the method, it will change the value at address 3000 and won't impact anything at address 1000.

Now when a variable is passed as a reference it will look as if both variables, `counter` and `displayCount,` are both pointing to address 2000. As soon as the method starts executing, memory can look like the following:

Address	Variable Name	Value
1000	adMessage	Sale Today!
2000	counter, **displayCount**	5
3000	memory	Sale Today!

Figure 8.17 Variable counter and displayCount pointing to same address.

Any change to the `displayCount` variable inside the method is going to change the value at address 2000. After the method execution, memory can look like the following:

Address	Variable Name	Value
1000	adMessage	Sale Today!
2000	counter, displayCount	7
3000	memory	Sale Today!

Figure 8.18 Changing value of displayCount to 7, changes the value of variable counter as well.

The variable `displayCount` inside the method has been changed to 7. The `counter` variable is also pointing to address 2000 and thus the value of the `counter` variable declared inside the **Main** method becomes 7.

DEFAULT

Oftentimes methods have a bunch of parameters. Some of the parameters are required but some may be required only when the caller wants to change the default behavior of something in the method. So far we have learned that if a method has two parameters then the caller of the method is required to pass two parameters when invoking the method.

Create a Console Application called **MessageFancy**. Add a method called `ShowMessage` to display a message on the console.

```
static void ShowMessage(string message, bool makeFancy)
{
  if (makeFancy)
  {
    Console.WriteLine("!!!{0}!!!", message);
  }
  else
  {
    Console.WriteLine(message);
  }
}
```

The `ShowMessage` method takes two parameters (`message` and `makeFancy`). The `message` parameter contains the message that will be displayed on the console. The `makeFancy` parameter is a `bool` type to tell the method to add a set of exclamations before and after the message when the value of the `fancy` variable is `true`.

Most of the time when we invoke the `ShowMessage` method we want the exclamations along with the message in the fancy style.

At the beginning of this book we showed "HelloWorld" to the console. Add the following statement in the **Main** method to display a fancy message on the console:

```
ShowMessage("Hello World", true);
```

The output of the program would look like the one shown in **Figure 8.19**.

```
static void Main(string[] args)
{
  ShowMessage("Hello World", true);
```

```
  Console.ReadKey();
}
static void ShowMessage(string message, bool makeFancy)
{
  if (makeFancy)
  {
    Console.WriteLine("!!!{0}!!!", message);
  }
  else
  {
    Console.WriteLine(message);
  }
}
```

```
!!!Hello World!!!
```

Figure 8.19 MessageFancy.

We want to simplify calling the `ShowMessage` method where we want to pass only the message parameter and have it display the message in the fancy style. The following code does not specify any value for the second parameter:

```
ShowMessage("Hello World");
```

In cases where we want to display a simple message we can pass the second parameter of `makeFancy` with a value of `false`.

```
ShowMessage("Hello World", false);
```

We can achieve this goal by making the second parameter of `makeFancy` optional by providing it a default value in the method signature as follows:

```
static void ShowMessage(string message,
bool makeFancy = true)
```

In the previous statement, `bool fancy = true` assigns a `true` value to the variable when it is not passed by the caller.

Add one more `ShowMessage` call in the **Main** method so the **Main** method looks like the following code:

```
static void Main(string[] args)
{
  ShowMessage("Hello World", true);
  ShowMessage("Hello World");
}
```

Both the `ShowMessage` statements in the **Main** method are essentially doing the same thing. In the first call we are explicitly providing a value for the parameter of `makeFancy` as `true`. In the second `ShowMessage` call we are not providing anything for the second parameter of `makeFancy`. Since the `makeFancy` parameter has a default value of `true`, `makeFancy` will be implicitly assigned `true` and the execution of the method would be the same as if `true` was passed as the second parameter.

Executing the program would look like **Figure 8.20**.

```
!!!Hello World!!!
!!!Hello World!!!
```

Figure 8.20 MessageFancy default parameter.

Lab 8.2: Parameters

Skill Check 1: Create a Console Application called **Fullname**. Write a method called `CreateFullname` which takes two input parameters of `firstName` and `lastName` and a third output parameter of `fullName`. Output parameter `fullName` should concatenate `firstName` and `lastName` with a space in between.

Try your program with the following **Main** method code:

```
static void Main(string[] args)
{
  string fullName;
  CreateFullname("John", "Doe", out fullName);
  Console.WriteLine(fullName);
  Console.ReadKey();
}
```

Output of the program should look like the one shown in **Figure 8.21**.

```
John Doe
```

Figure 8.21 Fullname.

Skill Check 2: Create a Console Application called **NumberSwap**. Write a method called `Swap` which takes two `int` parameters and swaps the values for both the variables.

Try your program with the following **Main** method code:

```
static void Main(string[] args)
{
  int x = 10, y = 20;
  Console.WriteLine("X={0} Y={1}", x, y);
  Swap(ref x, ref y);
  Console.WriteLine("X={0} Y={1}", x, y);
  Console.ReadKey();
}
```

Output of the program should look like the one shown in **Figure 8.22**.

```
X=10 Y=20
X=20 Y=10
```

Figure 8.22 NumberSwap.

Answer Code: The C# answer code for this lab is located in the downloadable files inside the Projects folder within the BeginningCS2012CompanionFiles.zip file.

Points to Ponder - Parameters

1. Simple data type input parameters are passed as a value to the method.
2. Passing a parameter as a value type won't change the value of the variable declared in the calling code.
3. The `struct` types are also known as value types.
4. Use the `ref` keyword for a method parameter when we want the method to change the value of a parameter declared in the calling code.
5. Using the `out` keyword for method parameters can be used to get more than one value from a method.
6. When a parameter is `out` type, it is required to be assigned a value inside the method.
7. To make a parameter optional, assign a default value to the parameter.
8. Optional parameters are required to be defined last in a method.

Review Quiz - Chapter Eight

1.) If x is 10 and y is 20, what will the GetSum method return?

```
static void GetSum(int x, int y)
{
  int sum = x + y;
  return;
}
```

O a) 30
O b) 10
O c) Nothing
O d) 20

2.) Which keyword is used to get back more than one value from a method?

O a) int
O b) out
O c) back
O d) return

3.) Is the following an example of method overloading?

```
static long Add1(int x, int y)
{
  return x + y;
}
static long Add2(int x, int y)
{
  return y + x;
}
```

O a) Yes
O b) No

4.) What will be the number displayed on the console based on the following code?

```
static void Main(string[] args)
{
  int number = 30;
  Add10(number);
  Console.WriteLine(number);
  Console.ReadKey();
}
static void Add10(int x)
{
  x = x + 10;
}
```

O a) 10
O b) 20
O c) 30
O d) 40

5.) What will be the number displayed on the console based on the following code?

```
static void Main(string[] args)
{
  int number = 30;
  Add10(ref number);
  Console.WriteLine(number);
  Console.ReadKey();
}
static void Add10(ref int x)
{
  x = x + 10;
}
```

O a) 10
O b) 20
O c) 30
O d) 40

Answer Key

1.) The GetSum method has a void return type so it returns nothing. The correct answer is option (c).

2.) Any method can return a maximum of one value. To get back more values from a method you can use out type parameters. The correct answer is option (b).

3.) Method overloading is a concept of having two or more methods with the same names that use different signatures. In this case Add1 and Add2 are different methods and cannot be categorized as method overloading. The correct answer is (b).

4.) The number variable is a value type and any changes done to the variable inside the method is not reflected on the passed parameter. The initial value of the variable will be maintained (i.e. 30), making option (c) the correct answer.

5.) Here, the parameter of the Add10 method is a ref type so any changes done to the parameter variable will be permanent. In this case the number variable started with a value of 30 and 10 got added to it by calling the Add10 method. The value of the number after the method call becomes 40, making option (d) the correct answer.

[NOTES]

Chapter 9 Classes

How would you characterize an employee in a company? An employee should have an employee ID, name, date of birth, hire date, etc. If we want to represent an employee we can create a couple of variables for employee ID, name, date of birth, hire date, etc. These variables are independent and have no relation between them. The following pseudo code is a good example of how to make the associations stronger than just independent variables:

```
//These variable values have no relation between them
int EmployeeID = 575;
string Name = "Tom Jones";
string DOB = "3/7/1978";
string.HireDate = "8/7/1999";
```

```
//These values are related to Tom (of the Employee class).
Tom.EmployeeID = 575;
Tom.Name = "Tom Jones";
Tom.DOB = "3/7/1978";
Tom.HireDate = "8/7/1999";
```

Classes provide a way to house these independent variables together. This example does so in an Employee class. In other words, classes act as a container to group various properties and attributes of an object.

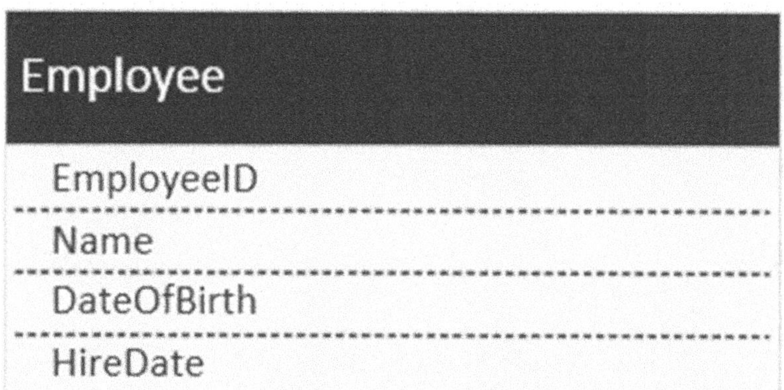

Figure 9.1 Employee Class.

READER NOTE: *Before doing the steps in this section you need to have the following folder structure on your hard drive C:\Joes2Pros\C# 2012\Chapter 9. Within the Chapter 9 folder there should be two more folders called Lab 9.1, Lab 9.2, and Lab 9.3. In order to follow along with the examples, you will need to have some version of Visual Studio 2012 installed.*

9.1 Creating Classes

Creating and using classes are integral to any object oriented language. Creating a class is very similar to creating a `struct`. The following code has the `Employee` class with fields of `EmployeeID` and `Name`:

```
class Employee
{
  public string EmployeeID;
  public string Name;
}
```

When we want to create an object of the `Employee` class we can use the `new` keyword as follows:

```
Employee emp1 = new Employee();
```

The `new` keyword creates an object in the computer's memory with all the defined members (like the `EmployeeID` and `Name` fields). At this point `emp1` can be used to set these fields. This process of creating objects is also called creating an instance of a class. Here `emp1` is an instance of the `Employee` class.

What if we just declared a variable from the class without the `new` keyword? The following code declares but does not instantiate `emp1`.

```
Employee emp1;
```

In the previous code sample the variable `emp1` is occupying no memory and doesn't even exist. If we try to access the fields of the `emp1` variable we will get a `null` error.

To set the field values of an object, the object should have been instantiated using the `new` keyword. The following code instantiates `emp1` and shows that the values are accessed using the object name then a dot and then the field name:

```
Employee emp1 = new Employee();
emp1.EmployeeID = "001";
emp1.Name = "John Doe";
```

Constructors

In the previous section we instantiated an object of the `Employee` class using `Employee emp1 = new Employee();`. In this section we are going to learn the ways to instantiate objects and how to provide some starting or default values for the class members.

Create a Console Application called **EmployeeManagement**. Usually it is a good practice to have a separate file for each class definition. To create a new class, right-click on the project inside **Solution Explorer** and click **Add** and then choose **Class**.

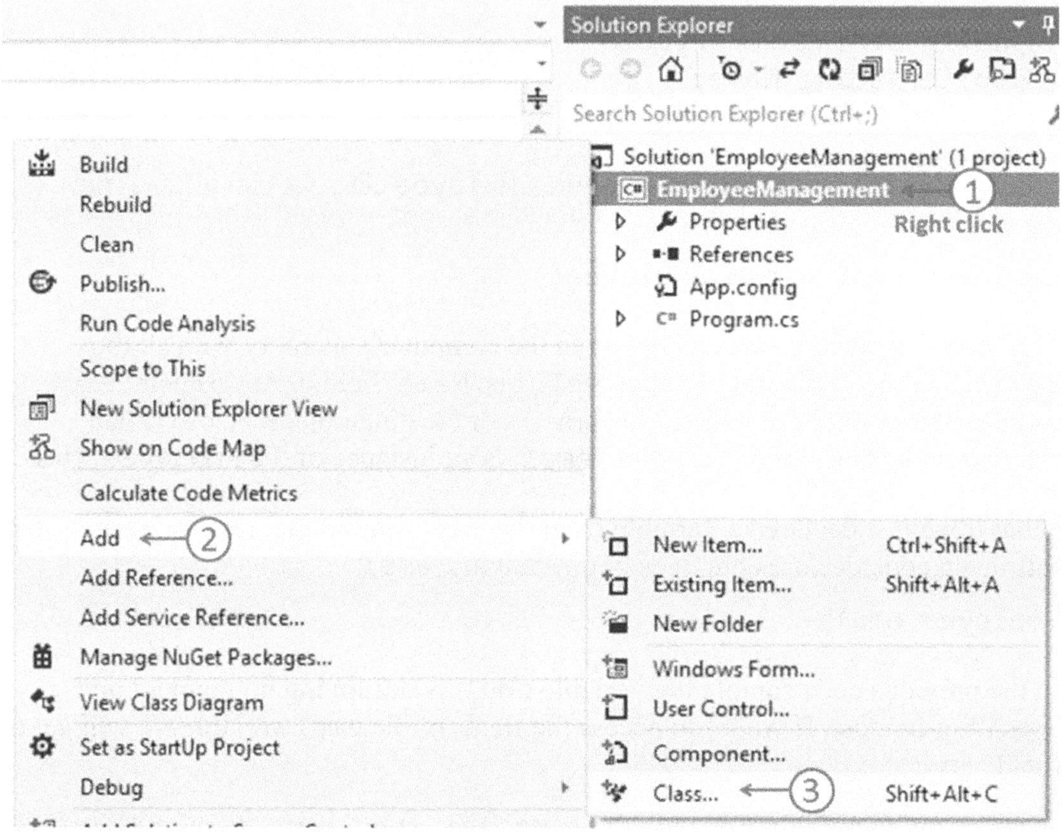

Figure 9.2 Add Class…

Now the **Add New Item** dialog will open where we will be required to provide a name for the class. Create a class called `Employee`.

The new file created is called **Employee.cs** and it contains the definition for the `Employee` class as follows:

```
namespace EmployeeManagement
{
  class Employee
  {
  }
}
```

Add two fields to `Employee` to match the following code:

```
class Employee
{
  public string EmployeeID;
  public string Name;
}
```

Build the solution and make sure there are no compiler errors (**Figure 9.3**).

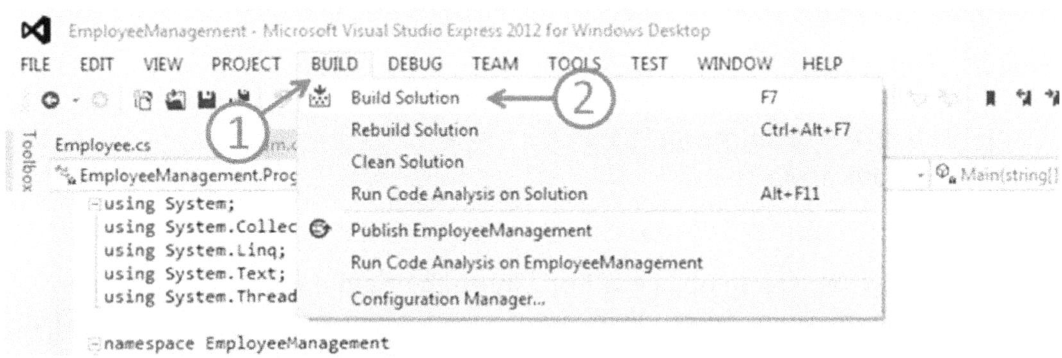

Figure 9.3 This shows the steps to build the solution.

In the Program.cs file create an object of `Employee` class inside the **Main** method, as seen in the following code:

```
static void Main(string[] args)
{
  Employee employee = new Employee();
}
```

The previous statement created an instance of the `Employee` class. Another way to state this is that we created an object of the `Employee` class. In the previous chapter we learned that methods are called using parentheses. If that is the case then `Employee()` appears to be a method. What type of method is called when we specify `Employee()` while we instantiate the `Employee` object? It is a special type of hidden method called a default constructor. A default constructor is present for each class. Explicitly write a constructor for the `Employee` class, as seen in the following code sample:

```
class Employee
{
  public string EmployeeID;
  public string Name;
  public Employee()
  {

  }
}
```

A constructor is a special type of method which doesn't have any return type. One reason to explicitly define the constructor is to initialize or assign default values to the field member variables. The following code assigns the default values of "Unknown" to all the field members of the `Employee` class.

```
public Employee()
{
  EmployeeID = "Unknown";
  Name = "Unknown";
}
```

Now anytime we create an object of `Employee` the field members have some default values rather than just nulls.

To check if the default constructor is working let's print the fields of the `Employee` object declared inside the **Main** method. We will be printing the field values of the `Employee` object a couple of times. To make this easier it would be a good idea to create a method in the `Program` class which takes an `Employee` object as a parameter and displays the field member values of the `Employee` parameter on the console. Use the following code to create the `DisplayEmployee` method of the `Employee` class:

```
static void DisplayEmployee(Employee emp)
{
  Console.WriteLine("EmployeeID: {0}", emp.EmployeeID);
  Console.WriteLine("Name: {0}", emp.Name);
}
```

Call the `DisplayEmployee` method from the **Main** method to display the field member values of the `Employee` object that we already declared within the **Main** method.

```
static void Main(string[] args)
{
  Employee employee = new Employee();
  DisplayEmployee(employee);
  Console.ReadKey();
}
```

In the previous code we declared an object of the `Employee` type and called the `DisplayEmployee` method by passing the employee object. The `DisplayEmployee` method will display the field values and the output of the program will look like the one shown in **Figure 9.4**.

```
EmployeeID: Unknown
Name: Unknown
```

Figure 9.4 Default constructor.

If we don't set the values, they were already set to "Unknown" at the time of instantiation by the constructor of the `Employee` class. If we want to assign proper values to the fields of the `Employee` object, we can set the values to the fields just like any other variable. Then we can use the `DisplayEmployee` method to display them on the console, as seen in the following code:

```
Employee employee = new Employee();
employee.EmployeeID = "001";
employee.Name = "John Doe";
DisplayEmployee(employee);
```

All fields now have some values assigned and these values are no longer just the default ones. The output of the program should look like the one shown in **Figure 9.5**.

```
EmployeeID: 001
Name: John Doe
```

Figure 9.5 Employee John Doe.

CONSTRUCTOR OVERLOADING

In the previous example when the `Employee` object was instantiated, the `Employee()` constructor was called. When the constructor was called then the fields all got assigned a default value. After the object was instantiated we explicitly assigned our own values to the fields of the `Employee` object.

Just like methods can be overloaded, we can also overload a constructor. To do this we can create one extra constructor which takes in the field values as parameters. Adding another constructor would make the `Employee` class look like the following code:

```
class Employee
{
  public string EmployeeID;
  public string Name;

  public Employee()
  {
    EmployeeID = "Unknown";
    Name = "Unknown";
  }
  public Employee(string empID, string name)
  {
    EmployeeID = empID;
    Name = name;
  }
}
```

Now we have two constructors for the `Employee` class. We can use either one to create objects of the `Employee` class. If we use the default constructor we are not required to pass in any parameters for the fields while creating an instance of the `Employee` class. If we leave the constructor call empty then we would get the default value of `"Unknown"` for the fields. We can use the second constructor (which takes two parameters) to create an object of `Employee` to set the fields of the `Employee` object at the time it is created. To do this we will provide the parameter values for `EmployeeID` and `Name`.

Let's create another employee using the parameterized constructor inside the **Main** method with the following code sample:

```
Employee employee2 = new Employee("002", "David");
```

Now we don't have to set the field values anymore since we were able to combine the object creation and field settings in one call using the parameterized constructor.

Call the `DisplayEmployee` method on the `employee2` object and the output of the program will look like the one shown in **Figure 9.6**.

```
static void Main(string[] args)
{
  Employee employee = new Employee();
  DisplayEmployee(employee);
  Employee employee2 = new Employee("002", "David");
  DisplayEmployee(employee2);

  Console.ReadKey();
}
```

```
EmployeeID: 001
Name: John Doe
EmployeeID: 002
Name: David
```

Figure 9.6 Parameterized constructor.

One thing to keep in mind is that when we define a constructor in a class it no longer has a default constructor. If we only define the parameterized constructor and not the default constructor then we can't make a call using the empty set of parameters. In other words, the following code will not run:

```
class Program
{
  static void Main(string[] args)
  {
    Employee employee = new Employee();
    Console.ReadKey();
  }
}

class Employee
{
  public string EmployeeID;
  public string Name;
```

```
  public Employee(string empID, string name)
  {
    EmployeeID = empID;
    Name = name;
  }
}
```

In the previous example we defined the `Employee` constructor to take an `empID` and a `name`. In the **Main** method we called on this with no parameters. Since a constructor is defined, there is no more implied default constructor. At this point nobody can create objects of that class using a default constructor and the only option would be to use the parameterized constructor. If the class author would like to provide a mechanism to create objects using a default constructor then an explicit default constructor should be present in the class definition.

READ ONLY FIELDS

In the previous section we created some `Employee` objects and we were allowed to set any values for the `EmployeeID` and `Name` fields after the creation of the object. There are times when we don't want field values to be changed after they were first set. To have that functionality we can define the field members as `readonly`. This will allow the variable to be set at initialization time (declaration time) inside the constructor.

We can modify the `Employee` class and make the `EmployeeID` field as `readonly` using the following code:

```
class Employee
{
  public readonly string EmployeeID;
  public string Name;
}
```

Now if we try to change the value of the `EmployeeID` field (which is defined as `readonly`) we will get the error, that is shown in **Figure 9.7**.

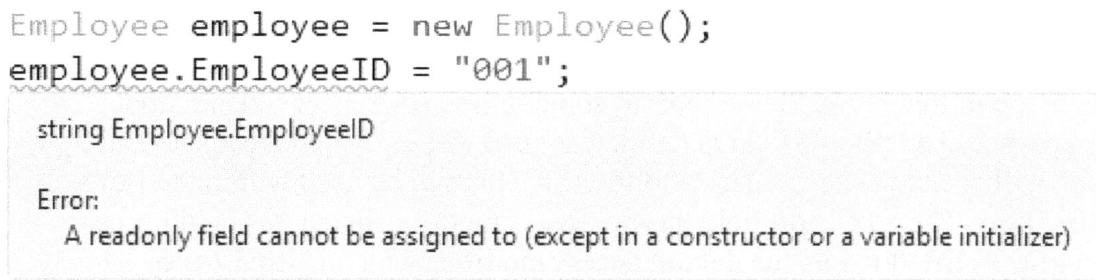

Figure 9.7 Readonly field.

ACCESS MODIFIERS

In the previous section we learned how to prevent a field value from being changed after the object was created. This was achieved by using the `readonly` keyword. This `readonly` option allows the caller to read the field value but not change it. In this section we will learn how to control the access of class field members in order to prevent the caller from even reading field values.

There are 4 types of access modifiers:

- public
- internal
- protected
- private

Whenever we define a field variable inside a class, we provide the access modifier along with the data type and variable name. Some of the examples are as follows for the class called `Person`.

```
class Person
{
  public string Name;
  internal string City;
  protected string state;
  private string phone;
  string zipCode;
}
```

The `Name` field is defined as `public` which means it can be modified freely. The `City` field is defined as `internal` which means it can be modified freely inside the assembly (DLL or EXE) where the `Person` class is defined. In other words, if somebody wrote the `Person` class and gave us the assembly to use in our application we wouldn't be able to see the `City` field portion of the `Person` class. The `state` field is defined as `protected` which means classes that inherit from the `Person` class will have access to that field. Inheritance is beyond the scope of this book. Please refer to some online references to learn about inheritance. The `phone` field is defined as `private`, which means no calling code will be able to see it. The `phone` field can only be used within the `Person` class itself. The `zipCode` field has no access modifier listed. When no access modifier is listed it gets the default access modifier which is `private`. Therefore, the `zipCode` field is set to `private`.

<u>There are 4 types of access modifiers:</u>

- Public - can be modified freely
- Internal - can be modified freely inside the assembly (DLL or EXE)
- Protedted - classes that inherit from the Person classes will have access to that field
- Private - no calling code will be able to see it. Ther phone field can only be used within the Person class itself.

If we create an object of the `Person` class then IntelliSense would only show two fields, as shown in **Figure 9.8**.

```
Person person = new Person();
person.
```

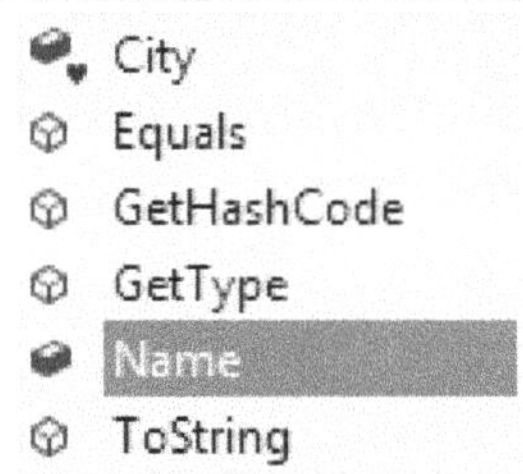

Figure 9.8 Access Modifier.

In **Figure 9.8** the `Name` and `City` fields are shown since the other fields are secured by using more restrictive access modifiers. The `Name` field is `public` and is available all the time. The `City` field is `internal` and is only available within the same assembly.

Lab 9.1: Creating Classes

Skill Check 1: Create a Console Application called **Products**. Create a new class called `Product` with the following fields:

- ProductID (`int`)
- ProductName (`string`)
- RetailPrice (`double`)

Skill Check 2: Modify the application created in Skill Check 1 and create an instance of `Product` in the **Main** method. Assign values to the fields and display the field values on the console, as shown in **Figure 9.9**.

```
Product ID  : 1001
Product Name: Cell Phone
Retail Price: 49.99
```

Figure 9.9 Products.

Skill Check 3: Modify the application in Skill Check 2 to add a default and parameterized constructor in the `Product` class. Create another object of `Product` type in the **Main** method and display it on the console, as shown in **Figure 9.10**. The second product object should be created using the following statement:

```
Product prod = new Product(1002, "Laptop", 499.99);
```

```
Product ID : 1001
Product Name: Cell Phone
Retail Price: 49.99
Product ID : 1002
Product Name: Laptop
Retail Price: 499.99
```

Figure 9.10 Parameterized Product.

Skill Check 4: Create a Console Application called **Orders**. Create a class called `Order` with the following fields and constructor:

```
class Order
{
  public readonly long OrderID;
  public readonly string Product;
  public readonly string Customer;

  public Order(long id, string prod, string cust)
  {
    OrderID = id;
    Product = prod;
    Customer = cust;
  }
}
```

In the **Main** method create an object of type `Order`. Keep in mind only a parameterized constructor is available for instantiating objects of the `Order` type. Verify that object creation happens, but when we try to change any field value we get an error, as shown in **Figure 9.11**.

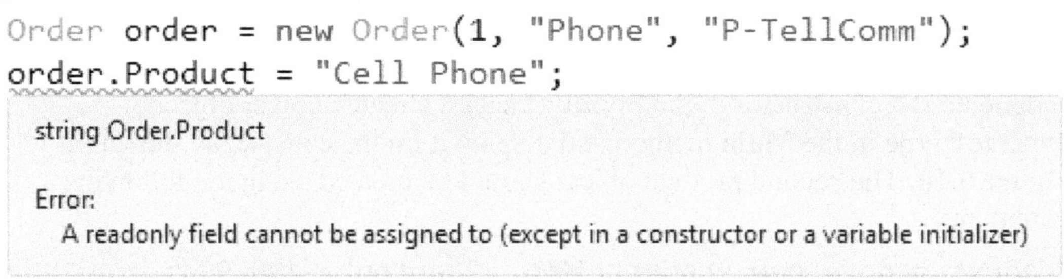

Figure 9.11 Read only error.

Answer Code: The C# answer code for this lab is located in the downloadable files inside the Projects folder within the BeginningCS2012CompanionFiles.zip file.

Points to Ponder - Creating Classes

1. Classes act as a container to group various properties and attributes of an object.
2. It is a good practice to create each class in its own separate file.
3. When no constructor is defined for a class the default constructor is still present.
4. Class constructors can be overloaded to have various constructors for different purposes.
5. When a field is defined as `readonly` its value can only be set at declaration time or inside the constructor.
6. When a parameterized constructor is present an implicit default constructor is no longer present.
7. To create an instance of a class type the `new` keyword is required.
8. There are four types of access modifiers, namely `public`, `internal`, `protected` and `private`.
9. All non-public field members should follow Camel casing to name the variables.
10. Class members can be referred to using the `this` keyword, as shown in the following code:

```
class Order
{
  public readonly long OrderID;
  public readonly string Product;
  public readonly string Customer;

  public Order(long id, string prod, string cust)
  {
    this.OrderID = id;
    this.Product = prod;
    this.Customer = cust;
  }
}
```

9.2 Methods

In the previous chapter we learned that methods help us break down a big piece of source code into smaller reusable modules. Until now we have created methods inside the `Program` class alongside the **Main** method. One example is the `Add` and `Subtract` methods to add and subtract two numbers. The code for the `Add` and `Subtract` method would look like the following code:

```
class Program
{
  static void Main(string[] args)
  {
    long total = Add(40, 30);
    long difference = Subtract(40, 30);
  }
  static long Add(int x, int y)
  {
    return x + y;
  }
  static long Subtract(int x, int y)
  {
    return x - y;
  }
}
```

In the previous example we created two methods inside the `Program` class. In this lab we will learn how to create methods inside our own custom classes.

Class Methods

Create a Console Application called **ClassMethods**. Add an `Employee` class which has three fields named `EmployeeID`, `Name`, and `hireDate`. Make sure `hireDate` is a `private` field. Define a constructor which takes in `EmployeeID` and `Name` as parameters. It is considered good practice to make private members as Camel case which is why we named it `hireDate` it instead of `HireDate`.

The code of the `Employee` class looks like the following:

```
class Employee
{
  public int EmployeeID;
  public string Name;
  private DateTime hireDate;
  public Employee(int empID, string name)
  {
    EmployeeID = empID;
    Name = name;
    hireDate = DateTime.Now;
  }
}
```

Inside the constructor the `hireDate` field is set to the current date and time. Notice that `hireDate` is a `private` field and is not visible outside the `Employee` class.

Create an object of `Employee` type inside the **Main** method.

```
Employee john = new Employee(1, "John Doe");
```

When we use IntelliSense to look at the fields available for the object `john` we only see `EmployeeID` and `Name`. The `hireDate` field is not shown since it has its access modifier set to be a `private` field.

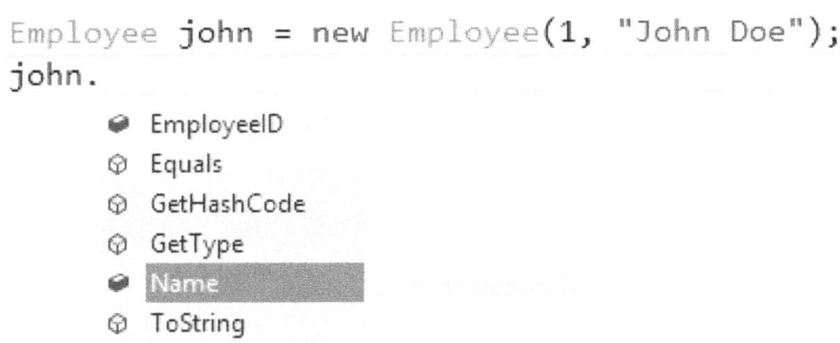

Figure 9.12 Employee HireDate private field.

Currently there is no way to get the value of the `hireDate` field from the object of the `Employee` type. We can create a method inside the `Employee` class to return the value of `hireDate`. Methods written inside the `Employee` class will be the only ones that have access to `private` fields like the `hireDate` field.

Use the following code to write a method called `GetHireDate`, which is inside the `Employee` class, to use the `public` access modifier.

```
public DateTime GetHireDate()
{
  return hireDate;
}
```

The return type of `GetHireDate` is `DateTime` and it returns a `hireDate` field value to the caller. `john` is an instance of the `Employee` class. The `GetHireDate` method is an instance method and should be called on the instance `john`. We can't call `GetHireDate` from the `Employee` object. See the comments in the following code for an example of how to call this method correctly:

```
DateTime hireDate = john.GetHireDate(); //This works
DateTime hireDate = Employee.GetHireDate(); //This fails
```

In the **Main** method write the following code to capture the `hireDate` from the object `john`:

```
Employee john = new Employee(1, "John Doe");
DateTime hireDate = john.GetHireDate();
```

We invoked the `GetHireDate` method on the `john` instance (which is an object of `Employee` type). The GetHireDate method is an instance method and needs to be called on by the instance `john` of the `Employee` type (class).

In the **Main** method write the following three statements at the bottom to display the field values of `john` on the console:

```
Employee john = new Employee(1, "John Doe");
DateTime hireDate = john.GetHireDate();

Console.WriteLine("EmployeeID: {0}", john.EmployeeID);
Console.WriteLine("Name: {0}", john.Name);
Console.WriteLine("Hire Date: {0}", hireDate);
```

Build and execute the program. The output will look like the one shown in **Figure 9.13**.

```
EmployeeID: 1
Name: John Doe
Hire Date: 12/12/2012 1:16:15 PM
```

Figure 9.13 Employee John.

We can create one more `Employee` object named `david` and display his information on the console using the following statement:

```
Employee david = new Employee(2, "David");

Console.WriteLine("EmployeeID: {0}", david.EmployeeID);
Console.WriteLine("Name: {0}", david.Name);
Console.WriteLine("Hire Date: {0}", david.GetHireDate());
```

In the previous code we used the field member variables to display the `EmployeeID` and `Name`. To display the `hireDate` we invoked the `GetHireDate` method on the `david` instance of the `Employee` class.

It looks like after creating an employee we want to have the ability to display the employee details on the console. Since this task is so common, it would be a good idea to create a method to display employee details on the console. Previously when we created a method to display the details of an object, we created a method in the `Program` class alongside the **Main** method, which is seen as follows:

```
class Program
{
  static void Main(string[] args)
  {}

  static void ShowEmployeeDetails(Employee emp)
  {
    Console.WriteLine("EmployeeID: {0}", emp.EmployeeID);
    Console.WriteLine("Name: {0}", emp.Name);
    Console.WriteLine("Hire Date: {0}", emp.GetHireDate());
  }
}
```

In the previous `ShowEmployeeDetails` method we need to pass an `Employee` object as the parameter to the method. For this, the `Program` class developer needs to know what fields to display and how to get other fields like `hireDate`. There might be other `private` fields which only the `Employee` class has access to. A good idea would be to create a `ShowDetails` method inside the `Employee` class. With the `ShowDetails` method inside the `Employee` class it will have access to all `private` field members of `Employee`.

Add a `public ShowDetails` method inside the `Employee` class using the code as follows:

```
public void ShowDetails()
{
  Console.WriteLine("EmployeeID: {0}", EmployeeID);
  Console.WriteLine("Name: {0}", Name);
  Console.WriteLine("Hire Date: {0}", hireDate);
}
```

The return type of the `ShowDetails` method is `void`. This means it is not going to return any value when it is invoked. Inside the `ShowDetails` method the `hireDate` field is directly referred to as any other field. If we are outside of the `Employee` class then it would be accessed through the `GetHireDate` method.

Modify the **Main** method to use the `ShowDetails` method for `john` and `david` in the code as follows:

```
Employee john = new Employee(1, "John Doe");
john.ShowDetails();

Employee david = new Employee(2, "David");
david.ShowDetails();
```

In this code the **Main** method looks much cleaner and more readable compared to the previous code involving multiple `Console.WriteLine` statements for each employee. Execute the program and the output will look like the one shown in **Figure 9.14**.

```
EmployeeID: 1
Name: John Doe
Hire Date: 12/12/2012 2:03:19 PM
EmployeeID: 2
Name: David
Hire Date: 12/12/2012 2:03:19 PM
```

Figure 9.14 Employee ShowDetails method.

STATIC METHODS

In the previous section we created two methods called `ShowDetails` and `GetHireDate`. These methods are instance methods and are required to be invoked on the instances of the `Employee` object which is seen as follows:

```
Employee john = new Employee(1, "John Doe");
john.ShowDetails();
```

If we try to invoke these methods on the `Employee` class itself we will get an error, as shown in **Figure 9.15**.

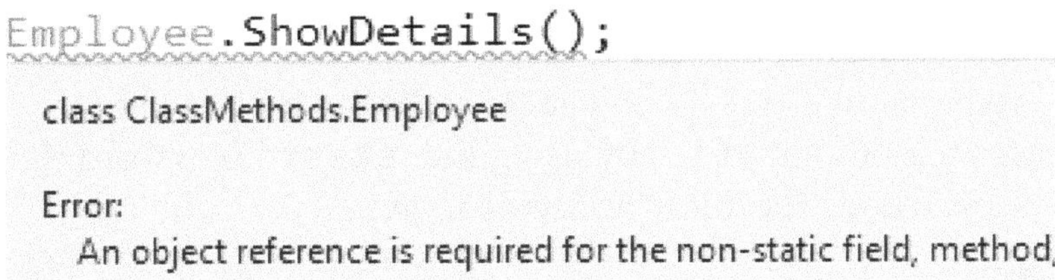

Figure 9.15 Error invoking instance method.

In **Figure 9.15** we tried to invoke the `ShowDetails` method as if it belonged to the `Employee` class. This assumption of accessing from the class name would mean the method has nothing to do with a particular instance like `david` or `john`. There is a way to make a method belong to a class and not to a particular instance. Methods that don't belong to any instance are called `static` methods. These `static` methods are generally utility methods to provide the developer with some common tools.

To demonstrate `static` methods in detail create a Console Application called **StaticMethods**. Create a class called `MyMath` and define methods that will add, subtract, multiply and divide two numbers. The code for the `MyMath` class is shown in the following example:

```
class MyMath
{
  public long Add(int x, int y)
  {
    return x + y;
  }

  public long Subtract(int x, int y)
  {
    return x - y;
  }

  public long Multiply(int x, int y)
  {
    return x * y;
  }

  public long Divide(int x, int y)
  {
    return x / y;
  }
}
```

Currently all these methods defined in the `MyMath` class are instance methods and we would be required to create an object of the `MyMath` class to invoke them. We can make these methods `static` by using the `static` keyword right before the return type. The code for this is seen as follows:

```
class MyMath
{
  public static long Add(int x, int y)
  {
    return x + y;
  }
  public static long Subtract(int x, int y)
  {
    return x - y;
  }
  public static long Multiply(int x, int y)
  {
```

```
        return x * y;
    }
    public static long Divide(int x, int y)
    {
        return x / y;
    }
}
```

Now we can invoke these methods on the `MyMath` class. IntelliSense on `MyMath` class also shows the availability of these methods (**Figure 9.16**).

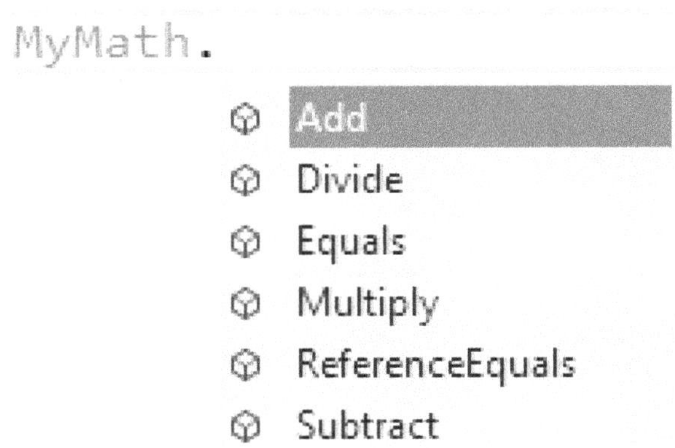

Figure 9.16 MyMath Methods.

Write the following statements in the **Main** method to invoke the `static` methods of the `MyMath` class and to display the return values on the console:

```
int num1 = 100;
int num2 = 50;

long add = MyMath.Add(num1, num2);
long sub = MyMath.Subtract(num1, num2);
long mul = MyMath.Multiply(num1, num2);
long div = MyMath.Divide(num1, num2);

Console.WriteLine("{0} + {1} = {2}", num1, num2, add);
Console.WriteLine("{0} - {1} = {2}", num1, num2, sub);
Console.WriteLine("{0} * {1} = {2}", num1, num2, mul);
Console.WriteLine("{0} / {1} = {2}", num1, num2, div);
```

Output of the program will look like the one shown in **Figure 9.17**.

```
100 + 50 = 150
100 - 50 = 50
100 * 50 = 5000
100 / 50 = 2
```

Figure 9.17 Static Methods.

Once a method is defined as `static` it no longer belongs to the instances of the class objects but instead to the class itself. **Figure 9.18** shows that the `MyMath` object doesn't have any of these four `static` methods.

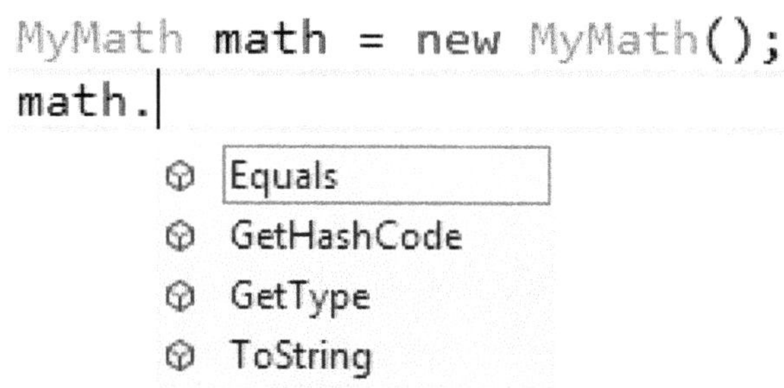

Figure 9.18 Static Methods Not Listed.

Lab 9.2: Methods

Skill Check 1: Create a Console Application called **PurchaseActivity**. Add a class named `Order` with the following fields and constructor:

```
class Order
{
  public readonly int OrderID;
  public string ProductName;
  public string CustomerName;
  private DateTime orderDate;

  public Order(int ordID, string pName, string cName)
  {
    OrderID = ordID;
    ProductName = pName;
    CustomerName = cName;
    orderDate = DateTime.Now;
  }
}
```

Define a method called `ShowOrder` to display the order details on the console inside the `Order` class. Verify the code by creating two objects in the **Main** method as follows:

```
Order order1 = new Order(101, "Phone", "John Doe");
order1.ShowOrder();
Order order2 = new Order(102, "Laptop", "Sally");
order2.ShowOrder();
```

Output of the program should look like the one shown in **Figure 9.19**.

```
101: Phone ordered by John Doe on 12/12/2012 4:03:48 PM
102: Laptop ordered by Sally on 12/12/2012 4:03:48 PM
```

Figure 9.19 PurchaseActivity.

Skill Check 2: Create a Console Application called **FancyBoard**. Add a class called `Board` which has three static methods to display a message differently on the console. The following code in the **Main** method should output messages on the console like the ones shown in **Figure 9.20**.

```
Board.WriteToSimpleBoard("Hello");
Board.WriteToDashBoard("Hello");
Board.WriteToHashBoard("Hello");
```

```
Hello
--Hello--
##Hello##
```

Figure 9.20 FancyBoard.

Answer Code: The C# answer code for this lab is located in the downloadable files inside the Projects folder within the BeginningCS2012CompanionFiles.zip file.

Points to Ponder - Methods

1. Classes can have methods defined inside them.
2. Methods can be overloaded.
3. Methods that are not defined as `static` are called instance methods.
4. Methods defined as `static` are invoked on a class.
5. A method's access can be controlled using various access modifiers like `public`, `internal`, `protected` and `private`.

9.3 Properties

So far in this chapter we have covered creating classes, adding field member variables, and adding class methods. We used a class method (like `GethireDate`) to access private class fields (like `hireDate`). This section is an extension of class methods used to handle private field members in a better way. Let's review the method way one more time and then see the easier counterpart.

Create a Console Application called **Persons**. Add a new class to the project called `Person`.

```
namespace Persons
{
  class Person
  {
  }
}
```

Add two `private` member variables called `name` and `age` for the `Person` class which is seen as follows:

```
namespace Persons
{
  class Person
  {
    private string name;
    private byte age;
  }
}
```

The `Person` class only has `private` fields. We need to create a parameterized constructor to assign values to the `name` and `age` fields.

```
public Person(string personName, byte personAge)
{
  name = personName;
  age = personAge;
}
```

Inside the constructor the `private` field members are getting assigned with the values passed as the parameter (`personName` and `personAge`) to the constructor.

We can now go back to the **Main** method inside the **Program.cs** file and create an object of `Person` type.

```
Person john = new Person("John Doe", 24);
```

The previous statement will create the `Person` object `john` with the name as "John Doe" and the age as "24". Looking at the fields and methods available to the `john` object from the **Main** method of the `Program` class we see that `name` and `age` are not showing up. This is because the fields are in the `Person` class and have their access modifiers set to being `private`. So another class (like `Program`) can't access them.

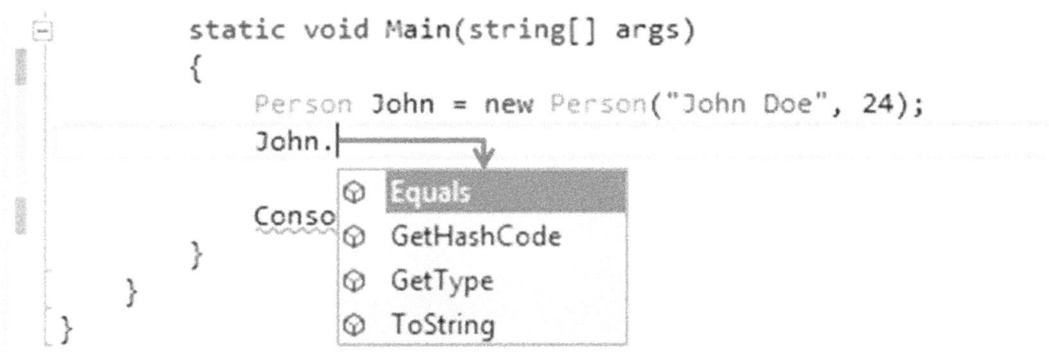

Figure 9.21 Person object not showing private field.

We should create a method in the `Person` class to display the name and age of an instance of the `Person` class on the console. Create a method called `ShowPerson` inside the `Person` class which is seen as follows:

```
public void ShowPerson()
{
  Console.WriteLine("Name: {0}", name);
  Console.WriteLine("Age: {0}", age);
}
```

Invoke the `ShowPerson` method on the `john` object instantiated inside the **Main** method to see the details of the newly created object on the console.

```
static void Main(string[] args)
{
  Person john = new Person("John Doe", 24);
  john.ShowPerson();

  Console.ReadKey();
}
```

Build and execute the program and the output will look like the one shown in **Figure 9.22**.

```
Name: John Doe
Age: 24
```

Figure 9.22 Person John.

By invoking the `ShowPerson` method we were able to display the field values for `name` and `age` on the console. We don't have a way to access the `name` and `age` variables individually. If we try to access the `name` and `age` fields like `public` members of the `Person` class we will get an error (**Figure 9.23**).

```
john.name;
```

```
string Person.name

Error:
  'Persons.Person.name' is inaccessible due to its protection level
```

Figure 9.23 Private fields inaccessible.

We can add a `GetName` method inside the `Program` class to return the name and also create a `GetAge` method to return the age. Add the following methods inside the `Person` class:

```
public string GetName()
{
  return name;
}
public byte GetAge()
{
  return age;
}
```

The `GetName` and `GetAge` methods are `public` and can be accessed inside the **Main** method of the `Program` class.

Add the following statements inside the **Main** method before the `Console.ReadKey` statement. This will display the name and age of `john` to the console using the `GetName` and `GetAge` methods.

```
static void Main(string[] args)
{
  Person john = new Person("John Doe", 24);
  john.ShowPerson();
  Console.WriteLine("Name from GetName: {0}
    ",john.GetName());
  Console.WriteLine("Name from GetAge : {0}
    ",john.GetAge());
  Console.ReadKey();
}
```

Execute the program and the output of the program should look like the one shown in **Figure 9.24**.

```
Name: John Doe
Age: 24
Name from GetName: John Doe
Age from GetAge : 24
```

Figure 9.24 GetName and GetAge returning private fields.

In our code, the first set of names and ages are displayed using the `ShowPerson` method defined inside the `Person` class. The second set of names and ages are displayed using individual get methods for `name` and `age`.

We now have a way to read the value of the `name` and `age` members defined inside the `Person` class. We do this by accessing the `public` methods of `GetName` and `GetAge`. We currently don't have a way to set or assign values to the `name` and `age` fields. We can add the `SetName` and `SetAge` methods inside the `Person` class to provide this functionality.

Write `SetName` and `SetAge` methods in the `Person` class which is seen as follows:

```
public void SetName(string personName)
{
  name = personName;
}
```

```
public void SetAge(byte personAge)
{
  age = personAge;
}
```

Now we can call the `SetName` and `SetAge` method on `john` inside the **Main** method to change the name to "John Dow" and the age to "45".

```
john.SetName("John Dow");
john.SetAge(45);
```

We can invoke the `ShowPerson` method again to check if the methods changed the field values. The code of the **Main** method would look like this:

```
static void Main(string[] args)
{
  Person john = new Person("John Doe", 24);
  john.ShowPerson();

  Console.WriteLine("Name from GetName: {0} ",
    john.GetName());
  Console.WriteLine("Age from GetAge: {0} ",
    john.GetAge());

    john.SetName("John Dow");
    john.SetAge(45);
    john.ShowPerson();

  Console.ReadKey();
}
```

Executing the program will output six lines on the console (i.e. three sets of name and age), as shown in **Figure 9.25**.

```
Name: John Doe
Age: 24
Name from GetName: John Doe
Age from GetAge: 24
Name: John Dow
Age: 45
```

Figure 9.25 Name and Age changed using set methods.

The first set of names and ages comes from calling the ShowPerson method. The second set comes from the GetName and GetAge methods. The last set is displayed by invoking the ShowPerson method. After calling GetName and GetAge, his name is now “John Dow” (instead of John Doe) and his age is “45” (instead of 24).

This works great and we can access the private fields of name and age using the get and set methods. If we want to set and get the values of the name and age fields without using these methods we could have made the name and age fields public and saved us the hassle of creating these four methods. So, is creating a private field and then to creating access to them extra work? No, there is a great potential benefit. We created these methods so we can put constraints on the field values.

By using the SetAge method, the caller is free to set any value for the age up to the limit of a byte (which is 255). We want to put a constraint so that if somebody tries to set the age greater than 130 we should not allow that entry.

Update the code for the SetAge method of the Person class which is seen as follows:

```
public void SetAge(byte personAge)
{
  if (personAge <= 130)
  {
    age = personAge;
  }
}
```

Inside the **Main** method change the parameter value of the SetAge method to 100 and execute the program.

```
john.SetName("John Dow");
john.SetAge(100);
john.ShowPerson();
```

```
Name: John Doe
Age: 24
Name from GetName: John Doe
Age from GetAge: 24
Name: John Dow
Age: 100
```

Figure 9.26 Age Set to 100.

Figure 9.26 shows that the value of the `age` field was changed successfully to 100. Now we will modify the `SetAge` parameter to 140 and see if the value of the `age` field changes.

```
john.SetName("John Dow");
john.SetAge(140);
john.ShowPerson();
```

Execute the program. **Figure 9.27** shows that the value of the `age` field didn't change to 140 since the value passed as a parameter was greater than 130.

```
Name: John Doe
Age: 24
Name from GetName: John Doe
Age from GetAge: 24
Name: John Dow
Age: 24
```

Figure 9.27 The age field value didn't change.

We would not have been able to set constraints on the `age` field value by changing the access modifier to `public`. The `set` and `get` methods on field variables allow us to check conditions before accepting and assigning the values to the `private` field members.

Setters and Getters

In the previous example we created four methods to provide access to two private class member variables, `name` and `age`. In this section we are going to talk about an easier way to achieve the similar functionality with far less coding. Our goal remains the same, to provide access to private field members with support to use logic or constraints on the acceptable values.

Start by creating a Console Application called **PersonProperties**. Add a class called `Person` with two `private` fields as `name` and `address`.

```
class Person
{
  private string name;
  private byte age;
}
```

Add a parameterized constructor with `personName` and `personAge` as the constructor parameters. The code for the `Person` class would look as follows:

```
class Person
{
  private string name;
  private byte age;

  public Person(string personName, byte personAge)
  {
    name = personName;
    age = personAge;
  }
}
```

In the earlier example we created `set` and `get` methods to provide access to the `name` and `age` member variables. There is something better than creating two methods for each private field. It is known as a property (and not a method). Properties are nothing but condensed `set` and `get` methods to access private field members.

Add the following code inside the `Person` class to create a property called `Name`.

```
public string Name
{
  get { return name; }
  set { name = value; }
}
```

The `Name` property has a `get` block and a `set` block. The `get` block is used to return a value to the caller and the `set` block is used to assign a value to the field variable. The `value` keyword in a `set` block acts like a parameter of the `set` method. Notice we have the `private` field `name` and the `public Name` property. It's a good practice to Pascal case the `public` members and Camel case the `private` members.

The best part about using properties is that they are used just like field variables when accessing them. In the **Main** method, add the following statements to create an instance of a `Person` object and display the person's name on the console.

```
Person john = new Person("John Doe", 24);
Console.WriteLine("Name :{0}", john.Name);
Console.ReadKey();
```

The object `john` is of the `Person` type and gets instantiated with the `name` field as "John Doe" and the `age` field as "24". In the next statement we used the `Name` property to display John's name on the console. In other words, we used the `Name` property to access the `name private` field member variable.

Build and execute the program and the output will look like the one shown in **Figure 9.28**.

```
Name: John Doe
```

Figure 9.28 Person Name property.

Here we used the property like a field to get the value. Likewise to set or assign the value we can use the `Name` property like a field member which is seen as follows:

```
john.Name = "John Dow";
```

Add another statement to display the changed name on the console. Execute the program and the output will look like the one shown in **Figure 9.29**.

```
Console.WriteLine("Name :{0}", john.Name);
```

```
Name :John Doe
Name :John Dow
```

Figure 9.29 Name changed using Property.

Now add another property for the `age` field inside the `Person` class. The code for this is seen as follows:

```
public byte Age
{
  get { return age; }
  set { age = value; }
}
```

We now have a way to read the value of the `name` and `age` members defined inside the `Person` class. We do this by accessing the `public` properties of `Name` and `Age`.

In the **Main** method use the `Age` property to display it on the console. Assign "45" as the age for object `john` and then display it on the console. The code for the **Main** method would look like the following:

```
Person john = new Person("John Doe", 24);

Console.WriteLine("Name:{0}", john.Name);

john.Name = "John Dow";
Console.WriteLine("Name:{0}", john.Name);
Console.WriteLine("Age:{0}", john.Age);

john.Age = 45;
Console.WriteLine("Age:{0}", john.Age);
Console.ReadKey();
```

Execute the program and the output should look like **Figure 9.30**.

```
Name :John Doe
Name :John Dow
Age :24
Age :45
```

Figure 9.30 Person Name and Age.

So far we have seen how to set and get values of a private field variable using properties. Now we will see how to add constraints similar to what we did using the `SetAge` method earlier.

To set constraints while setting a value we can modify the `set` block of the property. In the `Person` class, modify the `set` block of the `Age` property to put a constraint that ensures nobody can assign an `age` greater than 130.

```
public byte Age
{
  get { return age; }
  set
  {
    if (value <= 130)
    {
        age = value;
    }
  }
}
```

After the `if` block is in place, build and execute the program. At first we will find no change in the execution of the program and the output will look like the one shown in **Figure 9.30**. In the **Main** method, modify the assignment value of 45 to 140 and execute the program.

```
john.Age = 140;
```

As shown in **Figure 9.31** the age of `john` didn't change to 140 and remained the same at 24.

```
Name :John Doe
Name :John Doe
Name :John Dow
Age :24
Age :24
```

Figure 9.31 Property constraints.

The properties are much easier and cleaner to implement compared to writing the `set` and `get` methods to access `private` field members.

AUTOMATIC PROPERTIES

So far we have seen that to create a property we need to create `private` fields and then create `public` properties to provide access to the `private` fields. It is considered bad practice to create `public` field member variables (even if no constraints are required). Creating properties is the preferred way to provide access to class members.

It is a common practice to create properties for field variables. In C# 3.0 an Auto-Implemented Property concept was created. Auto-Implemented Properties are also known as Automatic Properties.

When creating Automatic Properties, field variables are not required. The following is the code example to create a regular property with a member variable:

```
private string name;

public string Name
{
  get { return name; }
  set { name = value; }
}
```

The previous code can be replaced with one statement, which is seen as follows:

```
public string Name { get; set; }
```

In Automatic Properties, empty `get` and `set` blocks are present and there is no need to declare a member variable. This time savings comes with one drawback. In the case of Auto-Implemented Properties, constraints cannot be set. Remember the age limit of 130 like we did with the `Age` property in the previous example? That is not possible with Automatic Properties

READ OR WRITE ONLY PROPERTIES

Until now we have created properties with both read and write access. In other words, we can read a value of the field via the `get` block and we can assign a value to the field using the `set` block of the property. There are times when we don't want the caller to set or assign any value to the field via a property. Likewise there are times where we would like to provide "set only" functionality. This way no caller is allowed to look at the field value via a property.

Currently the `Name` property code is defined as read-write, as shown here:

```
private string name;

public string Name
{
  get { return name; }
  set { name = value; }
}
```

There are two ways to make the `Name` property defined as read-only. First we can make the `Name` property read-only by getting rid of the `set` block, which is seen as follows:

```
private string name;

public string Name
{
  get { return name; }
}
```

We can achieve the similar functionality by making the `set` block `private`, which is seen as follows:

```
private string name;
```

```
public string Name
{
  get { return name; }
  private set { name = value; }
}
```

In case of Auto-Implemented Properties we can make a property read-only by making the `set` block `private`, which is seen as follows:

```
public string Name { get; private set; }
```

Using the same approach we can make properties write-only by getting rid of the `get` block or making the `get` block `private`, which is seen as follows:

```
// #1 - Write Only Property
private string name;

public string Name
{
  set { name = value; }
}

// #2 - Write Only Property
private string name;

public string Name
{
  private get { return name; }
  set { name = value; }
}

// #3 - Write Only Property
public string Name { private get; set; }
```

The write-only properties are not very common but, it is common to define properties read-only with a `private set` block.

Lab 9.3: Properties

Skill Check 1: Create a Console Application called **Products**. Create a class called `Product` with the following properties (Auto-Implemented) and default constructor:

- ID (`int`)
- Code (`string`)
- ReleaseDate (`DateTime`)

Instantiate two objects of the `Product` type. Assign values to the properties of these two objects and display the property value on the console, as shown in **Figure 9.32**.

```
ID:1 Code:LT-3030 Released:2/2/2012 12:00:00 AM
ID:2 Code:CP-1010 Released:1/1/2013 12:00:00 AM
```

Figure 9.32 Products.

Skill Check 2: Modify Skill Check 1 to add a parameterized constructor where ID, Code and ReleaseDate are the parameters. Change the properties to be read-only and display the product objects on the console, as shown in **Figure 9.33**.

```
ID:1 Code:LT-3030 Released:2/2/2012 12:00:00 AM
ID:2 Code:CP-1010 Released:1/1/2013 12:00:00 AM
```

Figure 9.33 Product read only properties.

Answer Code: The C# answer code for this lab is located in the downloadable files inside the Projects folder within the BeginningCS2012CompanionFiles.zip file.

Points to Ponder - Properties

1. Properties are created to provide access to the `private` class member variables.
2. Properties help us put constraints on the values of `private` class member variables.
3. The read-only property can only be created with a `get` block.
4. The read property can be created with a `private set` block.
5. The write-only property can only be created with a `set` block.
6. The write property can be created with a `private get` block.
7. Properties can be defined without a `private` field member.
8. Automatic Properties are also known as Auto-Implemented Properties and do not require a class field variable to be created.
9. The `private` field variables follow Camel casing.
10. The properties should be defined using Pascal casing (start first word with a capital case and capitalize the first letter for each subsequent word).

Review Quiz - Chapter Nine

1.) Will the following code compile?

```
class Person
{
  public int Id { get; set; }
  public string Name { get; set; }

  public Person(int id, string name)
  {
    Id = id;
    Name = name;
  }
}

class Program
{
  static void Main(string[] args)
  {
    Person p1 = new Person();
    p1.Id = 100;
    p1.Name = "John Doe";
  }
}
```

O a) Yes
O b) No

2.) Will the following code compile?

```
class Person
{
  public int Id { get; set; }
  public string Name { get; set; }
}

class Program
{
  static void Main(string[] args)
  {
    Person p1 = new Person();
    p1.Id = 100;
    p1.Name = "John Doe";
  }
}
```

O a) Yes
O b) No

3.) Will the following code compile?

```
class Order
{
  public readonly Guid OrderId;
  public Order()
  {
    OrderId = Guid.NewGuid();
  }
}
class Program
{
  static void Main(string[] args)
  {
    Order order = new Order();
    order.OrderId = Guid.NewGuid();
  }
}
```

O c) Yes
O d) No

4.) Which of the following is not an access modifier?

O a) internal
O b) private
O c) personal
O d) protected

5.) Methods marked as static cannot be overloaded.

O a) True
O b) False

6.) A property can be made readonly in the following way.

```
public readonly string Name { get; set; }
```

O a) True
O b) False

Answer Key

1.) In this code sample the Person class is defined with a parameterized constructor only. In the Main method, object p1 is declared using a default constructor. A default constructor is not available to the Person class and the compiler will throw an error, making option (b) the correct answer.

2.) In this case, the Person class has no explicitly defined constructor. When there is no constructor defined a default constructor is always present in the background. Inside the Main method the Person object is created using a default constructor, which is valid, making option (a) correct.

3.) In the Main method the order.OrderId = Guid.NewGuid(); statement is trying to assign a new OrderId to a readonly field. Readonly fields can be initialized only at declaration time or inside the constructor. The code will not compile, making option (b) the correct answer.

4.) Options (a), (b) and (d) are valid access modifiers. Option (c) is not a valid C# keyword, making it the correct answer.

5.) A static method in every respect is the same as an instance method and supports all features available to instance methods including the overloaded feature. Option (b) is the correct answer.

6.) The readonly keyword can only be used for fields and not properties, making option (b) the correct answer. A property can be made readonly using private before the set keyword, as follows:

```
public string Name { get; private set;}
```

[NOTES]

Chapter 10 Collections

When I go to a grocery store I like to carry a list of items to buy. This list is very dynamic. My wife can call me while driving to the store or while I'm there and tell me to add a few more items. Sometimes another item can pop up in my mind while walking the aisles. In this chapter we are going to learn about lists and list type collections which are provided as part of the .NET library.

READER NOTE: *Before doing the steps in this section you need to have the following folder structure on your hard drive C:\Joes2Pros\C# 2012\Chapter 10. Within the Chapter 10 folder there should be two more folders called Lab 10.1 and Lab 10.2. In order to follow along with the examples, you will need to have some version of Visual Studio 2012 installed.*

10.1 Lists, Stacks and Queues

In previous examples when we were required to create more than one variable of a similar type we created arrays. For example, to create a list for five grocery items we would create a `string` array of size 5, which is seen as follows:

```
string[] groceryItems = new string[5];
```

After that we would assign items to the array, as seen here:

```
groceryItems[0] = "Milk";
groceryItems[1] = "Bread";
groceryItems[2] = "Butter";
groceryItems[3] = "Eggs";
groceryItems[4] = "Chicken";
```

The array is of size 5 and five items have been assigned to it. If we want to add one more item to the `groceryItems` array we can't. This is because the array size is fixed. We would have to create another array of size 6, then copy the items from the previous array and assign one more item to the array at index 5 (which is the 6th item of 0 to 5). Again, to add yet one more item to an array of size 6 we would have to create another array of size 7 and repeat the steps to copy items and assign a new item at index 6.

This looks like a lot of work to simply add one item to an array. Arrays are not very helpful when we don't know how many items are expected to be part of the array. Dynamic sizing of an array is not possible, but this concept can be easily achieved by using a `List` data structure.

LISTS

Lists are sometimes called "dynamic arrays". With lists we are not required to specify the size at declaration time. To illustrate lists let's create a Console Application called **GroceryList**.

To declare a list type of strings we can create `List<string>` inside the **Main** method, which is seen as follows:

```
List<string> groceryList = new List<string>();
```

Specifying `string` in `<>` brackets tells the compiler we want to create a `List` which can only contain `string` items. This is a good thing since we don't want integers or any other data type to be stored inside a `string List`.

To add items to the `List` we can use the `Add` method of the `groceryList` object which is seen as follows:

```
groceryList.Add("Milk");
groceryList.Add("Bread");
groceryList.Add("Butter");
groceryList.Add("Eggs");
groceryList.Add("Chicken");
```

To add more items we can call the `Add` method again and again. Let's add two more items to the `List` using the following code:

```
groceryList.Add("Cheese");
groceryList.Add("Coffee");
```

If we had used an array we would be required to create another array and then copy the items from the previous `List` and then add the new items. With this `List`, we called the `Add` method again to add more items to the `List`.

To display the `List` items on the console we can use the `foreach` loop to iterate through all the items. The code sample for this is seen as follows:

```
foreach (string item in groceryList)
{
  Console.WriteLine(item);
}
```

We specified in the `foreach` loop that each item is a `string`. We also specified that for each iteration one item from the `List` is assigned to the item variable of the loop. Using the `Console.WriteLine` statement, the item variable is displayed on the console, as shown in **Figure 10.1**.

```
Milk
Bread
Butter
Eggs
Chicken
Cheese
Coffee
```

Figure 10.1 GroceryList.

We could have achieved a similar output using the `var` type as compared to using the `string` type in the `foreach` loop. The `var` type itself is not a type while you are coding, but at compile time the compiler checks that the `List` is of type `string`. At that time, internally, the `var` is treated like a `string`. The loop code would look as follows:

```
foreach (var item in groceryList)
{
  Console.WriteLine(item);
}
```

To remove an item from the `List` we can call the `Remove` method on the `List` object. Add the following statement right before the `foreach` loop:

```
groceryList.Remove("Chicken");
```

Build and execute the program. The output of the execution will look like the one shown in **Figure 10.2**.

```
Milk
Bread
Butter
Eggs
Cheese
Coffee
```

Figure 10.2 GroceryList (no chicken).

To sort items in the `List` we can call the `Sort` method of the `List` object. Call the `Sort` method right before displaying the items. Complete the code of the **Main** method and it will look like the following code:

```
List<string> groceryList = new List<string>();

groceryList.Add("Milk");
groceryList.Add("Bread");
groceryList.Add("Butter");
groceryList.Add("Eggs");
groceryList.Add("Chicken");
groceryList.Add("Cheese");
groceryList.Add("Coffee");

groceryList.Remove("Chicken");
groceryList.Sort();
```

```
foreach (string item in groceryList)
{
  Console.WriteLine(item);
}
Console.ReadKey();
```

Executing the previous code would look like **Figure 10.3**. Items in the `List` were sorted alphabetically before being iterated using a `foreach` loop.

```
Bread
Butter
Cheese
Coffee
Eggs
Milk
```

Figure 10.3 Sorted GroceryList.

The `List` type is a very useful and powerful data structure for storing items of different types. Following are a few `List` examples for storing different data types:

```
List<int> intList = new List<int>();
List<double> doubleList = new List<double>();
List<Person> personList = new List<Person>();
```

STACKS

If you are at a buffet and want to grab a plate from the stack, do you take it from the top of the stack or reach to the bottom? The one on the top is the easiest to get and most people will take a plate from there. When the stack of plates gets low the staff put more plates on top. The last plate they put on top will be the first one the next customer takes off. In other words, last-in first-out (LIFO).

So what is common with a stack of plates and a stack of paper? With both the stacks an item placed last on the stack is picked up first. It might sound funny but the term is you "pop the top one off first". If you refill, then you push new items on the top of the stack. In other words, in the last-in first-out (LIFO) stack terminology, the last item pushed in is popped out first.

Creating a `Stack` is similar to creating a `List`. Here we also need to specify the data type of the items to be stored in the `Stack`. A `Stack` of `string` names would look like the following:

```
Stack<string> names = new Stack<string>();
```

To illustrate other important methods of `Stack`, create a Console Application called **StackOfNumbers**. Declare a `Stack` of type `int` inside the **Main** method to store numbers in the `Stack`.

```
Stack<int> numbers = new Stack<int>();
```

In a `List` data structure we used the `Add` method to insert items into the `List`. Here we will use the `Push` method to push items into the `Stack`, as shown.

```
numbers.Push(1000);
numbers.Push(2000);
numbers.Push(3000);
numbers.Push(4000);
numbers.Push(5000);
```

Visually, each `Push` into the stack would look like **Figure 10.4**. The number 5000 is on the top of the `Stack`.

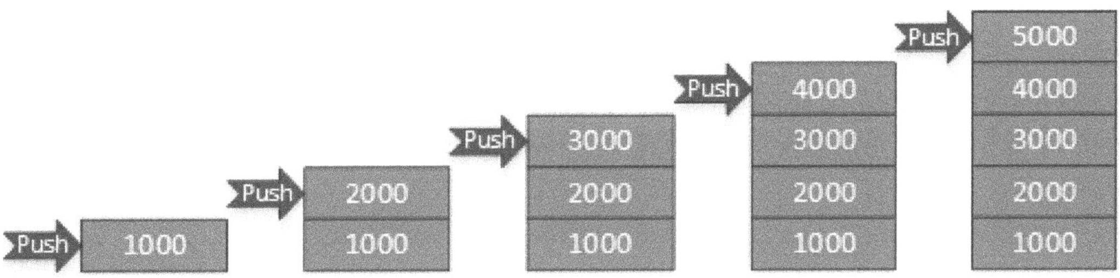

Figure 10.4 Stack Push Action.

To check the number of items in the `Stack`, we can use the `Count` method. Add the following statement to capture the size of the `Stack`:

```
int size = numbers.Count();
Console.WriteLine("Stack Size: {0}", size);
```

To display the items in the `Stack` along with its size add a few more statements to the **Main** method. The code for doing this would look like the following:

```
Stack<int> numbers = new Stack<int>();

numbers.Push(1000);
numbers.Push(2000);
numbers.Push(3000);
numbers.Push(4000);
numbers.Push(5000);
```

```
int size = numbers.Count();
Console.WriteLine("Stack Size: {0}", size);

foreach (var item in numbers)
{
  Console.WriteLine(item);
}

Console.ReadKey();
```

The number 5000 was pushed last and is on the top of the `Stack`. The output of the execution will look like **Figure 10.5**.

```
Stack Size: 5
5000
4000
3000
2000
1000
```

Figure 10.5 Stack output.

When we take (pop) a plate from a stack of plates the plate is removed from the top of the stack. Similarly, when we use the `Pop` method on a `Stack` object an item is removed from the `Stack`, as shown in **Figure 10.6**.

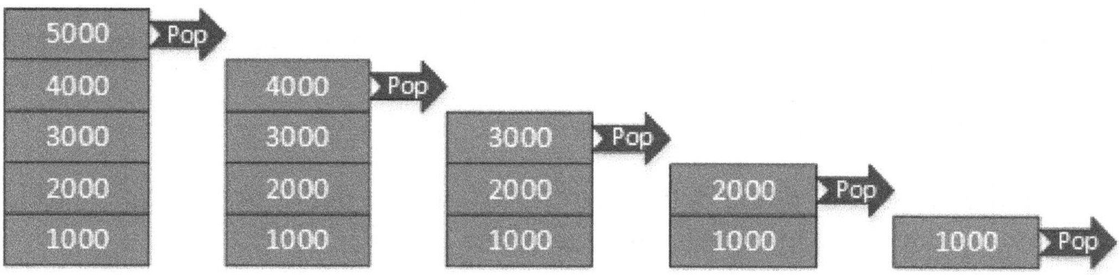

Figure 10.6 Stack Pop action.

The `Pop` method returns the topmost item and also removes the item from the stack. To `Pop` 5000 from the `Stack` and display it on the console, along with the current `Stack` size, add the following statements to the end of the **Main** method:

```
int poppedItem = numbers.Pop();
size = numbers.Count();
Console.WriteLine("PopItem:{0} Size:{1}", poppedItem, size);

Console.ReadKey();
```

```
Stack Size: 5
5000
4000
3000
2000
1000
PopItem:5000 Size:4
```

Figure 10.7 Stack Size after Pop.

As shown in **Figure 10.7,** after the Pop call, the `Stack` size became 4. There are some scenarios where we only want to look at the topmost item and but not pop it off the stack. We can use the `Peek` method to accomplish this task.

Currently the `Stack` contains four items and 4000 is the topmost item. Add the following statements to get the topmost `Stack` item and display it on the console:

```
int topItem = numbers.Peek();
size = numbers.Count();
Console.WriteLine("TopItem:{0} Size:{1}", topItem, size);

Console.ReadKey();
```

The output of execution should look like **Figure 10.8**.

```
Stack Size: 5
5000
4000
3000
2000
1000
PopItem:5000 Size:4
TopItem:4000 Size:4
```

Figure 10.8 Peek method.

QUEUES

Often times when I go to buy coffee, there are a few people in the line before me. The first person that got in the line is served first and then the second, and so on. People made a queue in front of the checkout counter and it follows the old saying "first come first served". In programming languages a `Queue` data structure is First-In First-Out (FIFO).

Adding an item to the Queue is called enqueue and removing the item is called dequeue. The Queue and the Stack are different in one major aspect. In a Stack, the last item pushed is popped out first. In a Queue, the first item enqueued is dequeued first. A Queue data structure (just like the Stack data structure) takes in a data type at declaration time. A few examples of a Queue can be seen in the following code sample:

```
Queue<long> queue = new Queue<long>();
Queue<Person> queue = new Queue<Person>();
```

The Queue of **Figure 10.9** and **Figure 10.10** shows the Enqueue and Dequeue in action respectively.

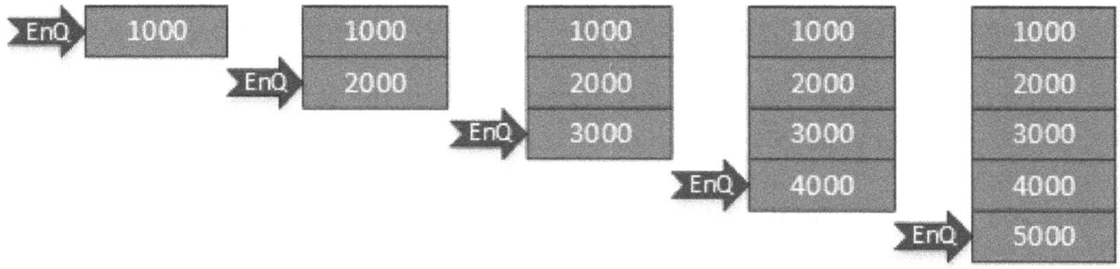

Figure 10.9 EnQueue In Action.

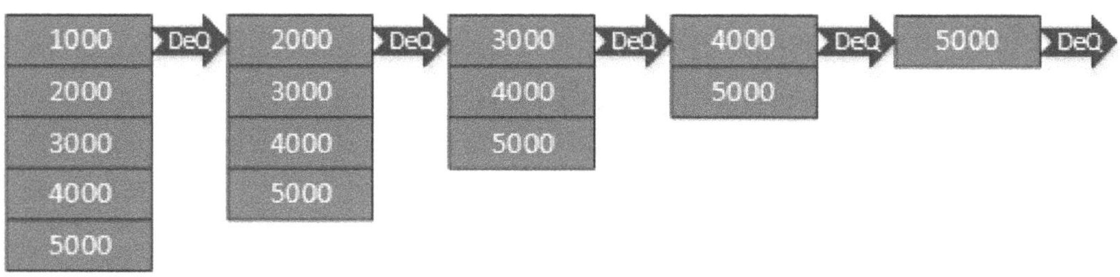

Figure 10.10 DeQueue in action.

Any time a new item is added to the Queue, the item is added to the end of the Queue. Also, any time an item is removed from the Queue the item is removed from the beginning of the Queue.

To illustrate a Queue in more detail, create a Console Application called **QueueOfNumbers**. Inside the **Main** method declare a Queue data structure to hold the int data type, as shown in the following example:

```
Queue<int> queueOfNumbers = new Queue<int>();
```

Now, to add items to the Queue use the Enqueue method on the Queue object.

```
queueOfNumbers.Enqueue(1000);
queueOfNumbers.Enqueue(2000);
queueOfNumbers.Enqueue(3000);
queueOfNumbers.Enqueue(4000);
queueOfNumbers.Enqueue(5000);
```

Here we added five items to the Queue. In other words, we Enqueued five items. To display the items in the Queue to the console, iterate the items in the Queue using a foreach loop as a var or variable type. The executing output is shown in **Figure 10.11**.

```
foreach (var item in queueOfNumbers)
{
  Console.WriteLine(item);
}
```

```
1000
2000
3000
4000
5000
```

Figure 10.11 QueueOfNumbers.

The items are shown in the same order as they got Enqueued in the Queue. To remove an item from the Queue, the Dequeue method is used. The Dequeue method returns the first item of the Queue and also removes it from the Queue. Write the following statements to Dequeue an item from the Queue and display the item on the console.

```
int firstItem = queueOfNumbers.Dequeue();
Console.WriteLine("First: {0}", firstItem);
```

Here we are capturing the first item of the Queue in a variable and displaying it to the console.

The complete code of the **Main** method would look as follows:

```
static void Main(string[] args)
{
  Queue<int> queueOfNumbers = new Queue<int>();
  queueOfNumbers.Enqueue(1000);
  queueOfNumbers.Enqueue(2000);
  queueOfNumbers.Enqueue(3000);
  queueOfNumbers.Enqueue(4000);
  queueOfNumbers.Enqueue(5000);

  foreach (var item in queueOfNumbers)
  {
    Console.WriteLine(item);
  }

  int firstItem = queueOfNumbers.Dequeue();
  Console.WriteLine("First: {0}", firstItem);

  Console.ReadKey();
}
```

Build (F6) and execute (F5) the program for the output to look like **Figure 10.12**.

```
1000
2000
3000
4000
5000
First: 1000
```

Figure 10.12 Item Dequeued.

The `Queue` data structure also supports many other methods. Some of the important methods are as follows:

- Peek
- Reverse
- Count

Lab 10.1: Lists, Stacks and Queues

Skill Check 1: Create a Console Application called **NameList**. Add the following names to a `List` data structure and display it on the console, as shown in **Figure 10.13**.

- John
- David
- Megan
- Roger
- Steven

```
John
David
Megan
Roger
Steven
```

Figure 10.13 NameList.

Skill Check 2: Modify the **NameList** application created in Skill Check 1 to sort the list in alphabetical order before displaying the items on the console. The output of the program should be like **Figure 10.14**.

```
David
John
Megan
Roger
Steven
```

Figure 10.14 Sorted NameList.

Skill Check 3: Create a Console Application called **CandyHolder**. Use a `string Stack` data structure to define a holder for storing candies. Every time a candy is added to the holder it is placed on the top and every time a candy is taken out the topmost candy is returned.

Add candies to the holder in the following order:

1. Red Candy
2. Green Candy
3. Blue Candy
4. Green Candy
5. Yellow Candy
6. Green Candy

Pop each candy from the holder until all candies are gone. Display each popped candy on the console, as shown in **Figure 10.15**.

```
Green Candy
Yellow Candy
Green Candy
Blue Candy
Green Candy
Red Candy
```

Figure 10.15 CandyHolder.

Skill Check 4: Create a Console Application called **TicketCounter**. Just like a real ticket counter, people are going to make a queue. One-by-one the attendant is going to cater the first person in the queue. Create a `Person` class that contains the following properties (Auto-Implemented).

Person Class
Name
Age
ZipCode

Figure 10.16 Use these properties when creating the Person class.

Declare a `Queue` of type `Person` to enqueue the following people in the `Queue`.

#	Name	Age	ZipCode
1	Roger	24	11111
2	Megan	25	22222
3	Sonam	26	33333
4	David	27	44444

Figure 10.17 Enqueue these people.

Dequeue each `Person` from the `Queue` and display the person's details on the console, as shown in **Figure 10.18**.

```
Name:Roger Age:24 ZipCode:11111
Name:Megan Age:25 ZipCode:22222
Name:Sonam Age:26 ZipCode:33333
Name:David Age:27 ZipCode:44444
```

Figure 10.18 Ticket counter.

Answer Code: The C# answer code for this lab is located in the downloadable files inside the Projects folder within the BeginningCS2012CompanionFiles.zip file.

Points to Ponder - Lists, Stacks and Queues

1. List<> types are dynamic and can hold any number of items.
2. List<> types are also called generic lists since the list type can be customized to store any data type provided in the <>.
3. Usually to iterate through the `List<> a foreach` loop is used. List<> items can also be referred to using an index just like an array.
4. The Stack<> type is a type of List which supports Last-In First-Out (LIFO).
5. The Queue<> type is a type of List which supports First-In First-Out (FIFO).

10.2 Dictionary and HashSet Types

Books have a table of contents and page numbers to help us get to a specific topic quickly. If there were no table of contents or index we would have to scan through the entire book to get to a specific topic. A `Dictionary` data structure acts like a `List` which. It supports features that are like having a table of contents or an index of a book.

Sometimes we don't want a lookup feature of a `Dictionary` but the requirement is to ensure uniqueness of items in the `List`. The `HashSet` data structure ensures items stored in it are unique. The first section of this chapter will look at the `Dictionary` data structure and the second section will look at the `HashSet` data structure.

DICTIONARY TYPES

As mentioned before, the `Dictionary` data structure supports a lookup feature and works like the index or table of contents in a book. In a table of contents, a section topic points to a page number where the actual section is present. The section name acts like a key and the actual section text acts like a value for that key. In other words, if the section is about Arrays and that is on page 56 then the key would be 56 and the pages you need to read would be the value. In the case of a `Dictionary` data structure there is a key-value concept defined. **Figure 10.19** shows a `Dictionary` of customers where the `CustomerID` acts like a key and the actual `Customer` object is the value stored somewhere else (which is pointed to by the key).

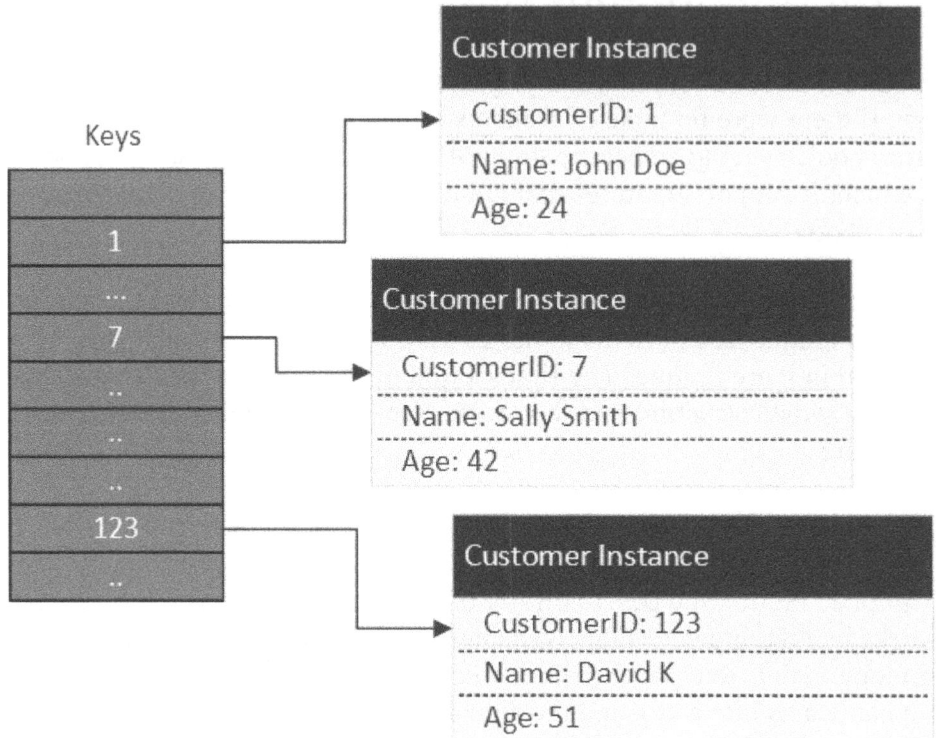

Figure 10.19 Customer Dictionary.

The Dictionary type also supports some generic behavior like other List types. The only difference between List types and a Dictionary type is that a List type requires one data type at declaration time but the Dictionary type requires two data types (one for the key type and the other one for the value type).

```
Dictionary<TKey,TValue> dict=new Dictionary<TKey,TValue>();
```

The TKey is the data type for the key (like int, double, string, etc.) and TValue is the data type for the value (like int, string, Person, etc.).

A Dictionary with an int key and a string value would look like the following code:

```
Dictionary<int, string> dict = new Dictionary<int, string>();
```

To add items to the Dictionary we can use the Add method, as shown in the following code sample:

```
dict.Add(100, "Laptop");
dict.Add(200, "Mouse");
```

To retrieve a value back from the `Dictionary` we can use its key. To get the value for key 100 we can use the following code:

```
string val = dict[100];
```

If we just want to check that a particular key exists we can use the `ContainsKey` method.

```
if (dict.ContainsKey(100))
{
  Console.WriteLine(dict[100]);
}
```

Here, we are checking if key 100 exists in the `dict` object before retrieving the value for key 100 from the instance of the `Dictionary`. If we try to retrieve a value for a non-existent key, we will get a runtime error, as shown in **Figure 10.20**.

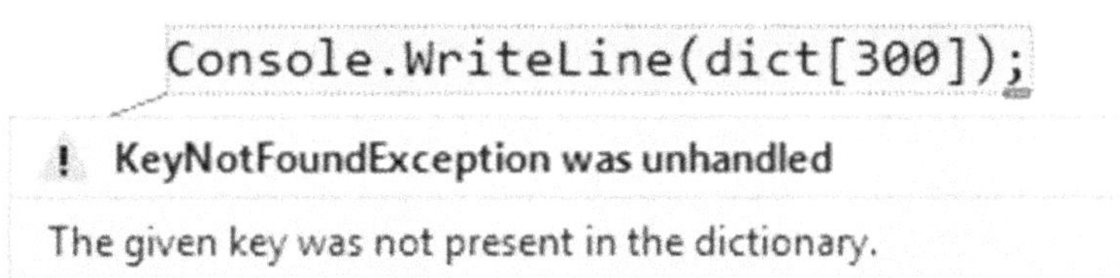

Figure 10.20 KeyNotFoundException.

Let's create a Console Application called **CustomerIndex** to illustrate the `Dictionary` data structure with a custom data type.

Add a class called **Customer** with `CustomerID`, `Name` and `Age` as the properties for the similarly named fields. The code for the `Customer` class would look like the following code:

```
class Customer
{
  public int CustomerID { get; private set; }
  public string Name { get; private set; }
  public byte Age { get; private set; }
```

```
  public Customer(int customerID, string name, byte age)
  {
    CustomerID = customerID;
    Name = name;
    Age = age;
  }
}
```

Add a method inside the `Customer` class to display customer details on the console as follows:

```
public void Show()
{
  Console.WriteLine("Customer ID:{0}", CustomerID);
  Console.WriteLine("Name:{0}", Name );
  Console.WriteLine("Age:{0}", Age);
  Console.WriteLine("~~~~~~~~~~~~~~~~~~~~~~~~~~~~");
  Console.ReadKey();
}
```

In the **Main** method declare four `Customer` objects as follows:

```
Customer customer1 = new Customer(1, "John", 20);
Customer customer2 = new Customer(2, "Sally", 30);
Customer customer3 = new Customer(3, "Rick", 40);
Customer customer4 = new Customer(4, "Sonam", 50);
```

Since all four customers are unique this data acts like a key for a `Dictionary` of customers. Declare an object of the `Dictionary` type with an `int` type as the key and `Customer` as the value type.

```
Dictionary<int, Customer> customerIndex = new
Dictionary<int, Customer>();
```

Add four `Customer` instances to the `Dictionary` with `CustomerID` as the key and a `Customer` object as the value.

```
customerIndex.Add(customer1.CustomerID, customer1);
customerIndex.Add(customer2.CustomerID, customer2);
customerIndex.Add(customer3.CustomerID, customer3);
customerIndex.Add(customer4.CustomerID, customer4);
```

To retrieve `CustomerID` 3 from the `Dictionary` we can use square brackets to provide the key.

```
Customer customer = customerIndex[3];
```

Invoke the `Show` method on the `customer` instance and execute the program. The output of the program should look like **Figure 10.21**.

```
customer.Show();
```

```
Customer ID:3
Name:Rick
Age:40
~~~~~~~~~~~~~~~~~~~~~~~~~~~~~~
```

Figure 10.21 Customer 3 from Dictionary.

If this would have been a `List`, we would be required to iterate through all the customers in the `List` and find `CustomerID 3` and then invoke the `Show` method on the found object. `Dictionary` types provide random or instant access to a value using a key.

To remove an item from the `Dictionary` we can invoke the `Remove` method. Remove `Customer 2` from the `Dictionary` using the following statement:

```
customerIndex.Remove(2);
```

To iterate through all the keys in the `Dictionary` we can use the `key` property and the `foreach` loop as follows:

```
Console.WriteLine("Displaying all Customers:");
foreach (var key in customerIndex.Keys)
{
  customerIndex[key].Show();
}
```

The `key` variable is used to retrieve a particular customer instance from `customerIndex`. Here we invoked the `Show` method on each retrieved `Customer` instance. The output of execution would look like **Figure 10.22**.

```
Customer ID:3
Name:Rick
Age:40
~~~~~~~~~~~~~~~~~~~~~~~~~~~~~~
Customer ID:1
Name:John
Age:20
~~~~~~~~~~~~~~~~~~~~~~~~~~~~~~
Customer ID:3
Name:Rick
Age:40
~~~~~~~~~~~~~~~~~~~~~~~~~~~~~~
Customer ID:4
Name:Sonam
Age:50
~~~~~~~~~~~~~~~~~~~~~~~~~~~~~~
```

Figure 10.22 All customers.

The loop iterated through all the customers remaining in the `customerIndex Dictionary`, `CustomerIDs:` 1, 3 and 4. The customer with `CustomerID 2` was removed from the `Dictionary`. The complete code inside the **Main** method would look like the following:

```
Customer customer1 = new Customer(1, "John", 20);
Customer customer2 = new Customer(2, "Sally", 30);
Customer customer3 = new Customer(3, "Rick", 40);
Customer customer4 = new Customer(4, "Sonam", 50);

Dictionary<int, Customer> customerIndex = new
Dictionary<int, Customer>();

customerIndex.Add(customer1.CustomerID, customer1);
customerIndex.Add(customer2.CustomerID, customer2);
customerIndex.Add(customer3.CustomerID, customer3);
customerIndex.Add(customer4.CustomerID, customer4);

Customer customer = customerIndex[3];
customer.Show();

customerIndex.Remove(2);
```

```
foreach (var key in customerIndex.Keys)
{
  customerIndex[key].Show();
}
Console.ReadKey();
```

One last thing about the `Dictionary` data structure is that adding the same key to the `Dictionary` will result in an error, as shown in **Figure 10.23**.

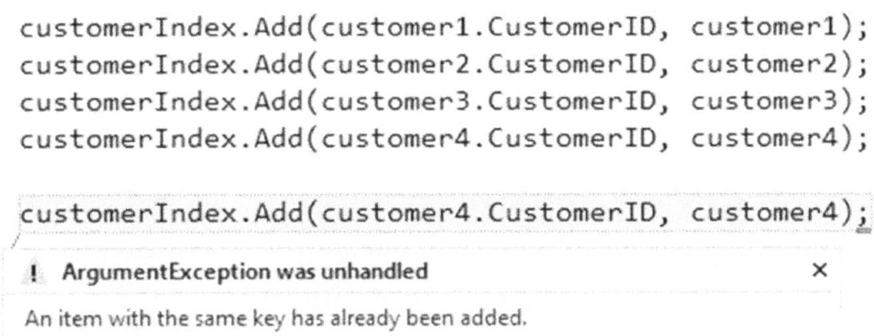

Figure 10.23 Same key exception.

HashSet Types

A `HashSet` is a special type of `List` which provides uniqueness to its items. In a regular `List` we can add the same number or same string again and it would be just fine. Adding the same item to the `HashSet` would be ignored. The `HashSet` also supports generic behavior like a `List` and is declared in the same way.

Create a Console Application called **UniqueNames**. Inside the **Main** method create an instance of a `string HashSet` and add two names to it.

```
HashSet<string> uniqueNames = new HashSet<string>();
uniqueNames.Add("John");
uniqueNames.Add("David");
```

Use a `foreach` loop to iterate through the `uniqueNames`, or the `HashSet`, and display the items on the console, as shown in **Figure 10.24**.

```
foreach (var name in uniqueNames)
{
  Console.WriteLine(name);
}
Console.WriteLine("==========================");
```

```
John
David
==========================
```

Figure 10.24 John and David in a HashSet.

The `Add` method of a `List` or a `Dictionary` returns nothing (i.e. return type of the `Add` method is `void`). In the case of the `HashSet`, the return type of the `Add` method is a `bool`. The `Add` method returns `true` when an item gets added to the `HashSet` and returns `false` when the item already exists in the `HashSet` and therefore, doesn't get added.

Add the following statements to try to add **John** again to the `HashSet`.

```
bool johnAdded = uniqueNames.Add("John");

if (johnAdded)
{
  Console.WriteLine("John added.");
}
else
{
  Console.WriteLine("John already present!");
}
```

Since **John** already exists in the `HashSet`, the `else` block will get executed and the output of the program will look like **Figure 10.25**.

```
John
David
==========================
John already present!
```

Figure 10.25 Add method returns false.

Add the following statements to insert a new name called **Susan** to the `HashSet`.

```
bool susanAdded = uniqueNames.Add("Susan");
```

```
if (susanAdded)
{
  Console.WriteLine("Susan added.");
}
else
{
  Console.WriteLine("Susan already present!");
}
```

The name **Susan** doesn't exist in the HashSet. This means **Susan** can be added. The Add method will return true and the if block will get executed, as shown in **Figure 10.26**.

```
John

David

===========================

John already present!

Susan added.
```

Figure 10.26 Susan added to HashSet.

The Remove method is used to remove an item from the HashSet. The Remove method also has a return type of bool and returns true if the item exists and therefore, gets removed.

Add the following statements to remove the existing name of **John** from the HashSet. In this case, the if block will execute.

```
if (uniqueNames.Remove("John"))
{
    Console.WriteLine("John removed.");
}
```

```
else
{
  Console.WriteLine("John does not exist!");
}
```

The following statements will try to remove a non-existing name of **Megan** from the `HashSet`. In this case, the `else` block will execute.

```
if (uniqueNames.Remove("Megan"))
{
  Console.WriteLine("Megan removed.");
}
else
{
  Console.WriteLine("Megan does not exist!");
}
```

Build and execute the program. The output of the program will look like **Figure 10.27**.

```
John
David
=========================
John already present!
Susan added.
John removed.
Megan does not exist!
```

Figure 10.27 HashSet remove method.

Lab 10.2: Dictionary and HashSet Types

Skill Check 1: Create a Console Application called **HeightChart**. Define a `Dictionary` type with a `double` key and a `string` value to store the following items:

#	Key	Value
1	5.5	John, Smith
2	5.7	Sally, Megan, Peter
3	6	Sam
4	5.10	Rose, Lilly, David

Figure 10.28 Store these items in a `Dictionary` type with a `double` key and `string`.

Retrieve height "5.10" from the `Dictionary` and display the value on the console, as shown in **Figure 10.29**.

```
Rose, Lilly, David
```

Figure 10.29 HeightChart.

Skill Check 2: Create a Console Application called **UniqueColors**. Add the following items to a `string HashSet`.

#	Items
1	Red
2	Blue
3	Green
4	**Red**

Figure 10.30 Add these items to a string HashSet.

Display all the `HashSet` items on the console, as shown in **Figure 10.31**.

```
Red
Blue
Green
```

Figure 10.31 UniqueColors.

Answer Code: The C# answer code for this lab is located in the downloadable files inside the Projects folder within the BeginningCS2012CompanionFiles.zip file.

Points to Ponder - Dictionary and HashSet Types

1. A `Dictionary` data structure creates a `List` with a key lookup.
2. Adding the same key again to the `Dictionary` will result in an error.
3. In a `Dictionary` data structure keys are required to be unique, but values can be repeated if required.
4. The `Dictionary<int, string>` can be iterated using a `foreach` loop.

   ```
   Dictionary<int,string> dict = new
   Dictionary<int,string>();
   foreach (var item in dict)
   {
   }
   ```

   (The `var` type is internally treated as `KeyValuePair<int, string>`).
5. A `HashSet` is a special type of `List` with unique items in the `List`.
6. Adding the same item to the `HashSet` will not result in an error.

Review Quiz - Chapter Ten

1.) How do you declare a List of numbers?

O a) List list = new List();
O b) List<int> list = new List<int>();
O c) ListOfNumbers list = new ListOfNumbers();
O d) List

2.) Can a List< > be created to store numbers and words at the same time?

O a) Yes
O b) No

3.) What will be the first number to come out of the stack?

```
Stack<int> numbers = new Stack<int>();
numbers.Push(100);
numbers.Push(200);
numbers.Push(300);
```

O a) 100
O b) 200
O c) 300

4.) Will the following code execute without errors?

```
Dictionary<int, string> numbers = new Dictionary<int,
string>();
numbers.Add(10, "Ten");
numbers.Add(20, "Twenty");
numbers.Add(10, "Ten");
numbers.Add(30, "Thirty");
```

O a) Yes
O b) No

ANSWER KEY

1.) A generic list List<> can be declared as an integer list to store numbers by providing int between < >, making option (b) the correct answer.

2.) The ultimate base class of all .NET objects is object. If we create a list as List<object> list = new List<object>();, it can store any type and the correct answer would be (a). Creating a list to store an object type is usually not a good idea and should be avoided.

3.) A stack follows the concept of last-in first-out. The last number to go in is 300 so the first number to be popped out of the stack would be 300, making option (c) the correct answer.

4.) In the case of a Dictionary, the same key cannot be added twice. Here key 10 is getting added twice and will cause an error at runtime, making option (b) the correct answer.

[NOTES]

Chapter 11 LINQ

In previous chapters we reviewed or learned about data structures called Lists, Stacks, Queues, Dictionaries and HashSets. If we have a `List` of 100 cities and we would like to select a few cities (which meet a particular search criteria) we would have to scan through the entire `List` object and check the condition by using an `if` statement. In this chapter we will learn how to query, or filter, a `List` type data structure using LINQ (Language Integrated Queries). One example can be to display all the cities starting with letter "S".

READER NOTE: *Before doing the steps in this section you need to have the following folder structure on your hard drive C:\Joes2Pros\C# 2012\Chapter 11. Within the Chapter 11 folder there should be two more folders called Lab 11.1 and Lab 11.2. In order to follow along with the examples, you will need to have some version of Visual Studio 2012 installed.*

11.1 Queries

The LINQ feature was introduced in C# 3.0 to query big or small data sets using "database like" SQL queries. In this section we will talk about querying simple and user-defined objects using LINQ.

FILTERING RESULTS

Let's start by creating a Console Application called **SpecificCities**. Inside the **Main** method create a `List` object named `cities`. Add a few cities to the `List`, as shown in the following code:

```
List<string> cities = new List<string>();
cities.Add("New York");
cities.Add("Los Angeles");
cities.Add("Chicago");
cities.Add("Houston");
cities.Add("Phoenix");
cities.Add("San Diego");
cities.Add("San Jose");
cities.Add("San Francisco");
cities.Add("Dallas");
cities.Add("Seattle");
cities.Add("Detroit");
cities.Add("Boston");
```

The code so far has a total of 12 cities in the `List` .To display the cities on the console add the following statements:

```
var selectedCities = cities;

foreach (var city in selectedCities)
{
  Console.WriteLine("{0}", city);
}

Console.ReadKey();
```

Build and execute the program. The output of execution will look like **Figure 11.1**.

```
New York
Los Angeles
Chicago
Houston
Phoenix
San Diego
San Jose
San Francisco
Dallas
Seattle
Detroit
Boston
```

Figure 11.1 All cities.

Look at the statement just before the `foreach` loop. These are all cities since we assigned the cities to the variable `selectedCities` with the following statement:

```
var selectedCities = cities;
```

What if we only want to select cities that start with the letter "S"? In other words, the requirement is "from all cities, select cities where city starts with S". We could loop through every city looking for that letter. Better yet we can write a LINQ query to do the same thing. Modify the variable `selectedCities` statement as follows:

```
var selectedCities = from city in cities
                     where city.StartsWith("S")
                     select city;
```

The variable `selectedCities` statement is now assigned to a query. A query is a request for specific data. Look at the query like it is a `foreach` loop where the `city` is a variable getting assigned a new value at each iteration. The `where` keyword is checking the condition, and if it is `true`, it returns that particular city to the `select` keyword. Running the program will generate an output like **Figure 11.2**.

```
San Diego
San Jose
San Francisco
Seattle
```

Figure 11.2 Cities starting with S.

Modify the query to display cities starting with "D".

```
var selectedCities = from city in cities
                     where city.StartsWith("D")
                     select city;
```

```
Dallas
Detroit
```

Figure 11.3 Cities starting with D.

The previous query can be written using a lambda expression. The lambda expression is an equal sign and then a greater than sign (like this `=>` together with no spaces). The lambda expression is a short hand approach for LINQ queries. Using the lambda expression for querying is a simpler way than the alternative but might take some getting used to.

The LINQ query using the lambda expression for cities starting with "D" would look like the following code:

```
var selectedCities =
cities.Where(city => city.StartsWith("D"));
```

In the previous query we used the `Where` clause (with a capital "W") to filter the results. It reads as "return cities where city starts with D".

We could use the same way to search for cities that start with the letter "N" (like New York). If we want to be more exact we can pick an exact city name. Modify the query to return "New York" with the following code:

```
var selectedCities = from city in cities
                     where city == "New York"
                     select city;
```

For the New York query, the lambda expression equivalent would be as follows:

```
var selectedCities = cities.Where(city => city == "New
York");
```

The pseudo code of the `Where` clause in the lambda expression looks like the following:

```
var items=
    <List Type>.Where(<ListItem> => <Boolean Condition>)
```

The `<ListItem>` checked against the `<Boolean Condition>` will be returned and assigned to the items.

The following lambda expression will return all the cities since the condition is hard-coded as `true`.

```
var selectedCities = cities.Where(city => true);
```

COMPLEX TYPE FILTERING

LINQ queries are not limited to simple data types and can be extended to user-defined types like classes. Create a Console Application called **PersonQueries** and add a class called `Person`. The code for the `Person` class looks like the following code:

```
class Person
{
  public string FirstName { get; private set; }
  public string LastName { get; private set; }
  public int Age { get; private set; }
  public string City { get; private set; }
  public string State { get; private set; }

  public Person(string firstName, string lastName, int age,
string city, string state)
  {
    FirstName = firstName;
    LastName = lastName;
    Age = age;
    City = city;
    State = state;
  }
}
```

Here we have defined properties with `private set` and the only way to assign the values to `Person`'s properties is through the constructor. The constructor takes five parameters to assign the values to the `FirstName`, `LastName`, `Age`, `City` and `State` properties.

In the **Main** method declare a `Person` list and couple of `Person` objects and add them to that `List` as follows:

```
List<Person> personList = new List<Person>();
personList.Add(new Person("John", "Doe", 24, "Seattle",
"WA"));
personList.Add(new Person("David", "Wing", 27, "Dallas",
"TX"));
personList.Add(new Person("Paul", "Young", 82, "San Diego",
"CA"));
personList.Add(new Person("Susan", "Ber", 45, "New York",
"NY"));
personList.Add(new Person("Richard", "King", 33, "Plano",
"TX"));
personList.Add(new Person("John", "Bee", 41, "Tacoma",
"WA"));
personList.Add(new Person("John", "Smith", 24, "Bellevue",
"WA"));
personList.Add(new Person("Sally", "Smith", 29, "Bothell",
"WA"));
```

To create a list of people from the state of “WA” we can write the following query:

```
var persons = from person in personList
              where person.State == "WA"
              select person;
```

The lambda equivalent of the query would look like the following:

```
var persons= personList.Where(person => person.State=="WA");
```

We are now checking the condition on the property of the `Person` object. To display selected people on the console write the following statements in a `foreach` loop:

```
foreach (var person in persons)
{
  Console.WriteLine("{0} {1}, {2}, {3}-{4}",
person.FirstName, person.LastName, person.Age, person.City,
person.State);
}
```

Build (F6 for VS Professional or F7 for VS Express) and execute (F5) the program. The output of the execution will look like **Figure 11.4**.

```
John Doe, 24, Seattle-WA
John Bee, 41, Tacoma-WA
John Smith, 24, Bellevue-WA
Sally Smith, 29, Bothell-WA
```

Figure 11.4 WA persons.

The `person` variable is a filtered list of items from the `personList` variable, meeting the criteria that the `State` is "WA".

Modify the query to return people with the `LastName` of "Smith".

```
var persons = from person in personList
              where person.LastName == "Smith"
              select person;
```

The lambda expression for this query would be:

```
var persons =

personList.Where(person => person.LastName == "Smith");
```

```
John Smith, 24, Bellevue-WA
Sally Smith, 29, Bothell-WA
```

Figure 11.5 LastName is Smith.

DEFERRED EXECUTION

Whenever we use a query to search for specific data it takes a certain amount of processing time. In the example where we defined the `persons` variable with an expression, the actual query didn't get processed until we used the `persons` variable for the first time in the `foreach` loop. In the case of LINQ queries the queries get executed or processed when they get used and not when they are defined. This process is called deferred execution.

To illustrate deferred execution, add one more person with a `LastName` of "Smith" both after the query is defined and right before the loop. The complete code inside the **Main** method would look like as follows:

```
List<Person> personList = new List<Person>();
personList.Add(new Person("John", "Doe", 24, "Seattle",
"WA"));
personList.Add(new Person("David", "Wing", 27, "Dallas",
"TX"));
personList.Add(new Person("Paul", "Young", 82, "San Diego",
"CA"));
personList.Add(new Person("Susan", "Ber", 45, "New York",
"NY"));
personList.Add(new Person("Richard", "King", 33, "Plano",
"TX"));
personList.Add(new Person("John", "Bee", 41, "Tacoma",
"WA"));
personList.Add(new Person("John", "Smith", 24, "Bellevue",
"WA"));
personList.Add(new Person("Sally", "Smith", 29, "Bothell",
"WA"));

var persons = from person in personList
                where person.LastName == "Smith"
                select person;


personList.Add(new Person("Roger", "Smith", 29, "Seattle",
"WA"));

foreach (var person in persons)
{
  Console.WriteLine("{0} {1}, {2}, {3}-{4}",
person.FirstName, person.LastName, person.Age, person.City,
person.State);
}

Console.ReadKey();
```

By the time we ran the query assignment there were only two `LastName` items with “Smith”. Then after the query was defined we added another person, “Roger Smith” to the list. If the `persons` variable is already processed then “Roger Smith” should not be part of the `persons` variable. Executing the program, as shown in **Figure 11.6** we see that “Roger Smith” became part of the `persons` list.

```
John Smith, 24, Bellevue-WA
Sally Smith, 29, Bothell-WA
Roger Smith, 29, Seattle-WA
```

Figure 11.6 Deferred Execution.

The `persons` variable was assigned the people only when it was used inside the loop.

Lab 11.1: Queries

Skill Check 1: Create a Console Application called **Gadgets**. Add the following gadgets to the `List` using these `string` items.

Gadget
Laptop
Phone
MP3 Player
Tablet 7
HeadPhones
Tablet 10
EarPhones

Figure 11.7 Add these gadgets to the List.

Using LINQ, display all the gadgets that start with the word "Tablet". The output of execution should look like **Figure 11.8**.

```
Tablet 7
Tablet 10
```

Figure 11.8 Tablets.

Skill Check 2: Modify Skill Check 1 to return the gadgets containing the word "Phone". The output of execution should look like **Figure 11.9**.

Hint: `gadget.Contains("Phone")`

```
Phone
HeadPhones
EarPhones
```

Figure 11.9 Phone.

Skill Check 3: Create a Console Application called **ProductCategory**. Create a `class` called `Product`. The code of the `Product` class will look like the following:

```
class Product
{
  public int ProducID { get; private set; }
  public string ProductName { get; private set; }
  public string Category { get; private set; }
  public double RetailPrice { get; private set; }

  public Product(int productID, string productName, string
category, double retailPrice)
  {
    ProducID = productID;
    ProductName = productName;
    Category = category;
    RetailPrice = retailPrice;
  }
}
```

In the **Main** method create a `List` of `Product` objects with the following property values:

ProductID	ProductName	Category	RetailPrice
100	Black Formal	Shoe	90
200	Red Boots	Shoe	140
300	White Sandals	Shoe	55
400	Laptop	Electronics	650
500	Smartphone	Electronics	450
600	E-Reader	Electronics	99
700	Tablet	Electronics	200
800	Mouse	Electronics	35
900	Keyboard	Electronics	60

Figure 11.10 Use these property values to create a list of products.

Using LINQ, filter the `List` to show all items in the "Electronics" category. Build and execute the program. The output should look like **Figure 11.11**.

```
400: Laptop (Electronics) $650
500: Smartphone (Electronics) $450
600: E-Reader (Electronics) $99
700: Tablet (Electronics) $200
800: Mouse (Electronics) $35
900: Keyboard (Electronics) $60
```

Figure 11.11 Electronics.

Skill Check 4: Modify Skill Check 3 to display all products where `retailPrice` is less than $220. The output will look like **Figure 11.12**.

```
100: Black Formal (Shoe) $90
200: Red Boots (Shoe) $140
300: White Sandals (Shoe) $55
600: E-Reader (Electronics) $99
700: Tablet (Electronics) $200
800: Mouse (Electronics) $35
900: Keyboard (Electronics) $60
```

Figure 11.12 Products Less Than $220.

Answer Code: The C# answer code for this lab is located in the downloadable files inside the Projects folder within the BeginningCS2012CompanionFiles.zip file.

Points to Ponder - Queries

1. LINQ stands for Language Integrated Query.
2. A LINQ query helps us to query `List` type objects like a SQL database query.
3. Results are filtered using "where" in a LINQ query.
4. A LINQ query is not executed at declaration time. It is executed only when it gets used.

11.2 Refining Results

So far we have used LINQ queries to filter results from a `List`. We have not controlled the sorting order of the result set. LINQ is a powerful language and supports sorting of results. For example, we can filter a `List` of cities and also sort the filtered `List` using LINQ.

SORTING DATA

Create a Console Application called **SortList**. Add an `Employee` class with the following code:

```
class Employee
{
  public int EmployeeID { get; set; }
  public string Name { get; set; }
  public string Division { get; set; }
  public string City { get; set; }
  public string State { get; set; }

  public Employee(int employeeID, string name, string
division, string city, string state)
  {
    EmployeeID = employeeID;
    Name = name;
    Division = division;
    City = city;
    State = state;
  }

  public void Show()
  {
    Console.WriteLine("{0}\t{1}\t{2}\t{3}\t{4}", EmployeeID,
Name, Division, City, State);
  }
}
```

In the `Show` method we have used `\t` to introduce a tab after every field. In the **Main** method create an array of `Employee` objects and assign ten employees to their respective index as follows:

```
Employee[] employees = new Employee[10];
```

```
employees[0] = new Employee(1, "John Doe", "Tech",
"Seattle", "WA");
employees[1] = new Employee(2, "Peter King", "Tech",
"Redmond", "WA");
employees[2] = new Employee(3, "Sally Smith", "HR",
"Seattle", "WA");
employees[3] = new Employee(4, "David Peters", "HR",
"Tacoma", "WA");
employees[4] = new Employee(5, "Roger Singh", "Sales",
"Seattle", "WA");
employees[5] = new Employee(6, "Megan Hollow", "Tech",
"Dallas", "TX");
employees[6] = new Employee(7, "Paul Young", "Tech",
"Dallas", "TX");
employees[7] = new Employee(8, "Nick Beard", "Sales",
"Redmond", "WA");
employees[8] = new Employee(9, "Ronnie Kar", "Tech",
"Seattle", "WA");
employees[9] = new Employee(10, "Lisa Bird", "Sales",
"Dallas", "TX");
```

The array has ten employees belonging to various divisions, cities and states. To display all employees in the array to the console we can write the following statements:

```
var selectedEmployees = from employee in employees
                        select employee;

foreach (var employee in selectedEmployees)
{
  employee.Show();
}

Console.ReadKey();
```

The output of execution will look like **Figure 11.13**.

```
1         John Doe        Tech     Seattle WA
2         Peter King      Tech     Redmond WA
3         Sally Smith     HR       Seattle WA
4         David Peters    HR       Tacoma  WA
5         Roger Singh     Sales    Seattle WA
6         Megan Hollow    Tech     Dallas  TX
7         Paul Young      Tech     Dallas  TX
8         Nick Beard      Sales    Redmond WA
9         Ronnie Kar      Tech     Seattle WA
10        Lisa Bird       Sales    Dallas  TX
```

Figure 11.13 All employees.

Figure 11.13 shows all employees in the same order as they were created. To show all employees sorted by `State` we can modify the LINQ query as follows:

```
var selectedEmployees = from employee in employees
                        orderby employee.State
                        select employee;
```

In the previous example we used the `orderby` keyword to sort the results based on `employee.State`. Executing the program will show the employees in sorted order by `State`, as shown in **Figure 11.14**.

```
6         Megan Hollow    Tech     Dallas  TX
7         Paul Young      Tech     Dallas  TX
10        Lisa Bird       Sales    Dallas  TX
1         John Doe        Tech     Seattle WA
2         Peter King      Tech     Redmond WA
3         Sally Smith     HR       Seattle WA
4         David Peters    HR       Tacoma  WA
5         Roger Singh     Sales    Seattle WA
8         Nick Beard      Sales    Redmond WA
9         Ronnie Kar      Tech     Seattle WA
```

Figure 11.14 Employees sorted by State.

The same query using the lambda expression can be written as follows:

```
var selectedEmployees = employees.OrderBy(e => e.State);
```

In previous LINQ queries we have used more descriptive names for the parameter like **employee** or **city**. In this example we used the more readable parameter name **e**. If we would have done this same lambda query using the name emp for employee it would have looked like the following:

```
var selectedEmployees = employees.OrderBy(emp => emp.State);
```

SORTING AND FILTERING DATA

We can use the sorting feature along with the filtering feature. Let's say the requirement is to show employees from the "Tech" division sorted by `State`. Modify the query as follows:

```
var selectedEmployees = from employee in employees
                        where employee.Division == "Tech"
                        orderby employee.State
                        select employee;
```

The same query using a lambda expression can be written as:

```
var selectedEmployees = employees.Where(e=>e.Division ==
"Tech").OrderBy(e => e.State);
```

The lambda expression looks like a step-by-step approach where we filtered the results and then sorted the result set.

The output of execution will look like **Figure 11.15**.

```
6       Megan Hollow    Tech    Dallas  TX
7       Paul Young      Tech    Dallas  TX
1       John Doe        Tech    Seattle WA
2       Peter King      Tech    Redmond WA
9       Ronnie Kar      Tech    Seattle WA
```

Figure 11.15 Tech employees sorted by state.

Currently the result set is sorted based on `State`. There are many employees from WA but in different cities. What if we want to sort by `City` within a

State? In other words, sort by State and then by City. Modify the query as follows to sort by State and then by City:

```
var selectedEmployees =
  from employee in employees
  where employee.Division == "Tech"
  orderby employee.State, employee.City
  select employee;
```

In the orderby clause we specified to sort by State and then City using a comma. The lambda expression equivalent would look like the following code:

```
var selectedEmployees = employees.Where(e=>e.Division ==
"Tech").OrderBy(e => e.State).ThenBy(e=>e.City);
```

Here, after the OrderBy we used ThenBy to achieve multi-level sorting using a lambda expression.

Execute the program and the output would look like **Figure 11.16**.

```
6       Megan Hollow    Tech    Dallas  TX
7       Paul Young      Tech    Dallas  TX
1       John Doe        Tech    Seattle WA
2       Peter King      Tech    Redmond WA
9       Ronnie Kar      Tech    Seattle WA
```

Figure 11.16 Multi-level sorting.

To sort the objects in descending order we can use the descending keyword in the query as follows:

```
var selectedEmployees =
  from employee in employees
  where employee.Division == "Tech"
  orderby employee.State descending, employee.City
  select employee;
```

In this case State will be sorted in descending order and City within State sorted by ascending order. The lambda expression equivalent would be as follows:

```
var selectedEmployees = employees.Where(e=>e.Division ==
"Tech").OrderByDescending(e => e.State).ThenBy(e=>e.City);
```

The execution output will look like **Figure 11.17**.

```
2       Peter King      Tech    Redmond WA
1       John Doe        Tech    Seattle WA
9       Ronnie Kar      Tech    Seattle WA
6       Megan Hollow    Tech    Dallas  TX
7       Paul Young      Tech    Dallas  TX
```

Figure 11.17 Descending State sort.

State is sorted in descending order with "WA" as the topmost State. Within State we see City is sorted in ascending order with "Redmond" showing up before "Seattle".

CREATING ANONYMOUS TYPES

In all the previous examples wherever we have used a LINQ query, the resulting filtered or sorted List maintains the data type of the source List. For example, in the following example we applied a LINQ query to a List of Employee objects and the resulting filtered List is also a List of Employee types.

```
Employee[] employees = new Employee[10];

var selectedEmployees = from emp in employees
                        where emp.State == "TX"
                        select emp;
```

The selectedEmployees object is a List of Employee objects since in the select clause we selected emp which is of the Employee type. The lambda equivalent of the previous query would look like the following:

```
var selectedEmployees = employees.Where(emp => emp.State ==
"TX");
```

The `Employee` class contains a couple of properties like `EmployeeID`, `Name`, `Division`, `City` and `State`. The code of the `Employee` class looks like the following:

```
class Employee
{
  public int EmployeeID { get; set; }
  public string Name { get; set; }
  public string Division { get; set; }
  public string City { get; set; }
  public string State { get; set; }
}
```

Our goal is to create a `List` of a new type which contains two properties (namely `EmployeeID` and `Name`). Here we won't be creating a new class with two properties but will use something known as an anonymous type. Anonymous types won't have a name (like `Employee`) but can have any number of properties as desired. The following code will return a filtered `List` of new anonymous types with two properties (`EmployeeID` and `Name`).

```
var selectedEmployees = from emp in employees
  where emp.State == "TX"
  select new { emp.EmployeeID, emp.Name };
```

In the `select` clause we created a new anonymous type with `EmployeeID` and `Name` as the properties.

The lambda expression equivalent of the query would look as follows:

```
var selectedEmployees = employees.Where(emp => emp.State ==
"TX").Select(emp => new { emp.EmployeeID, emp.Name });
```

Previously in the lambda expression we have not used `select`. When we are required to create custom anonymous types using lambda we have to use `select`. In both cases the anonymous type is created using the following:

```
new { emp.EmployeeID, emp.Name }
```

Figure 11.18 shows that the new type has no name but has two properties.

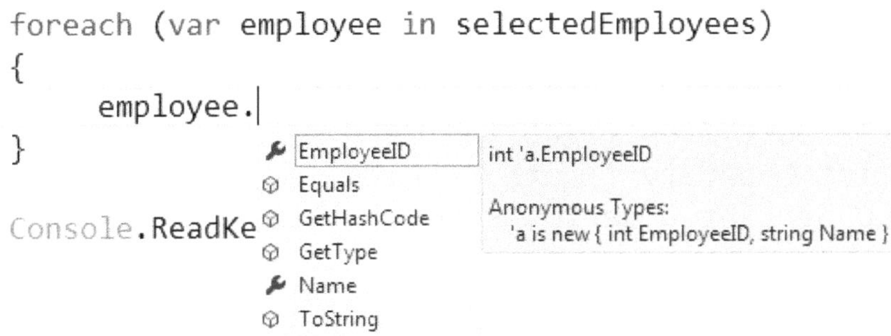

Figure 11.18 Anonymous Type.

To understand anonymous types in detail create a Console Application called **ProductSales**.

Add a class called `Product` to hold the product details. The code of `Product` class looks like the following:

```
class Product
{
  public int ProductID { get; set; }
  public string Name { get; set; }
  public double RetailPrice { get; set; }

  public Product(int productID, string name, double
retailPrice)
  {
    ProductID = productID;
    Name = name;
    RetailPrice = retailPrice;
  }
}
```

In the **Main** method create some `Product` instances as follows:

```
Product laptopPC = new Product(100, "LaptopPC", 500);
Product smartPhone = new Product(200, "SmartPhone", 200);
Product keyboard = new Product(300, "Keyboard", 100);
Product mousePad = new Product(400, "MousePad", 110);
Product tabletPC = new Product(500, "TabletPC", 600);
```

To store order information of a product we will create another class called `Order`. The code of the `Order` class will use the following code:

```
class Order
{
  public int OrderID { get; private set; }
  public Product Item { get; private set; }
  public int Quantity { get; private set; }
  public Order(int orderID, Product item, int quantity)
  {
    OrderID = orderID;
    Item = item;
    Quantity = quantity;
  }
}
```

The `Order` class has three properties. The `Order` class has a property called `Item` which is of the type `Product` to store which product was ordered. An order can be treated as a line in an invoice, as shown.

ID	Description	Price	Quantity
1			
2			
3			
4			
5			

Figure 11.19 The order is being treated as a line in an invoice.

The `Order` class contains all the information for each entry of the invoice. The ID and `Quantity` are direct properties of the `Order` class as `OrderID` and `Quantity`. The `Description` and `Price` are coming from the `Item` property of the `Order` class which is of the `Product` type that contains the `Name` and `RetailPrice` property.

In the **Main** method after the `Product` instances, create four `Order` instances like you see in the following:

```
Order order1 = new Order(1, laptopPC, 2);
Order order2 = new Order(2, smartPhone, 1);
Order order3 = new Order(3, tabletPC, 5);
Order order4 = new Order(4, mousePad, 3);
```

The `Order` constructor takes in `OrderID` as an `int`, `Item` as a `Product`, and `Quantity` as an `int` type. An invoice for a complete order can be looked at as a

List of Order instances. Create a List of Order types and add the Order instances to the invoice as follows:

```
List<Order> invoice = new List<Order>();
invoice.Add(order1);
invoice.Add(order2);
invoice.Add(order3);
invoice.Add(order4);
```

So far we have created Product instances, Order instances and a List of Order types called invoice. The complete code inside the **Main** method is seen as follows:

```
Product laptopPC = new Product(100, "LaptopPC", 500);
Product smartPhone = new Product(200, "SmartPhone", 200);
Product keyboard = new Product(300, "Keyboard", 100);
Product mousePad = new Product(400, "MousePad", 110);
Product tabletPC = new Product(500, "TabletPC", 600);

Order order1 = new Order(1, laptopPC, 2);
Order order2 = new Order(2, smartPhone, 1);
Order order3 = new Order(3, tabletPC, 5);
Order order4 = new Order(4, mousePad, 3);

List<Order> invoice = new List<Order>();
invoice.Add(order1);
invoice.Add(order2);
invoice.Add(order3);
invoice.Add(order4);
```

To display the invoice with the order details on the console write a foreach loop as follows:

```
Console.WriteLine("ID\tDescription\tPrice\tQuantity");

foreach (var order in invoice)
{
  Console.WriteLine("{0}\t{1}\t{2}\t{3}",
    order.OrderID,
    order.Item.Name,
    order.Item.RetailPrice,
    order.Quantity);
}

Console.ReadKey();
```

To get the values for `Description` and `Price` we accessed the `Item Name` and `RetailPrice` property respectively.

Build and execute the program, the output will look like **Figure 11.20**.

```
ID          Description          Price     Quantity
1           LaptopPC             500       2
2           SmartPhone           200       1
3           TabletPC             600       5
4           MousePad             110       3
```

Figure 11.20 Invoice from order list.

The `Item` property is of a `Product` type and contains another property called `ProductID`. Assume we don't want the invoicing system to have access to the `ProductID` or any other properties that the `Product` class might have had. Using LINQ we can create an invoice with an anonymous type `List` containing only the required fields for the invoicing system.

Inside the **Main** method remove the `foreach` loop and add the following code to create a new invoice list.

```
var secureInvoice = from order in invoice
                    select new {
                                    order.OrderID,
                                    order.Item.Name,
                                    order.Item.RetailPrice,
                                    order.Quantity
                                };
```

The `secureInvoice` object contains anonymous type objects with `OrderID`, `Name`, `RetailPrice` and `Quantity` as the properties. The lambda expression equivalent would look like the following:

```
var secureInvoice = invoice.Select(order =>
  new
{
  order.OrderID,
  order.Item.Name,
  order.Item.RetailPrice,
  order.Quantity
});
```

Using a `foreach` loop with the `secureInvoice` object, display the invoice on the console.

```
foreach (var order in secureInvoice)
{
  Console.WriteLine("{0}\t{1}\t{2}\t{3}",
    order.OrderID,
    order.Name,
    order.RetailPrice,
    order.Quantity);
}
```

The `order` object inside the `foreach` loop is directly accessing four available properties and has no access to any other properties. Hover the mouse pointer over `var` to validate the point again that the `order` object contains only four properties.

```
var secureInvoice = from order in invoice

interface System.Collections.Generic.IEnumerable<out T>
Exposes the enumerator, which supports a simple iteration over a collection of a specified type.

T is 'a

Anonymous Types:
   'a is new { int OrderID, string Name, double RetailPrice, int Quantity }
```

Figure 11.21 Invoice has anonymous items.

Build and execute the program, the output will look like **Figure 11.22**.

```
ID      Description     Price   Quantity
1       LaptopPC        500     2
2       SmartPhone      200     1
3       TabletPC        600     5
4       MousePad        110     3
```

Figure 11.22 Anonymous Type invoice.

Currently the anonymous type has properties named `OrderID`, `Name`, `RetailPrice` and `Quantity` but the `invoice` has headings like `ID`, `Description`, `Price` and `Quantity`. It would be a good idea to change the property names of the anonymous type to look the same as the heading in the invoice.

The property names of the anonymous types are easy to change by providing a property name and assigning them with a particular value inside the LINQ expression. Modify the LINQ query to have property names that are the same as the heading of the invoice.

```
var secureInvoice =
  from order in invoice
  select new {
               ID= order.OrderID,
               Description = order.Item.Name,
               Price = order.Item.RetailPrice,
               Quantity = order.Quantity
             };
```

The lambda equivalent would look as follows:

```
var secureInvoice = invoice.Select(order =>
  new {
        ID= order.OrderID,
        Description = order.Item.Name,
        Price = order.Item.RetailPrice,
        Quantity = order.Quantity
      });
```

Also modify the property names used in the `foreach` loop to reflect the change in the property name or else we will get compiler errors.

```
foreach (var order in secureInvoice)
{
  Console.WriteLine("{0}\t{1}\t{2}\t{3}", order.ID,
      order.Description, order.Price, order.Quantity);
}
```

Now we are using our desired property names for the anonymous type. The output of execution will look the same, as shown in **Figure 11.20** and **Figure 11.22**.

Lab 11.2: Refining Results

Skill Check 1: Create a Console Application called **Electronics**. Add the following electronics to a `List` of type `string`.

Electronics
Laptop
Desktop
MP3 Player
Tablet
E-Reader

Figure 11.23 Add this to a List of type string.

Using LINQ, display all the items sorted alphabetically. The output of execution should look like **Figure 11.24**.

```
Desktop
E-Reader
Laptop
MP3 Player
Tablet
```

Figure 11.24 Sorted items.

Skill Check 2: Create a Console Application called **PersonDetails**. Add a class called `Person` with the following code:

```
class Person
{
  public string FirstName { get; set; }
  public string LastName { get; set; }
  public int Age { get; set; }
  public string City { get; set; }
  public string State { get; set; }
}
```

Create objects of the `Person` type and add them to the list. The details for the `Person` objects are as follows:

FirstName	LastName	Age	City	State
John	Doe	52	Seattle	WA
David	Pole	23	Bellevue	WA
Sally	Smith	22	New York	NY
Megan	Lee	67	Dallas	TX
Paul	Young	29	Bothell	WA

Figure 11.25 Use this to create objects of the Person type.

Using LINQ, sort the list based on the `Age` property and display the details for each person, as shown in **Figure 11.26**.

```
Sally Smith     22      New York, NY
David Pole      23      Bellevue, WA
Paul Young      29      Bothell, WA
John Doe        52      Seattle, WA
Megan Lee       67      Dallas, TX
```

Figure 11.26 Sorted Persons.

Skill Check 3: Modify Skill Check 2 to create a `List` of anonymous types of two properties called `Fullname` and `Age`. Display the contents of the `List` to the console, as shown in **Figure 11.27**.

Hint: `Fullname = person.FirstName + " " + person.LastName`

```
Sally Smith      22
David Pole       23
Paul Young       29
John Doe         52
Megan Lee        67
```

Figure 11.27 Anonymous Person properties.

Answer Code: The C# answer code for this lab is located in the downloadable files inside the Projects folder within the BeginningCS2012CompanionFiles.zip file.

Points to Ponder - Refining Results

1. `List` type data can be sorted using the `orderby` clause.
2. To sort `List` type data in `descending` order, use the `descending` keyword along with the `orderby` clause.
3. The `select` clause can create new anonymous types.
4. The anonymous types can have user-defined named properties.

Review Quiz - Chapter Eleven

1.) Which keyword is used to filter results using LINQ?

O a) filter
O b) select
O c) linq
O d) where

2.) How many numbers will be displayed on the Console?

```
List<int> numbers = new List<int>();
numbers.Add(100);
numbers.Add(150);
numbers.Add(50);
numbers.Add(200);
var nums = numbers.Where(n => n > 125);
numbers.Add(160);
numbers.Add(400);
foreach (var n in nums)
{
  Console.WriteLine(n);
}
```

O a) 2
O b) 4
O c) 0
O d) 6

3.) The orderby clause can only be used on one field to sort a result set using LINQ.

O a) True
O b) False

4.) All types in .NET should have a name.

O a) True
O b) False

ANSWER KEY

1.) The where keyword is used to filter results in LINQ, making option (d) the correct answer.

2.) LINQ follows the concept of deferred execution where the statement var nums = numbers.Where(n => n > 125); didn't get executed until the nums variable is used for the first time inside the loop. So before the query gets executed numbers list had 6 numbers. Out of these 6 numbers, 4 are greater than 125, making option (b) the correct answer.

3.) The orderby clause can be used on more than one field where the fields are separated by a comma. The correct answer is option (b).

4.) The anonymous type allows us to create types without providing names, making option (b) correct.

[NOTES]

Chapter 12 Delegates and Anonymous Methods

Executives in companies don't do all the work themselves; they have people who act as delegates for them. Outside people or shareholders don't care who did the work as long as the work gets done. There can be many reasons to delegate a task. For example, the executive is busy or the executive doesn't have the expertise to do the work. In this chapter we will learn how to apply similar concepts in programming.

READER NOTE: *Before doing the steps in this section you need to have the following folder structure on your hard drive C:\Joes2Pros\C# 2012\Chapter 12. Within the Chapter 12 folder there should be two more folders called Lab 12.1 and Lab 12.2. In order to follow along with the examples, you will need to have some version of Visual Studio 2012 installed.*

12.1 Delegates

When we have a big pile of work we divide it into smaller chunks. In the programming world a big piece of code is divided into many smaller methods. Inside our smaller chunks of code are variables that are assigned to values. In the case of a reference variable they are pointing to values in memory. Can you create a variable and assign it to a method? Yes, that is called a delegate. A delegate in C# is nothing but a method pointer or method reference. We can create a variable pointing to a method just like we can create a variable to point to an object of any `class`.

METHOD SIGNATURES

Some methods have many parameters. This means that different methods can have different signatures. A method signature is defined by the type and the number of parameters along with the return type of the method. The method name has no impact on the method signature. The following example shows two different methods that are using the same method signature:

```
static void HelloMessage(string Hellomessage) {}
static void GoodbyeMessage(string Goodbyemessage) {}
```

Since the same return type, parameter type(s) and return values are being used, it makes both these example methods have matching signatures. If the parameters have any types that don't match then the signatures would not be matching. The following example shows two methods with different method signatures:

```
static void HelloMessage(string Message) {}
static void GoodbyeMessage(string Message, bool isFinal) {}
```

Both methods take a `string` parameter but the `GoodbyeMessage` method also takes a `bool` parameter. In a similar fashion the following two methods also are using different signatures:

```
static void HelloMessage(string message) {}
static void GoodbyeMessage(char message) {}
```

Both methods take one parameter but the `GoodbyeMessage` method needs a `bool` type parameter. In the next example will be two methods using the same exact parameter but they will have different method signatures:

```
static void HelloMessage(string message, bool isFinal) {}
static uint GoodbyeMessage(string message, bool isFinal) {}
```

Notice the return type for the `HelloMessage` method is `void` and the return type for the `GoodbyeMessage` method is `uint`. This means these two methods are using different method signatures.

Create a Console Application called **MethodPointers**. Add a method in the `Program` class called `ShowMessage`. The `ShowMessage` method displays a message on the console based on the parameter value it is passed. The code for the `ShowMessage` method is seen as follows:

```
static void ShowMessage(string message)
{
  Console.WriteLine(message);
}
static void Main(string[] args)
{
}
```

Inside the **Main** method invoke the `ShowMessage` method by passing "Hello There!" as the parameter to the method.

```
static void Main(string[] args)
{
  ShowMessage("Hello There!");
  Console.ReadKey();
}
```

The output of execution will look like **Figure 12.1**.

```
Hello There!
```

Figure 12.1 ShowMessage.

The `ShowMessage` method has just one parameter. Some methods have many parameters since methods can have different signatures. The `ShowMessage` method takes one `string` input parameter and has a `void` return type, which makes up the signature of this method. Method signatures are represented using a `delegate`. A `delegate` is usually created inside the namespace (and not inside of a class).

METHOD POINTERS

Add the following code inside the namespace to define a `delegate` that takes one input parameter and returns nothing (`void`):

```
public delegate void MessageDelegate(string anyMessage);
```

The `delegate` definition looks like a method definition, with the word `delegate` between the access modifier (`public`) and the return type (`void`). The `MessageDelegate` is a new type (like any other `class`) and can be used to create objects. To create an object of the `MessageDelegate` delegate we might think we need to pass in a regular parameter like a `string`. We need to pass the method to the constructor that matches the signature of this `delegate`. The `ShowMessage` method and the `MessageDelegate` both take a `string` parameter and return a `void`.

Inside the **Main** method create an object of type `MessageDelegate` with the `ShowMessage` method as the parameter of the constructor.

```
MessageDelegate del = new MessageDelegate(ShowMessage);
```

Because they have matching signatures the `ShowMessage` method can be passed into the constructor while creating an object of the `MessageDelegate` delegate. The **del** variable is of the `MessageDelegate` type which points to the `ShowMessage` method. To invoke (or call) the `ShowMessage` method we can invoke the **del** variable since **del** points to the `ShowMessage` method. The **del** object can be used like its underlying method, `ShowMessage`, by passing a `string` parameter inside the parentheses.

```
del("Using a delegate...");
```

The code of the **Main** method would look as follows:

```
static void Main(string[] args)
{
  ShowMessage("Hello There!");
  MessageDelegate del = new MessageDelegate(ShowMessage);
  del("Using a delegate...");

  Console.ReadKey();
}
```

In the **Main** method we invoked the `ShowMessage` method twice, one by directly invoking the `ShowMessage` method and "Hello There!" as a parameter and the other time by invoking the **del** variable which points to the same `ShowMessage` method.

The output of execution will look like **Figure 12.2**.

```
Hello There!
Using a delegate...
```

Figure 12.2 ShowMessage twice.

RETURNING VALUES

The delegate is a method pointer and methods can return values. This section talks about delegates that point to methods that return some values.

Create a Console Application called **DelCalculator**. In the **Main** method add the following statements to ask the user to input two numbers along with an operator like plus (+) or minus (-).

```
Console.Write("Please enter the first number: ");
double num1 = double.Parse(Console.ReadLine());

Console.Write("Please enter the second number: ");
double num2 = double.Parse(Console.ReadLine());

Console.Write("Please enter an operator(+ OR -): ");
string op = Console.ReadLine();
```

Add a class called `MatchCalc` to the project. This class will contain the methods to add and subtract two numbers. The code of `MatchCalc` is as follows:

```
class MatchCalc
{
  public static double Add(double number1, double number2)
  {
    return number1 + number2;
  }
```

```
  public static double Subtract(double number1, double
number2)
  {
    return number1 - number2;
  }
}
```

The `MatchCalc` class has the `static` methods of `Add` and `Subtract`. We can invoke these methods directly using the class name, with no need to create instance objects of the class. Both of these methods have a signature where there are two `double` parameters and a `double` return value. We can invoke these methods inside the **Main** method to calculate the sum and difference of the two numbers that the user inputs. The code for this is as follows:

```
double result = MatchCalc.Add(num1, num2);
```

To invoke the `Add` and `Subtract` methods of the `MatchCalc` class using a `delegate` we need to define a `delegate` above the `Program` class but still inside the namespace as follows:

```
public delegate double Calc(double x, double y);
```

An object of the `Calc` type can be created using any method signature that takes two `double` type input parameters and returns a `double` type. Declare an object of the `Calc` type after the code (that later will ask the user for an operator) inside the Main method as follows:

```
static void Main(string[] args)
{
  Calc del = null;
}
```

The **del** variable is not pointing to any method yet. The **del** variable will point to the `MatchCalc.Add` method if + is the operator or will point to `MatchCalc.Subtract` method if - is the operator. Add the following statements in the **Main** method to assign the correct method to the **del** variable based on the user selected operator.

```
static void Main(string[] args)
{
  Calc del = null;
  if (op == "+")
  {
    del = MatchCalc.Add;
  }
    else if (op == "-")
  {
    del = MatchCalc.Subtract;
  }
}
```

If the user input for the operator is + then the Add method would be assigned to the **del** variable. This means the **del** variable would behave like the Add method. If the user input for the operator is - then the Subtract method would be assigned to the **del** variable. In this case the **del** variable would behave like the Subtract method. If the user inputs something other than **+** or **-** then the program will error out at runtime since the **del** object will be null.

Lastly, add the following statements to invoke the delegate **del** and to display the result on the console.

```
double result = del(num1, num2);

Console.WriteLine("{0} {1} {2} = {3}", num1, op, num2,
result);
```

The complete code of the **Main** method would look as follows:

```
Console.Write("Please enter the first number: ");
double num1 = double.Parse(Console.ReadLine());

Console.Write("Please enter the second number: ");
double num2 = double.Parse(Console.ReadLine());

Console.Write("Please enter the operator(+ OR -): ");
string op = Console.ReadLine();

Calc del = null;
```

```
if (op == "+")
{
  del = MatchCalc.Add;
}
else if (op == "-")
{
  del = MatchCalc.Subtract;
}
double result = del(num1, num2);

Console.WriteLine("{0} {1} {2} = {3}", num1, op, num2,
result);

Console.ReadKey();
```

Build and execute the program and try out the program with different values, as shown in **Figure 12.3** and **Figure 12.4**.

```
Please enter the first number: 100
Please enter the second number: 40
Please enter the operator(+ OR -): +
100 + 40 = 140
```

Figure 12.3 Calculator + operation.

```
Please enter the first number: 200
Please enter the second number: 100
Please enter the operator(+ OR -): -
200 - 100 = 100
```

Figure 12.4 Calculator - operation.

Lab 12.1: Delegates

Skill Check 1: Create a Console Application called **CurrentTime**. Add the following methods in the `Program` class.

```
static void ShowLocalTime()
{
  Console.WriteLine("Local Time: {0}",DateTime.Now);
}
static void ShowUTCTime()
{
  Console.WriteLine("UTC Time: {0}", DateTime.UtcNow);
}
```

Define a `delegate` that matches the `ShowLocalTime` and `ShowUTCTime` methods. Create two instances of the `delegate` and make them point to each method. Invoke (or call) the delegates inside the **Main** method. The output should look like **Figure 12.5**. In the sample output the local time zone is PST.

```
Local Time: 3/7/2013 11:55:25 PM
UTC Time: 3/8/2013 7:55:25 AM
```

Figure 12.5 CurrentTime.

Skill Check 2: Create a Console Application called **Fullname**. Add the following methods in the `Program` class.

```
static string GetFullname(string f, string l)
{
  return f + " " + l;
}
static string GetFullnameFancy(string f, string l)
{
  return String.Format("Your full name is {0} {1}", f, l);
}
```

Define a `delegate` that matches the `GetFullname` and `GetFullnameFancy` methods. Create two instances of the `delegate` and make them point to each method. Invoke (or call) the delegates by passing "John" as the first parameter and "Doe" as the second parameter. Capture the method's return value and display it on the console.

Execute the program and the output should look like **Figure 12.6**.

```
John Doe
Your full name is John Doe
```

Figure 12.6 Fullname.

Answer Code: The C# answer code for this lab is located in the downloadable files inside Projects Folder within the BeginningCS2012CompanionFiles.zip file.

Points to Ponder - Delegates

1. A `delegate` is a reference type that points to a method.
2. A `delegate` type is nothing but a class.
3. The method that a `delegate` points to is specified in the constructor when instantiating a `delegate` type.
4. Delegates can pass a method as a parameter to a method.

12.2 Anonymous Methods

The word anonymous means, whose name is not known or not given. So far all the methods we have created have names. For example, we created `Add` and `Subtract` methods in the `MatchCalc` class in the last section of this chapter. There are times when we will want to perform a simple or small set of operations in just one place. Creating a separate method for each operation when we only intend to use one is overkill. These small methods can be created in-line along with other statements. These in-line methods are available to be used inside the method they were created in. These methods don't have names, hence they are called anonymous methods.

In-Line Methods

Create a Console Application called **AnonymousMethods**. We will be creating a method that displays the current date and time to the console. To do this, add a method called `DisplayDateTime` in the `Program` class with the following code:

```
static void DisplayDateTime()
{
  Console.WriteLine("Current Time: {0}", DateTime.Now);
}
```

Add a few statements in the **Main** method to invoke the `DisplayDateTime` method with the following code:

```
static void Main(string[] args)
{
  DisplayDateTime();
  Console.ReadKey();
}
```

Build and execute the program. The output of execution will look like **Figure 12.7**.

```
Current Time: 3/10/2013 12:48:34 PM
```

Figure 12.7 DisplayDateTime.

The output of the console displays just one time. We want it to display a total of three times. Invoke the `DisplayDateTime` method two more times in the **Main** method.

```
static void Main(string[] args)
{
  DisplayDateTime();
  DisplayDateTime();
  DisplayDateTime();
  Console.ReadKey();
}
```

Upon executing the program again the output looks like **Figure 12.8**. The program runs very fast and all the times shown to the console are the same.

```
Current Time: 3/10/2013 12:57:20 PM
Current Time: 3/10/2013 12:57:20 PM
Current Time: 3/10/2013 12:57:20 PM
```

Figure 12.8 DisplayDateTime three times.

If this program would run a little slower we would see that each line on the console can have different times. We can introduce an artificial delay (sleep) between the method calls as follows:

```
static void Main(string[] args)
{
  DisplayDateTime();
  System.Threading.Thread.Sleep(1000);
  DisplayDateTime();
  System.Threading.Thread.Sleep(1000);
  DisplayDateTime();

  Console.ReadKey();
}
```

The `Sleep` method takes a numeric parameter and we used 1000 (milliseconds). This will pause the execution of each statement for 1000 milliseconds (or 1 second). Execution of the program will look like **Figure 12.9**.

```
Current Time: 3/10/2013 1:00:54 PM
Current Time: 3/10/2013 1:00:55 PM
Current Time: 3/10/2013 1:00:56 PM
```

Figure 12.9 DisplayDateTime three times with the Sleep method.

The `DisplayDateTime` method can be expressed as a `delegate` that takes no parameters and returns nothing (`void`). Define a `delegate` inside the namespace (above the `Program` class) to represent the `DisplayDateTime` method.

```
public delegate void ShowDelegate();
```

Change the code inside the **Main** method to use `ShowDelegate` instead of a direct method call. The code of the **Main** method should be as follows:

```
static void Main(string[] args)
{
  ShowDelegate del = DisplayDateTime;

  del();
  System.Threading.Thread.Sleep(1000);
  del();
  System.Threading.Thread.Sleep(1000);
  del();

  Console.ReadKey();
}
```

The instance of `ShowDelegate` is called `del` and is assigned to the `DisplayDateTime` method. The `DisplayDateTime` method is used only inside the **Main** method and is very simple. Creating this method above **Main** with a proper name seems to be overkill. We can create a method with the same code as `DisplayDateTime` inside the **Main** method and avoid creating an extra method.

```
static void Main(string[] args)
{
  ShowDelegate del = delegate()
  {
    Console.WriteLine("Current Time: {0}", DateTime.Now);
  };
```

The variable **del** is created from `ShowDelegate` and is assigned to something known as an anonymous method. All anonymous methods have no names. This usage of the anonymous method takes no parameters and returns nothing (`void`). Anonymous methods are written like regular methods where the method name is replaced with the word `delegate`.

Now we no longer need the `DisplayDateTime` method as we replaced it with the anonymous method. The complete code of the program would look as follows:

```
namespace AnonymousMethods
{
  public delegate void ShowDelegate();

  class Program
  {
    static void Main(string[] args)
    {
      ShowDelegate del = delegate()
      {
        Console.WriteLine("Current Time: {0}",
DateTime.Now);
      };

      del();
      System.Threading.Thread.Sleep(1000);
      del();
      System.Threading.Thread.Sleep(1000);
      del();

      Console.ReadKey();
    }
  }
}
```

Executing the program would be same as before where the method `DisplayDateTime` was used instead of the anonymous method. Using the anonymous method we did not clutter the `Program` class with the extra isolated method `DisplayDateTime`.

INPUT PARAMETERS - RETURN VALUES

Anonymous methods (like regular named methods) can have input parameters and return types. Create a Console Application called **MethodParameters**. Define a `delegate` called `DoMath` inside the namespace (above the `Program` class) which takes two `int` parameters and returns a `long` type.

```
public delegate long DoMath(int x, int y);
```

The `DoMath delegate` can be used to refer to any (named or anonymous) method that takes two `int` parameters and returns a `long` value (i.e. matching signatures). For example, we can point an instance of the `DoMath delegate` to a method for adding two numbers, subtracting two numbers, or even a method to multiply two numbers.

Inside the **Main** method we can create an anonymous method to add two numbers and assign this anonymous method to an instance of the `DoMath delegate`.

```
static void Main(string[] args)
{
  DoMath addDelegate = delegate(int num1, int num2)
  {
    return num1 + num2;
  };
}
```

The **addDelegate** instance can be used to add two numbers. Invoke the **addDelegate** `delegate` inside the **Main** method and display the result on the console.

```
long result = addDelegate(20, 10);

Console.WriteLine("Result: {0}", result);
```

Here we achieved the same functionality of a named method without creating one. Likewise we can create another instance for subtracting two numbers in the following code:

```
DoMath subDelegate = delegate(int num1, int num2)
{
  return num1 - num2;
};
```

Add a few statements to invoke the **subDelegate** and to display the result on the console. The complete code of the **Main** method would be as follows:

```
static void Main(string[] args)
{
  DoMath addDelegate = delegate(int num1, int num2)
  {
    return num1 + num2;
  };
  long result = addDelegate(20, 10);
  Console.WriteLine("Add Result: {0}", result);
  DoMath subDelegate = delegate(int num1, int num2)
  {
    return num1 - num2;
  };
  result = subDelegate(20, 10);
  Console.WriteLine("Sub Result: {0}", result);
  Console.ReadKey();
}
```

Here, two anonymous methods were created and method references were assigned to `addDelegate` and `subDelegate` respectively. The output of the program execution would look like **Figure 12.10**.

```
Add Result: 30
Sub Result: 10
```

Figure 12.10 DoMath.

Lab 12.2: Anonymous Methods

Skill Check 1: Create a Console Application called **AnonymousFullname**. Change the following code to use an anonymous method for the `DisplayFullname` method.

```
class Program
{
  static void Main(string[] args)
  {
    DisplayFullname("John", "Doe");
    Console.ReadKey();
  }
  static void DisplayFullname(string fName, string lName)
  {
    Console.WriteLine("{0} {1}", fName, lName);
  }
}
```

The output of execution is shown in **Figure 12.11**.

```
John Doe
```

Figure 12.11 AnonymousFullname.

Skill Check 2: Create a Console Application called **AnonymousMessages**. Change the following code to use anonymous methods for all methods except the **Main** method.

```
class Program
{
  static void Main(string[] args)
  {
    ShowMessage1("Anonymous");
    ShowMessage2("Anonymous");
    ShowMessage3("Anonymous");
    ShowMessage4("Anonymous");
    Console.ReadKey();
  }

  static void ShowMessage1(string message)
  {
    Console.WriteLine("@@@@   {0}   @@@@", message);
  }

  static void ShowMessage2(string message)
  {
    Console.WriteLine("####   {0}   ####", message);
  }

  static void ShowMessage3(string message)
  {
    Console.WriteLine("$$$$   {0}   $$$$", message);
  }

  static void ShowMessage4(string message)
  {
    Console.WriteLine("%%%%   {0}   %%%%", message);
  }
}
```

The output of execution is shown in **Figure 12.12**.

```
@@@@    Anonymous    @@@@
####    Anonymous    ####
$$$$    Anonymous    $$$$
%%%%    Anonymous    %%%%
```

Figure 12.12 AnonymousMessages.

Answer Code: The C# answer code for this lab is located in the downloadable files inside Projects Folder within the BeginningCS2012CompanionFiles.zip file.

Points to Ponder - Anonymous Methods

1. Anonymous methods enable us to create small and simple methods in-line within other methods.
2. Anonymous methods can help reduce code bloating by avoiding local (specific to calling method) and small methods.
3. An anonymous method has access to the local variables of a method.
4. An anonymous method has no access to defining a method's `ref` and `out` type parameter variables.

Review Quiz - Chapter Twelve

1.) A delegate is a string pointer.

O a) True
O b) False

2.) A delegate can point to methods that return a value.

O a) True
O b) False

3.) Methods can take types like int and string. as parameters and other methods as well.

O a) True
O b) False

4.) All methods that a delegate points to should have a valid name.

O a) True
O b) False

5.) An anonymous method has access to the local variables of a method.

O a) True
O b) False

ANSWER KEY

1.) A delegate is not a string pointer but a method pointer, making option (b) the correct answer.

2.) A delegate is a method pointer and can point to any method, making option (a) correct.

3.) A delegate type can be a method parameter, making option (a) the correct answer.

4.) A delegate can point to anonymous methods, making (b) the correct answer.

5.) True, an anonymous method has access to local variables declared inside a method, making option (a) the correct answer.

[NOTES]

Index

Lightning Source UK Ltd.
Milton Keynes UK
UKHW031111140220
358738UK00006B/1029

9 781939 666192